D1266945

STOLEN YOUTH

STOLEN
YOUTH

HOW RADICALS ARE
ERASING INNOCENCE
AND INDOCTRINATING
A GENERATION

BETHANY MANDEL AND
KAROL MARKOWICZ

Stolen Youth: How Radicals Are Erasing Innocence and Indoctrinating a Generation

Copyright © 2023 by Bethany Mandel and Karol Markowicz

ISBN: 978-1-956007-08-4

Cover photos: Generated Media, Inc.

First Edition

Published by DW Books

DW Books™, a division of The Daily Wire®

Daily Wire
1831 12th Avenue South
Suite 460
Nashville, TN 37203

www.dailywire.com

PRINTED IN THE USA

DEDICATION

For our children.

CONTENTS

Introduction: *Bethany*   9

PART I: EDUCATION

CHAPTER 1   Totalitarians and Our Children: *Karol*   21

CHAPTER 2   Wokeness in the Time of Pandemic: *Karol*   47

CHAPTER 3   No Subject Is Safe: *Karol*   73

PART II: INSTITUTIONS IN TROUBLE

CHAPTER 4   When Mickey and Scholastic Went Woke: *Bethany*   105

CHAPTER 5   The Peril of Woke Medicine: *Bethany*   135

PART III: KIDS AS GUINEA PIGS

CHAPTER 6   The Transgender Crusade: *Bethany*   167

CHAPTER 7   Sexualized Childhood: *Bethany*   191

CHAPTER 8   Child Soldiers: *Karol*   207

PART IV: WHERE DO WE GO FROM HERE?

CHAPTER 9   In Praise of Resiliency: *Bethany*   225

CONCLUSION

How to Pull Your Kids Out: *Bethany*   243

How to Fight from Within: *Karol*   255

Acknowledgments   261

Endnotes   271

INTRODUCTION

"I never paid attention to politics or cultural issues; I was too busy raising my family. I spent my time volunteering at my kids' school, so I always thought I knew what was happening there. I thought it was enough. It wasn't. Not paying attention to these issues was the biggest mistake I made as a parent."

We heard variations of this lament from countless parents, parents who had no idea the danger lurking in every corner of their children's lives, from their schoolroom, to their library, to their smartphone, to their television, and beyond.

If you look at birth rates by ideological persuasion, you'll see that it's not progressives having kids; they're entrenched in anti-natalist propaganda. Their aim is ideological capture of a generation, but it's not their kids they're working to brainwash—it's ours.

They're not shy about their intentions: they want to turn *our* kids into their foot soldiers. In the baby board book *Antiracist Baby* by Ibram X. Kendi, which has been a bestseller on Amazon (we'll explain a bit how that happens later), the agenda is explicit. In the book Kendi writes, "Antiracist Baby is raised to make society transform. Babies are taught to be racist or antiracist—there's no neutrality."[1]

We named this book *Stolen Youth*, but we could have just as easily called it *Woke War on Families* because the assault on childhood is an all-out battle against the American family. The radical progressive Left—the woke—are trying to completely remake society and start a revolution. They know they can't accomplish that without ideologically capturing America's youth. After all, you can't start a revolution among happy and contented citizens. Their goal, thus, is to make our kids miserable, make them question every fundamental building block of society ("What is a woman?" "What is a man?"), and make them rebuild their entire sense of reality, concept of right and wrong, and vision for the future.

For woke revolutionaries, similar to the communist revolutionaries of the twentieth century, the goal is societal transformation, even if the cost is individual suffering. According to this ideology, the well-being and best interests of the individual are subjugated for the "collective good." Individual suffering is irrelevant; it's the pursuit of the collective societal shift that matters. That individual misery is in fact a feature, not a bug, for these revolutionaries.

When we began researching this book, stories from individual suffering families filled our inboxes, and we spent hours talking to parents who had watched the happy and contented homes they worked hard to build for their children pulled out from under them. Their children transformed into shells of their former selves, angry and disconnected from their parents, their sense of self, and their communities. (Out of respect for these individuals and their families, some names, locations, and identifying characteristics have been changed to protect the privacy of those referenced.) The trend was only accelerated by our mismanaged societal response to the COVID-19 pandemic.

Alison, a mother of three from the Boston area, was one of those parents. Her daughter, Elissa, was already struggling a bit academically and socially in 2019 when she started sixth grade. Her friend group wasn't filled with the most desirable characters, and she was beginning to show outward signs of rebellion, like dying her hair and dressing in darker clothing. It all took a turn when COVID hit. The school closed on her birthday, and her beloved uncle died (of non-COVID causes). Isolated in her room on her devices, she soon began to spiral. Alison said, "She stayed in her room all the time, and it was dark. We didn't know what she was doing online, but we thought, 'whatever keeps her busy,' while we were locked down." The return to school two days a week didn't improve the situation, and in October of 2020, Alison discovered that Elissa was not only cutting, but she was also suicidal. Every single outpatient program for troubled youth was on Zoom, even over six months into a pandemic that was widely understood not to put anyone under the age of forty at significant risk. Only one program was inpatient, and Alison compared it to "a prison" where they had to drop their daughter off outside at the gate, masked. Elissa was only supposed to be there for ten days but stayed for over three weeks.

Alison explained what happened next: "Our daughter looked like she was in a prison. She wouldn't really talk to us; the psychiatrist did all the talking for her. She was in a mask on Zoom with us. [In one session] the psychiatrist prompted her, 'Elissa, you have something to tell your parents?' Elissa sat silently, and the psychiatrist announced that she's 'nonbinary.' We asked, 'Where is this coming from?' We were dumbfounded. It didn't sound like her. We knew there were issues, but I don't know if she thought it was an escape or the cool thing to do because it's what she's watching on YouTube or TikTok."

It just so happened that eight other kids in that program were also nonbinary or gay. The psychiatrist kept recommending books and resources to "support" Elissa through the change.

Alison went on, venting, "She was groomed. We think she was groomed to be this way. This came out of the blue."

When Elissa came home, they faced another enemy in their fight to save their daughter: the school. Alison explained, "When she went back to school, the public school helped this process along. They helped groom her. They came to me and said Elissa wanted to change her name to Corey. 'We're going to look into changing it in her records.'" Alison refused, but it didn't matter. Alison explained, "They will do whatever the kids say. They don't care what the parents say. She was Corey, and they used [the pronouns] they/them. They didn't give a shit what I said."

After transferring their daughter to a charter school, things began to improve, both with Elissa's gender identity confusion and with her underlying mental health issues that had led her to the inpatient clinic that was more concerned with helping her gender transition along than treating her severe mental health issues that had spiraled out of control when she was isolated during COVID.

The key takeaway for Alison about what happened to her family is this: "The inpatient program started the whole thing, and the schools just went along. They don't care. The school is so involved in politics and pushing their agenda. It's sad. Us as parents, we feel like we have no control."[2]

Elissa's story is one that Charlie Jacobs hears frequently in her work with parents of children who are experiencing rapid-onset gender dysphoria (ROGD). Charlie's own daughter was one of those children, and Charlie shared the same sense of powerlessness that Alison did when every other authority figure in her daughter's life, from therapists to the school, were working to encourage her daughter's transition rather than dealing with the underlying issues that led to her gender confusion.

The Jacobs family is from the San Francisco Bay area, white, and relatively affluent by American standards, though not quite as wealthy as the neighborhood kids with private jets. Charlie explained, "These kids are exposed to all of this very liberal schooling, which I was clueless about. I thought I'd have my finger on the pulse of the school, but I missed a lot. The seed that started the transgender plant growing inside of her was in seventh-grade health class. It gave these kids highly sexualized labels. It was nonsense: polyamorous, bi-gender, etc., a whole list of made-up words. And the eleven- and twelve-year-old girls picked a label; it became cool. Nobody wanted to be the cis-basic kid; that's boring. And not only is it boring. For a white and affluent kid who wants for nothing, they don't want to be the oppressor, which is what they're being taught in school. They have to pick something that marginalizes them."

Charlie explained that kids then go down a rabbit hole. They start off at lesbian, then nonbinary, then transgender. "That's a pattern I see over and over with kids."

In her daughter's Girl Scout troop, eight out of eighteen kids came out as something after the health class. Charlie told me, "I didn't think anything of it, except the polyamorous, because it was disturbing that they were talking about sex. In the parent course for the health class, all of the parents were just [nodding] their heads in agreement. It was *The Emperor's New Clothes*, and everyone around us is very smart with PhDs, etc. But everyone just sat there, silently." She laughed wryly, "I didn't know I was a bigot or transphobe at the time."

After her daughter declared her transgender identity, the school was all-in, changing her name and pronouns. She went to a dark place: self-tattooing, piercing herself, darkening her room. Charlie asked the school to partner with her to monitor and limit her daughter's internet usage, but she was on a device all day long. She was doing high school on the internet during COVID.

It wasn't just the school working against Charlie and her daughter, either. All of the therapists said the Jacobses had to affirm their daughter's new identity or she'd commit suicide. It was because of Charlie's refusal to go along with the school and therapists—and working to find ones that would partner *with* her rather than work *against* her—that her daughter began to make progress. She no longer goes by a male name, but Charlie isn't sure if it'll stick. "Everything out there is trans, trans, trans. It's in every storefront window, trans people walking up the red carpet. It's a constant battle."[3]

It's a battle more and more parents are realizing they're fighting, not only to protect their children from being inducted into the gender ideology cult, but also to protect them from becoming collateral damage.

At sleepaway camps and programs across the country, children are increasingly being grouped into sleeping arrangements with children and counselors according to their "gender identity," not their biological sex. In Broward County, Florida, the guidelines state, "If students are to be based on gender, the transgender student should be allowed to room with peers that match their gender identity."[4]

It's not just a possibility. It's a reality that is happening nationwide. In February 2022, parents of fifth graders in Los Alamitos, California, received startling news about a sleepover their children participated in: students from Weaver Elementary School had been placed in cabins with camp counselors according to how they identified, resulting in biologically male counselors sharing a cabin with young girls. This wasn't illegal; in fact, it is what was—and is—required under California law, according to the Assistant Director of the camp, who explained they "place staff in cabins they identify with."[5]

After the trip, parents were sent an email by the school superintendent, Andrew Pulver, who explained, "Privacy rights protect disclosure of information about an individual's gender to the public, and thus, we do not have information to share about other individuals in your student's cabin."[6]

The message to parents was clear: everyone but your child has an expectation of privacy, and parents have no hope of being granted information about the people with whom their children are sharing a cabin. The email got worse. Pulver gaslit parents who objected to how the trip was handled by school administrators, writing, "As parents, you may not be aware of federal and state nondiscrimination laws that all employers must abide and operate under. This is consistent for all school activities, whether during the day, on field trips, or overnight. Please know that all individuals supervising students were appropriately vetted through background checks and that there have not been any allegations of sexual misconduct. Due to state and federal nondiscrimination laws, the District does not know, nor will we, if an individual was in fact the opposite biological identity than the students they were supervising."[7]

The school district *basically* told parents this: "We don't know whom we put in a cabin with your kids, and you won't ever get to know that, either. We're legally required to allow anyone in the cabin, as long as they tell us that they identify with a certain gender, and there's nothing you can do about it, nor do we even find your objections to be at all reasonable. In fact, you're a bigot if you do object!"

This is what happened to Hannah in Orange County, California, who sent her then-ten-year-old daughter to another nearby summer camp. Parents from her daughter's school had caught wind of what happened in Los Alamitos and confronted the camp and the school about sleeping and bathroom arrangements before they sent their children. When parents contacted the school and camp with their concerns, a Q&A was held and the legal language of the statute was sent. The email stated:

> Students who attend Outdoor Education have the right to partic-ipate, and use facilities, consistent with their gender identity, ir-respective of the gender listed on the student's record. (Ed. Code, § 221.5(f).) Similarly, the California Gender Nondiscrimination Law requires adults have access to facilities that align with their gender identity. (Cal. Civ. Code, § 51.) Privacy rights protect dis-closure of information about an individual's gender to the public, and thus, information about other individuals in your student's cabin cannot be shared, other than to clarify that all individuals in the "female" cabin primarily identify as female, and all indi-viduals in the "male" cabin primarily identify as male. To the extent an individual is non-binary, the individual must select a primary gender for the purpose of use of single-sex facilities.[8]

But Hannah didn't understand the legal jargon and was reassured that she was on the same page as the school, which told parents that the reporting about what happened to children in Los Alamitos was "fake news." Hannah explained in a subsequent email to school ad-ministrators, "I feel completely [misled] and what I find most con-cerning, is the lack of information divulged to parents on the matter when our principal was fully aware that this was a possibility. I spoke with the school after my daughter came home from camp. They in-formed me that out of 65 employees, about four of their staff members identify as non-binary. They said that the principal was perfectly aware that they could be sleeping with our children. She could have clarified this to parents, especially when she saw that this was a concern for several of us."[9]

Whom did Hannah's daughter spend the weekend with? A counselor named "Nick" with a neon green mohawk, arms covered in tattoos, two missing teeth, and other teeth that were visibly rotting. Nick had some facial hair and announced "their" pronouns as they/them, something Hannah's daughter didn't understand and felt too intimidated to ask about, due largely to a recent experience at her school.

The school's actions just weeks prior bullied Hannah's daughter into silence. Hannah's daughter was part of a group text chain where one child wished death on another because he was unvaccinated against COVID. The entire text chain was turned over to school authorities, and in that chain, they found a boy bullying Hannah's daughter, taunting her and calling her a "lesbian." As way of retribution and standing up for herself, as young children do, Hannah's daughter threw the insult right back, calling the bully a "gay boy." It was for this reason that Hannah's daughter was stripped of her title as class president, humiliating and devastating her. Hannah explained, "When I asked her why she didn't say anything to a teacher or the principal when she was uncomfortable at camp, she said it was because she was worried that she would get in trouble. She said that when she tried to explain her side of the story [during] the previous incident, the principal didn't listen." Why would she listen now? Hannah's daughter got the message loud and clear from the school: on issues related to gender and sexuality, you are to keep your mouth closed or risk retribution.

And the lesson Hannah herself learned? "I'm the kind of person that gives the benefit of the doubt and is too trusting. This is that wake-up call that I can't trust people, especially with my children. They're more concerned about the leaders being comfortable than my daughter being comfortable."[10]

After an extended fight with the school administration, Hannah's daughter was reinstated as class president, but the sleepaway camp policies remain unchanged because they are enshrined in state law.

In the long term, a generation of children, including Hannah's daughter, have learned that they must ignore their internal alarm that signals danger solely because they might offend someone. That fear of potentially offending someone comes at a cost, and the cost is their safety. Hannah's daughter wasn't the only person who quieted her internal alarm; the principal and every adult involved at the camp did as well. Nobody wanted to question the wisdom of putting someone who was sporting a green mohawk, a sleeve of tattoos, and facial hair in charge of a cabin of girls. It's the job of adults to take care of children, not the other way around.

How did these children come to be endangered in this way? How did we get here, and perhaps more importantly, how do we protect our own kids from a similar situation? Reading this book is the first step: you recognize there is a problem. It's even more pernicious than you could have possibly imagined.

It's not just gender identity indoctrination. Critical race theory (CRT) is taking over whole curricula, from social studies to math. But while CRT has been at the forefront of parental protests in 2021, it's still just one piece of the woke indoctrination puzzle.

This forced indoctrination extends into everything. It's not enough to teach kids the science behind climate change; we need to have them put on a protest, as schools across the country did in 2019. Instead of teaching actual science, science classes focused on learning bio-graphical information about climate-activist Greta Thunberg.[11]

The danger is this: While every librarian may not consider himself or herself to be woke (although many do), woke ideology sets the narrative currently sold by children's publishing houses. While every pediatrician isn't woke, wokeness sets the narrative in medical schools and profes-sional medical organizations. While there are many well-meaning teachers and mental health counselors, the woke narrative is uniformly dominant in their graduate programs and professional organizations across the country.

The same woke narrative is bleeding into our youth. This brain-washing into left-wing ideology for all children, even for those whose parents lean leftward politically, is potentially devastating to the health of our nation and the mental health of individual children. In this book, we set forth with a few objectives: expose how the woke are infiltrating American childhood, provide parents with the tools to fight back, and tell the cautionary tales of parents who didn't realize what was happening until it was too late.

This is a battle—for our own children and for all children. That's why we wrote this book, and hopefully why you're reading. It's time to fight back.

PART I

EDUCATION

There's good news and bad news.

The good news is leftism remains highly unpopular in America.

The bad news is woke autocrats have not backed down. Instead, they have captured institutions—from schools to corporations and beyond—and are using the same methods as their totalitarian predecessors to force their bad ideas on us all.

Like the despots of failed leftist regimes, the woke's goal is to target the children so their ideology spreads to parents. Enforced conformity is step one.

Schools are a key battleground. Leftists needlessly closed schools during COVID and dared anyone to challenge their authority. They silenced concerned parents through social consequences, just as history's villains have done before. The woke have targeted rigor and destroyed merit. They pretend that 2 + 2 does not always equal 4 and claim that this is somehow related to equity. They're forcing an agenda on our kids that steals their childhood and turns them into soldiers for the woke cause. The indoctrination they push is all-encompassing and merciless. They must be opposed. It is time to be brave.

1

TOTALITARIANS AND OUR CHILDREN

My great-grandfather, Aron Gelberg, died in a gulag near the Kuril Islands in eastern Russia sometime in the late 1930s. Gulag stands for Glavnoye Upravleniye Ispravitelno-Trudovykh Lagerey or Chief Administration of Corrective Labor Camps, a bureaucratic name for forced labor camps maintained during the time of the Soviet Union.[1] Aleksandr I. Solzhenitsyn, author of the three-volume book set *The Gulag Archipelago* chronicling his own time in the gulags, believed forty to fifty million people served time in the camps, though some estimates put that number at closer to sixty million.[2]

Aron and his wife, Chaya, had owned a bakery in Gomel, Belarus, when private enterprise became illegal under the rule of Joseph Stalin. Being Jewish in the Soviet Union had never been easy, but this was something different. They were no longer simply "other." Overnight, they became enemies of the state. Aron became a political prisoner. They hadn't stepped out of line; the line had shifted underneath them.

Other people in the gulags were politicians, intellectuals, artists or simply related to one of those objectionable persons. Some were there because they had said the wrong thing, others because they didn't say the right thing strongly enough. Solzhenitsyn, for example, was sentenced to eight years for criticizing Stalin in a private letter. Some prisoners were there for no discernable reason at all.

There were also children in the gulag. Solzhenitsyn writes, "Vera Inchik, the daughter of a charwoman, and two other girls, all aged fourteen, discovered (Yeisk, in 1932) that in the course of the liquidation of the 'kulaks,' little children were being thrown out to die. The girls ('like the revolutionaries earlier') decided to protest. They wrote out their protests in their own handwriting on sheets of paper taken from their school notebooks and posted them in the marketplace themselves, expecting immediate and universal indignation."[3] Instead, all the girls were eventually arrested and sent to the camps.

The girls discovered the hard way that protest was only allowable when it fit into the narrow confines of acceptable speech, a theme that carries to present day. Children who protest should be encouraged—unless they're protesting something the woke Left doesn't like. Of course, my great-grandfather didn't have to protest. Simply being himself was enough to get him sent to the gulag.

"Great-grandfather" sounds distant, but I always kept Aron's story very close to me, partly because I was raised by his daughters. Aron and Chaya had four children: two boys and two girls. The boys, Ilya and Abram, went missing in action during World War II and were never heard from again. The husband of the older daughter, Raya, died in that war, and she, a newlywed, never remarried or had children. The youngest daughter, Sarra, was my grandmother.

Sarra and Raya helped raise me while my parents worked intensely long hours to get our lives started in Brooklyn. The trauma of their lives was evident in everything they did. Solzhenitsyn quotes a girl, Svetlana Sedova, whose father was similarly taken away: "From the age of six I have been 'the daughter of a traitor to the Motherland.' And there can be nothing more awful in life than this."[4] My grandmother and her sister similarly carried their experience as traitors, always careful about what they said and to whom.

The four Gelberg siblings produced only one descendent, my father. Their family was torn apart by circumstance, yes: war and displacement, disasters that have upended people's lives since the beginning of time. But at the core of their family's decay was the oppression of a tyrannical state, a dedication to sameness and forced equality. My grandmother and her siblings were children when their father was taken away, but they learned the lesson: obey.

I was raised with the knowledge that the freedom I have gotten to experience in the United States should not, for a single moment, be taken for granted. None of it is promised. Sometimes the slide toward an authoritarian society is slow. Other times, it's very fast. America is in danger. People are not being carted off to work camps, that's true, but that was also true for much of the Soviet Union as well. Gulags only existed for about thirty of the USSR's sixty-nine years. And yet the stifling of speech, the fear of committing a crime today that wasn't a crime yesterday, the indoctrination, the censorship, all persisted in Soviet society until the USSR's last day.

In the 1980s, a slow loosening had begun in the Soviet Union. We had arrived in America in 1978, and a few years later my mother's mother could actually come visit us. This was somewhat groundbreaking. My mother's father had a low-level government job and could never be allowed out, but the fact that his wife could even make the trip was novel and exciting. Even then, my grandmother barely spoke, convinced she was being followed and would be in danger if she told us anything at all. It had been more than thirty years since they had closed the gulags, but all the lessons of fear and compliance remained.

America is in a conformist moment of its own, and the signs are all too familiar for families like mine.

There are a lot of terms associated with this time: "wokeness," "cancel culture," and "indoctrination" are all front and center. The commercials start, "We believe . . ." and the assumption is that only the worst people could possibly not be included in that "we." There is a push from schools, corporations, media, and elsewhere for one woke monoculture, and they are targeting ever-younger children in this mission. They are on a march through our institutions.

The term "woke" was once used by the black community to describe someone who stays alert to racism in society. But once it spread to larger use, woke thought became more than just social awareness or just espousing leftist doctrine or even just having the "right" beliefs. Wokeness became the enforcement of a narrow set of values and a policing of language. It is now a method to shut down any alternate opinions, even those within the same general range. It's a system characterized by intolerance and showing one's own superiority by denouncing those who step out of line. And though woke ideology centers a very different set of people than the USSR did, the methods are eerily similar.

Merriam-Webster defines "woke" as "aware of and actively attentive to important facts and issues (especially issues of racial and social justice)," but that's the old definition.[5] They have not updated the definition. Yet this avoidance to update "woke" is not because the publication is unwilling to revise definitions. For example, after the October 2020 Senate Judiciary Committee hearing, Judge Amy Coney Barrett used the term "sexual preference" in what the Left deemed an "offensive" manner, so *Merriam-Webster* rewrote the definition of the term as "offensive" to correspond with left-wing criticism.[6] They have also added people who oppose vaccine mandates to the definition of "anti-vaxxer." But no update to the word "woke" has been forthcoming despite a real shift in how the word is used. *Merriam-Webster* is careful to cater to a very Left audience. Why? Because even *Merriam-Webster* is woke.

After the November 2021 election where Democrats lost the gubernatorial race in Virginia, and nearly lost it in New Jersey, longtime Democratic political consultant James Carville said "stupid wokeness" was responsible.[7] Alexandria Ocasio-Cortez, the reigning queen of woke, shot back that "wokeness is a term almost exclusively used by older people these days, so that should tell you all you need to know."[8] Liberal television host Bill Maher then noted that "woke" was *The Guardian*'s word of 2020 and that it was exactly people like AOC who introduced it to our lives. The term is no longer seen as an undeniable positive. *The Guardian* newspaper was complaining "how the word woke was weaponised by the right" as early as January of 2020,[9] while linguist John McWhorter covered in the *New York Times* in August of 2021 how the term became an insult.[10] It's understandable why the Left is trying to drop it. Maher asked, "What word would you like us to use for the plainly insane excesses of the Left, that are not liberalism, but something completely different? Because you can't have that word 'liberal,' from us, and think it should cover things like canceling Lincoln and teaching third graders they are oppressors. That's all your new thing."[11]

Throughout this book we will discuss "wokeness" as a new version of leftism that is directly aimed at your child. Wokeness has infected everything. The right way of looking at wokeness and woke culture is as a set of deeply toxic ideas that are force-fed to the populace, in particular to children.

Part of the philosophy, and indeed the definition of staying awake to offenses, is to always be seeking new targets for reeducation. Racism, sexism, and general wrongthink are always lurking somewhere and must be rooted out.

The insidiousness of wokeism is a phenomenon most American parents likely never picked up on, or never fully realized the extent of, until recently. That insidiousness isn't a twist of fate; it's a strategy of brainwashing that has affected every corner of our culture. The woke are our moral betters, and while they imagine they understand human nature and our children better than we do, they also know that their message isn't necessarily appreciated or welcomed, and as a result, it is often slipped in like an Easter egg for our kids to discover in books, movies, and everyday interactions.

In fact, leftism is deeply unpopular in America, which is why this woke language and behavior gets enforced through social and political pressure. A *Gallup* poll released in early 2022 showed "37% of Americans described their political views as moderate, 36% as conservative and 25% as liberal." Only 7% described themselves as "very liberal." Only about half of Democrats describe themselves as "liberal." The rest call themselves "moderate" or "conservative."[12]

The majority of Americans are not woke, and yet, wokeness has an outsized influence at the top of academia, culture, business, and across media. The result: the power of this narrative vastly outstrips its actual popularity and general level of acceptance. Wokeism's permeation into every aspect of our lives as parents has the potential not just to reverse all of our hard work raising our children as upstanding young people, but to strip them of their innocence and resiliency as well.

Conservatives have long been worried about indoctrination of young adults on college campuses. David Horowitz's *Indoctrination U: The Left's War Against Academic Freedom* came out in 2009. Ben Shapiro wrote *Brainwashed: How Universities Indoctrinate America's Youth* in 2010. But what's happening today starts far earlier. *A is for Activist* is a board book. So are *No!: My First Book of Protest* and *Woke Baby*.

But the ubiquity and power of the woke worldview extends far past the influences of childhood. From cradle to college, from the big moments to the small, parents are subject to its influence on our kids. And worse yet, the woke want to turn our children into not just automatons but active child soldiers in their fight to remake our society at its most basic level.

All of this indoctrination and conformity comes with the backing of plenty of money. After George Floyd's death and the ensuing Black Lives Matter (BLM) protests that erupted in the summer of 2020, companies and organizations reworked their organizational missions to include "racial equity" and "social justice." Brands posted black squares on their social media and pledges to "do better" in hiring and showcasing diversity. "Please continue to buy our stuff" was unsaid. It was the "new normal," and we were going to have to get on board or be left behind.

The pageantry was important. It applied the pressure on businesses to say all the right things and for organizations to pay up.

Amazon donated a minimum of 550 copies of the book *Stamped: Racism, Antiracism, and You* as well as the accompanying study guide, to Wakefield High School in Arlington, Virginia, in February of 2021.[13] Amazon also funded $8,000 for the fee of one of the book's co-authors, Jason Reynolds, to give a talk virtually to faculty and students.[14] Various foundations—JPMorgan Chase & Co., Ford Foundation, Bill & Melinda Gates Foundation, and others—spent more than $23 billion (compared to a mere $3.3 billion for the nine years previous) funding racial equity nonprofits in 2020 and 2021.[15] Open Society Foundations, a group founded by George Soros, is one of the funders of the 1619 Freedom School, an after-school program based on the widely discredited 1619 series by Nikole Hannah-Jones. Soros funds a variety of groups that reporter Luke Rosiak in 2019 called "The 'Equity' Industrial Complex."[16] They fund local political races, pinpoint where "equity" education can be helpful, and also provide that equity education themselves. And while the very mention of Soros funding all of this sounds like a conspiracy theory, Rosiak points out that it's all out in the open. "At least three of these groups—Center for Social Inclusion, PolicyLink and the Center for American Progress—are funded by Soros through his Foundation to Promote Open Society, according to tax records available through CitizenAudit.org."[17]

The obscene money spent on this indoctrination is important because it conveys to parents, and the public at large, that this is what we are doing now. If you don't like it, you're racist, sexist, or worse. The conformity they demand is instrumental to the leftist cause.

Conformity is easier to achieve than it may seem. We all hope we'd stand up for what's right but, generally, people want to be accepted by their peers and will cover up their real opinions to ensure they are. In the 1950s, a psychologist named Solomon Asch conducted the Asch conformity experiments. Each had one real participant and several actors, who were all asked to match a line to another line of similar length. The actors would knowingly give the same wrong answer. About 5 percent of the participants always went with the group answer and around a quarter of the participants always gave the correct answer, unswayed by the answers of the actors. But the rest would sometimes go along and other times not.[18]

A similar experiment conducted on children in 2017 by scientists Emma Flynn, Cameron Turner, and Luc-Alain Giraldeau found "that children are sensitive to the contextual cues of the domain in which they are witnessing norms and vary their own conformity based on such cues."[19] They also found that younger children were more likely to conform than older ones.[20] A study out of the School of Psychology, Center for Studies of Psychological Application and Key Laboratory of Mental Health and Cognitive Science of Guangdong Province found "sustained conforming behaviors among children in situations of relatively low social pressure."[21] In other words, kids wouldn't just conform to the opinions of their peers in the present situation; they would continue to conform to those opinions even the following day, and even under minimal social pressure to do so.

Preference falsification occurs because of societal pressure, even without overt threats. In his 1997 book *Private Truths, Public Lies: The Social Consequences of Preference Falsification*, economist Timur Kuran writes about "preference falsification," people covering up their true beliefs and instead representing what they know to be the correct opinion to the outside world. A Czech friend asks him whether he had ever lived under totalitarian rule to experience this kind of "preference falsification." Kuran has not but writes, "despotic government is not the only source of fear, the only obstacle to overt and candid discourse. A more basic factor is public opinion . . . Even in democratic societies, where the right to think, speak, and act freely enjoys official protection, and where tolerance is a prized virtue, unorthodox views can evoke enormous hostility."[22] People often falsify their preference to conform or risk being ostracized—or worse.

We're seeing it happen in America today. It's not crazy. We're social creatures, and we want to fit in with our friends and neighbors. And now, social media has opened the door to a forced conformity that we largely haven't experienced in this country before. We know each other's opinions and ideas in a way we couldn't have twenty years before. We know who stands out as different. We click "like" to send the message that we're on the same side. And we see who dares to dissent.

Children are no different. They want to please, and they will repeat the lessons being pushed on them from every direction. Parents have to identify and stop the onslaught, and they have to do it now.

While wokeness might be new, forced conformity and targeting children to push obedience to that conformity are not new concepts at all. It was the Italian dictator Benito Mussolini who coined the term totalitarian, or "totalitario" in Italian. "Everything within the state, nothing outside the state, nothing against the state," he said.[23] No dissent could be allowed. Individualism was impossible if a truly cohesive culture was to be achieved.

The conformity of totalitarian regimes, whether fascist or communist, always had to begin with children. Children were the great hope of the realized utopian future. They belonged to all of society—not just the family to which they were born. If they could lead the children to righteous thought, they could become the idealized society. If children could be convinced into the ideas the totalitarians wanted, their parents would follow. And if not, the disobedient parent could easily be removed from the equation.

In *Mussolini's Children: Race and Elementary Education in Fascist Italy*, Eden K. McLean writes on the importance of children, and messaging to children, in upholding the fascist state. "Children's magazines were especially adept at highlighting the youth contributions" to various fascist programs, she writes.[24] "Propaganda measures and other initiatives within the education system were used to combat what one author in *Motherhood and Childhood* [a magazine put out by Opera Nazionale Maternità e Infanzia, a national network of clinics that delivered childcare instructions to parents] termed 'egotistical individualism.'"[25]

But even in totalitarian societies, people frown on the indoctrination of kids. "Efforts to revolutionize childhood were among the most reviled of Soviet experiments in the realm of culture," writes Lisa A. Kirschenbaum in her book examining Soviet childhood, *Small Comrades: Revolutionizing Childhood in Soviet Russia, 1917-1932*.[26] It's a bright line, not to be crossed, and that's why today, in America, it's done so insidiously.

Nevertheless, revolutionizing childhood under fascism was still successful. The process went on for generations. But separating kids from their parents proved somewhat harder. In the first years after the Russian Revolution, the communist Bolsheviks built kindergartens at a fast clip. The idea was to separate children from their families, and as Kirschenbaum writes, in general they anticipated a "withering away" of the family.[27] But Kirschenbaum notes that by the late 1920s, the Bolsheviks "were questioning both the possibility and the wisdom of speeding the withering away of the family . . . It soon became clear that far from replacing parents, kindergartens would have to rely on their active material and financial support."[28] What happened in schools had to be bolstered by what happened at home, and vice versa.

For so long, parental involvement in education has been seen as the key factor to student success in America. But as the critical race theory (CRT) battles gained prominence, that shifted. Once parents became concerned about CRT in the classroom, the idea that parents should get involved in their kids' education was seen as a "right-wing" idea.

We used to know that involving parents in their child's education was a good thing. A 2010 study called "Parent Involvement and Student Academic Performance: A Multiple Mediational Analysis" by researchers at the Warren Alpert Medical School of Brown University and the University of North Carolina at Greensboro noted that parent involvement in student success had long been a given: "Parent involvement in a child's early education is consistently found to be positively associated with a child's academic performance. Specifically, children whose parents are more involved in their education have higher levels of academic performance than children whose parents are involved to a lesser degree. The influence of parent involvement on academic success has not only been noted among researchers, but also among policy makers who have integrated efforts aimed at increasing parent involvement into broader educational policy initiatives."[29]

However, only eleven years later, in November 2021, Virginia gubernatorial candidate Democrat Terry McAuliffe said, "I don't think parents should be telling schools what they should teach."[30] The remark was offhand and, as McAuliffe would later tell it, the audience applauded it.[31]

But parents across the state heard something very different, and they responded at the ballots. When Republican Glenn Youngkin won that gubernatorial election in Virginia, the outcome was widely seen as revenge of the parents. Youngkin's win represented an answer to the question: who do the children belong to? McAuliffe's brazen attempt to cut the parents out of the education process had shocked even liberal parents into action.

It's not a new concept to separate children from parents for the purpose of indoctrination. It was just shocking that it was being attempted so openly in America.

A good friend of ours, who, like so many we talked to for this book, requested to remain anonymous, offered a cutting analysis of this woke attack on the family: "The effort to sow gender and racial confusion among little kids, and to impose on little kids a bunch of theories and ways of looking at the world that are totally unnatural and at odds with what little kids understand around them, should be situated I think as part of the leftist mission to destroy the nuclear family. The Left hates normalcy because normalcy is happy and bourgeois and resists change and revolution, and the great enforcer of normalcy in a society is the family. It takes men off the streets and domesticates them in homes, caring for wives and children. It creates sacred bonds and loyalties between people that come before politics, the state, or anyone's ideology. . . . And the Left hates this. Passionately. So, their new attack on the normalcy of the family is to convince six-year-olds not to believe what they see. You have a penis, but really, you're a girl. You see mommy and daddy, but really there's no such categories and instead there's a gender spectrum." What does this woke attack on the family dynamic do to the children?

Our friend continues, "Kids are left confused and damaged by this. And that's what the Left wants. Both because they hate it when kids see normalcy as normal and because they know that the revolution will fail unless they can build a large class of people in our society who believe that they hate the way things are and that it would be good to tear down established ways of living. Promoting alienation and grievance has always been a central part of the groundwork for leftist revolution."[32]

＼ In Mao's China, for example, kids were instrumental in pushing the totalitarian state. In a 1995 piece for the *Los Angeles Times*, writer Rone Tempest lays out how the family stood in the way of that: "The late Chinese leader Mao Tse-tung, although himself a member of a strong Hunanese family clan, realized that political reform was not possible unless people placed the interests of the state above those of the family, which up to that point had been by far the most powerful institution in China . . . Communist leaders were instructed to 'draw a clear line' between themselves and their families. During the Cultural Revolution, youths were encouraged to love Chairman Mao more than their parents and were sent to the countryside to learn from the peasants. Parents were attacked by their own children in struggle sessions. Collective daycare centers became the norm."[33]

Indoctrination was happening at every stage of childhood. Little Red Guards were the children of China's Communist Party, foot soldiers in the idea that the state should be paramount. This devotion amounted to children turning in their parents. Zhang Hongbing was sixteen when he turned in his mother for criticizing Chairman Mao. "He called for her to be shot as a counter-revolutionary," Tania Branigan of *The Guardian* writes. "He last saw her as she knelt on stage in the hours before her death."[34]

In the Soviet Union, the Communists kept trying to push the idea that family was secondary to the state. Communist youth groups were a staple of Soviet Russia. Children would become "Little Octobrists" at seven years old, "Young Pioneers" at nine, and at fourteen they would join the Komsomol, short for Kommunisticheskiy Soyuz Molodyozhi, or Communist Soviet Youth.

Kids were taught to be like the hero child Pavlik Morozov, who had discovered his father was hoarding grain and informed on him to the authorities. This propaganda tale was told to children to illustrate expectations, but according to a *Los Angeles Times* piece from 2002, the story wasn't, as many believed, entirely made up. There was a real boy named Pavlik whose death was repurposed as a heroic tale: "Pavlik's story wasn't really a fairy tale, though. A real 13-year-old boy named Pavel Morozov was killed along with his little brother on the outskirts of this Siberian village on Sept. 3, 1932. Four members of his family—his grandfather, grandmother, cousin and godfather—were convicted of the murders in a show trial two months later and shot. Within weeks of his death, Pavlik became a powerful icon in the new pantheon of Communist saints, a child-martyr worshiped for his feat of heroism: informing on his father."[35]

Statues of Pavlik were erected all over Russia. Poems and songs were written about him. He was referred to as Pioneer #001.[36] Children were taught to be like Pavlik, to put the state above all, even their family. *Especially* their family. It was an understandably powerful lesson. Do the right thing, listen to authority, believe what we believe, act how we want you to act, and you will be celebrated like Pavlik. Don't, and you'll end up in a ditch like his accused family members.

Writing on the *Forbes* magazine site about her Soviet childhood, Katya Soldak recalls, "As part of our school curriculum, we discussed the young martyr, praising his bravery and loyalty to communism, absorbing his story through poems and schoolbooks." Soldak believed the propaganda and would write poems to the great leader Vladimir Ilyich Lenin. A year before the collapse of the Soviet Union, Soldak was feeling jaded. Things were not going as swimmingly as they had to pretend they were. "One day, moved by the rebellious sentiment in the air, I arrived at school without my Red Pioneer tie. Had I been a lousy pupil, that might not have been such a big deal to our teachers. But in the seventh grade, I had a reputation as a straight A-student and an activist, and my teacher publicly lynched me in order to teach others a lesson. 'You are a flaky, slimy person,' the teacher repeatedly told me in front of the entire class. 'Your mother and your aunt were good, trustworthy individuals,' (they had attended the same school) 'but you didn't take after them,' the teacher

continued. '. . . You are a traitor.' You have betrayed our Pioneer organization, our Fatherland, the teacher said."[37]

As Soldak's story illustrates, stepping out of line is always severely
punished under totalitarianism. It has to be. If someone is seen as
doing their own thing—being independent, thinking for themselves—it might lead to others doing the same, and a breakdown of
society will follow.

Soldak also describes the erasing of history she experienced in Soviet
schools: "The Soviet version of history omits many facts: the Holocaust,
various famines, massacres, labor camps, mass executions, as well as
this agreement between Stalin and Hitler. Since Soviet textbooks never
mentioned the pact, I and many other young people in the USSR grew
to adulthood before learning of its existence. For the people of the
Soviet Union, World War II started on June 22, 1941, when Hitler invaded the USSR and the Great Patriotic war began."[38]

The erasing of problematic aspects of the past is a typical feature of
those seeking to stifle dissent. If we have nothing in common, no shared
experiences or familiar rituals and ideas, we are easier to sway and
control. One feature of this is that what we believed in the recent past
can no longer be allowed. Words we used or ideas we held must be discarded, and anyone who doesn't comply is suspect.

During the Cultural Revolution in China, launched in 1966 and
lasting a decade, leadership erased anything of the former culture. Arts
and music had to be specifically socialist in nature. Denunciation of
anyone disobeying was common. According to Christian Caryl writing
in *Foreign Policy* magazine, "A central part of the Cultural Revolution
was Mao Zedong's campaign against intellectualism, book learning, and
the 'Four Olds' (old habits, old ideas, old customs, and old culture)."[39]
Kathrin Hille writes in the *Financial Times* about Mao Zedong's cultural
revolution, "Several former Red Guards, those who followed Mao's ral-
lying cry to destroy China's traditional culture and build a new socialist
society, have publicly apologised during the past few months for turning
against their teachers, cadres and even their own families. But this

remains an exception."[40] When the past gets erased, it's rare that that erasure is acknowledged at all.

In Cambodia, Pol Pot and the Khmer Rouge took power in the mid-1970s and restarted history at "year zero." A 2019 Reuters piece described the mission: "The extremist ideology of the 1975-79 regime sought to turn Cambodia back to 'year zero' in its quest for a peasant utopia."[41] That utopia always requires destruction of the past. Children, again, were the main target. The British government's Holocaust Memorial Day Trust website describes the Khmer Rouge ideologies: "In order to enforce loyalty to the state, the Khmer Rouge broke peoples' ties to religion and family. All political and civil rights were abolished. Formal education ceased and from January 1977, all children from the age of eight were separated from their parents and placed in labour camps, which taught them that the state was their 'true' parents. For the Khmer Rouge, children were central to the revolution as they believed they could be easily moulded, conditioned and indoctrinated. They could be taught to obey orders, become soldiers and kill enemies. Children were taught to believe that anyone not conforming to the Khmer laws were corrupt enemies."[42] The denouncements came fast and furious. Kids learned that some people were in and others were out. They learned to fear being caught on the wrong side of that line, lest they be erased from history too.

This history erasure has come to America. In January of 2021, at the height of the pandemic and with schools still closed across the city, the San Francisco Board of Education decided by a vote of 6-1 to rename many of the city's public schools. As the Associated Press reported, "The approved resolution calls for removing names that honored historical figures with direct or broad ties to slavery, oppression, racism or the 'subjugation' of human beings. In addition to Washington and Thomas Jefferson—former presidents who owned slaves—the list includes naturalist John Muir, Spanish priest Junipero Serra, American Revolution patriot Paul Revere and Francis Scott Key, composer of the 'Star Spangled Banner.'" It also included Democratic

Senator Dianne Feinstein. Her crime wasn't exactly clear. An Associated Press article about the schools' name changes notes that Feinstein "embraced Republican Sen. Lindsey Graham at the end of heated confirmation hearings for U.S. Supreme Court Judge Amy Coney Barrett" but also "replaced a vandalized Confederate flag that was part of a longstanding flag display in front of City Hall. When the flag was pulled down a second time, she did not replace it." "I want to ensure people this in no way cancels or erases history," San Francisco Board of Education President Gabriela Lopez said, while doing exactly that.[43]

This isn't the only way leftists across the country have attempted to delete anything uncomfortable or imperfect in American history. Christopher Columbus was an Italian voyager, funded by Spanish royalty, who crossed the Atlantic on four separate occasions at a time when that seemed impossible. But in new woke America, he does not get credit for discovering the new world (since he never landed in what today would be the United States) while somehow still getting all the blame for the displacement and killing of Native Americans. At least thirty-three Christopher Columbus statues in the United States have been removed, including one in Columbus, Ohio, a city named after the explorer which, as of yet, has not been renamed.[44] Many states no longer celebrate Columbus Day and instead celebrate Indigenous Peoples' Day or a combination of both days. It's unclear why Indigenous People would want to share a day with Columbus if he is responsible for their displacement and destruction, but much about woke culture continues to escape logic.

It's not just Columbus, of course. In the riots after the George Floyd killing, removing Confederate statues was the order of the day, but plenty of non-Confederates were dragged in along with them. Several statues of George Washington were torn down[45] or defaced,[46] and Thomas Jefferson's statue was torn down in Portland, Oregon.[47] Statues of Abraham Lincoln and Theodore Roosevelt were removed or defaced.[48] All of them are terrible, but the last two make no sense at all. Lincoln is widely credited with ending slavery, and Roosevelt is unrelated to slavery or the Confederacy at all. But when history cleansing gets going, it's hard to stop it.

Woke politicians and institutions didn't want to be left out of the action, so they began their own decontamination. Thomas Jefferson's bust was removed after a century in New York's City Hall.[49] An "equestrian monument to [Theodore] Roosevelt, which has stirred protests as a symbol of colonialism and racism," as described by the *New York Times*, was removed from the American Museum of Natural History in New York City because the statue also featured a Native American leading Roosevelt's horse.[50]

Boston took down an Abraham Lincoln statue with a freed slave at his feet. It didn't matter that, as NPR reported, "The statue, which stood in Park Square since 1879, is a copy of Thomas Ball's monument that still stands in Washington, DC's Lincoln Park. The original work, which came to be known as the Emancipation Group, was purchased through donations by freed enslaved people and black veterans of the Union Army. A copy was then erected in Boston, Ball's hometown."[51] Former slaves had wanted this statue displayed, but they were no match for the "everything is offensive" wokesters of today. The statues were deemed unacceptable and problematic by today's purified standards, so they had to go.

Across the country, statues of George Floyd popped up. His imperfections were not up for debate. His brutal death, captured on video, had shocked Americans. We had united in disgust and grief over what had happened to him, but even that unity, in our totalitarian-mimicking moment, was simply not enough. "Black lives matter" is an idea as uncontroversial as "the Earth is round." But because everyone already agreed with it, it couldn't simply be believed. You had to put a sign in your window to signal support for an idea that everyone already favored. You had to imagine there were people to convert to the cause, those who didn't believe strongly enough or didn't use the exact right words like "anti-racist" to describe it. And you had to badger them into walking the very narrow line of acceptable speech on the issue, lest you not be fully identified as an "ally."

It wasn't just statues either. In March of 2021, as we'll explore later in the book, the estate of Dr. Seuss pulled six books from future publication due to potentially offensive images. Dr. Seuss Enterprises released a statement saying, "These books portray people in ways that are hurtful and wrong."[52] The books were outdated because some of them were from the late 1930s.[53] Not only were the books pulled from Amazon and big box stores, but secondhand versions were suddenly not available on eBay.[54] It was full erasure.

It had all been done before.

This conformist culture, and the idea that you have to be active in finding someone doing wrong somewhere, requires new pressure points, and so it must keep spreading. Part of this is because the signature features of wokeness are conformity and spectacle. There are correct positions, correct words, correct behaviors, correct responses. But the more outlandish the accusation, and the more normal people you can get to agree with it, the better.

Tyrannical societies have always demanded conformity and spectacle in the same way. Aron died in that gulag, but his family had to learn to endure. When Stalin's death was announced, Aron's two daughters immediately got to work making a scrapbook of Stalin's glorious life. They were no fools. The spectacle was survival.

It's not surprising, then, that much of our current woke thought has its origins in Marxist thought. The ideology of Karl Marx, a foundation of Soviet society, focused on the struggle within organizational structures and power systems. It's these exact ideas that teachers are force-fed at their universities before passing these concepts onto our children. The same failed ideas from over a hundred years ago are circulating in our schools today—ideas involving spectacle and conformity.

But the problem of wokeism isn't just conformity; it's acceptance to that conformity. It's also the consequences parents face for daring to object. The Joe Biden administration, for example, used the Justice Department to target parents who spoke up at school board meetings. The National School Board Association sent a letter to the Justice Department saying parents at these meetings "could be the equivalent to a form of domestic terrorism."[55] The attorney general, in turn, directed the FBI to investigate "a disturbing spike in harassment, intimidation and threats of violence against school administrators, board members, teachers and staff who participate in the vital work of running our nation's public schools."[56] Be quiet, parents, or we will get you.

This enforced conformity also extended to a number of issues around COVID-19 policies. When schools stayed closed, mostly in Democratic strongholds across the country, and it became clear that the closures were entirely political and not scientific, parents in these blue areas did not feel like they could speak out, lest someone mistake them for being aligned with the "wrong" side. Some were afraid for their jobs, that someone would call their boss and inform on them for supporting something that was the standard in other countries around the world, but many others were simply afraid of reputational damage. To want schools open meant that you were on the wrong team. That was even more important than your own children's well-being.

Woke compliance is easier to instill in children than in adults. Adults have fully formed personalities, if not opinions, and it's much harder to cow them into obedience. Wokeness is black and white, right and wrong—exactly the kind of thing that appeals to children and why they are so susceptible to being brainwashed in the name of wokeness.

What does raising children to be woke do to their value system and inherent sense of curiosity? Childhood anxiety and mental health challenges are at all-time highs.[57] Is it any wonder, when we're teaching children to be anxious?

In December of 2021, Elon Musk told the satirical website, the *Babylon Bee*, "At its heart, wokeness is divisive, exclusionary and hateful. It basically gives mean people a shield to be mean and cruel, armored in false virtue."[58] When you aim that behavior at children, it teaches them never to speak up or speak out unless they do so along authorized lines. It stunts their creativity and intelligence and creates malleable robots who parrot what they are told.

The encroachment of leftism into every single facet of American life, from academia to Hollywood to corporate boardrooms, has been going on for decades. But wokeism is something novel. Wokeism demands subservience and conformity. There is only one correct answer to any given question. Any stepping outside the lines, any questioning of official positions, gets you kicked off the team. Curiosity is discouraged. It is leftism on steroids, and it is taking over everything. It's important to remember that, just like wokesters say they're actually fighting racism, sexism, anti-LGBTQ+, etc., so, too, did the totalitarians throughout history say they were enforcing their will on the people for the people's own good. No one ever says they're going to remake society for the worse. Every tyrant believes they are doing good. That's why it's so important to recognize the pattern. The leaders of the Soviet Union told my parents they were going to usher in a more impartial, just, equitable world. Many people had to die, my great-grandfather among them, for that cause.

The United States is not a totalitarian country. We elect our leadership. We can criticize our government. But the forced conformity of unfree countries has arrived at our shores, and wannabe totalitarians are enforcing it with zeal. Everything is being politicized, just like in totalitarian countries. We're in danger, and our kids are in danger. It might not be government agencies enforcing sameness *yet*, but it is enforced just the same.

The narrow wokeness of our time is boxing us in while removing our shared understanding of history. Ideological purity necessitates destroying the past, and it's happening in the U.S. today just as it has happened in places like China. How can anyone fully embrace Maoist ideas when they may have believed competing ideas in the past? No growth or change can be permitted, only a restart.

The past isn't that far away. Totalitarian-forced conformity isn't just something from long ago. In China today, the Chinese Communist Party (CCP) makes sure that its message is central in all of the arts. The China Media Project, which conducts "specialized research and engagement around developments in the Chinese media landscape"[59] at the University of Hong Kong's Journalism and Media Studies Centre, describes this as the "main melody."[60] "The term 'main melody,' or zhu xuanlü (主旋律), is frequently found in contemporary Chinese Communist Party discourse to describe activity in the cultural sphere, including media and journalism, that sticks to the main political line of the CCP. Emerging in the 1980s to refer to developments in film, the phrase can now refer more generally to the need to ensure the Party's voice is dominant in media and the arts, and leads the chorus."[61]

A "main melody" has appeared in so many different facets of American life: one tune, one chord. Once you hear the melody, you start noticing it everywhere.

It's why cancel culture has accompanied wokeness on its ascent. One error or misplaced word can easily harm a child's life forever. In December of 2020, the *New York Times* featured a story by Dan Levin called "A Racial Slur, a Viral Video, and a Reckoning." In it, an eighteen-year-old sociopath, Jimmy Galligan, is allowed to destroy the life of a classmate, Mimi Groves, for using a racial slur when she was fifteen years old. Groves had not directed the slur at anyone but had used it for excited emphasis upon getting her driver's license. Galligan held on to the video until the time when it would do the most damage: "'I wanted to get her where she would understand the severity of that word,' Mr. Galligan, 18, whose mother is black and father is white, said of the classmate who uttered the slur, Mimi Groves. He tucked the video away, deciding to post it publicly when the time was right." And get her, he did. Levin notes, "Ms. Groves, in a public Instagram post, urged people to 'protest, donate, sign a petition, rally, do something' in support of the Black Lives Matter movement."[62] It didn't matter. She had sinned against the gods of woke, and she would be punished.

The *New York Times* running a story about non-famous teenagers is the same kind of ideological policing done by totalitarians: behave how we want or we pummel you. Groves was kicked off her cheerleading squad and withdrew from attending the University of Tennessee after immense pressure.

It was not enough that Galligan got to be the hero of the *New York Times* story. He was also a Pavlik, proudly denouncing his family for the cause. Levin writes, "Shortly after his 18th birthday in July, Mr. Galligan asked his father, a former law enforcement officer, what he thought about white privilege. 'The first thing he said to me is that it doesn't exist,' Mr. Galligan recalled. He then asked his father if he had ever been scared while walking at night, or while reaching into the glove box after getting pulled over by the police. He said his father had not. 'That is your white privilege,' Mr. Galligan said he told hi[s father]."[63]

We have always been a very second-chance country, liking nothing more than "the comeback," whether by a fallen Hollywood star or a bankrupt businessman. But this new woke religion does not have a mechanism for forgiveness or compassion. There are no do-overs. People get canceled with speedy efficiency, a drastic departure from traditional American values and beliefs.

Interestingly, loneliness is often a precursor to totalitarianism. In her 1951 book *The Origins of Totalitarianism*, Hannah Arendt writes, "What prepares men for totalitarian domination in the non-totalitarian world is the fact that loneliness, once a borderline experience usually suffered in certain marginal social conditions like old age, has become an everyday experience of the ever-growing masses of our century."[64] In many ways, our society has moved in the direction of segmentation, with loneliness being the effect of today's world.

America is ripe for totalitarianism because of this, just like the societies Arendt covers. In writing about Arendt's book in his own 2020 book *Live Not by Lies*, Rod Dreher notes, "The political theorist wrote those words in the 1950s, a period we look back on as a golden age of community cohesion. Today, loneliness is widely recognized by scientists as a critical social and even medical problem."[65] We are told we have nothing in common with each other and no shared culture. We move ever further away from each other and pretend there is no bond between us.

Even worse, our kids are led to believe they have nothing in common with their fellow countrymen. The message is that nothing about

America or its founding should be celebrated. No American history may be acknowledged as respectable. Wokeness mocks the idea of American greatness. Everything about us is bad. Christopher Columbus is bad. George Washington is bad. We can no longer celebrate our first president.

Certain schools across the country have cut out the Pledge of Allegiance. My own kids did not say it at their public schools in Brooklyn, despite it being New York State law for schools to say it daily. It seems like a small thing and, after all, aren't we concerned about the state enforcing sameness? But saying the Pledge is not mandatory.[66] If a child chooses not to, their parents will not be dragged before a tribunal. It is the wonder of free countries that patriotism can come so naturally and without coercion. But it is coercion of a different kind when schools separate the children from their country.

When I learned my children were no longer saying it at their school in Brooklyn, I wrote a letter to the school asking them to reinstate it. I was told that because the school had kids from many cultures, they did not want anyone to feel left out. I was born in the Soviet Union, and the Pledge of Allegiance was the first English I learned. Saying it with my classmates as an immigrant child growing up in Brooklyn made me feel like I was a part of something. Wokeness shuns patriotism, teaching that our American experiment is not worth celebrating, that only our individual races and past cultures matter.

American traditions are in trouble too. Columbus Day went first, but the attack on Thanksgiving has been brewing for years. It's already not an idea limited to the fringe. "Revisiting the racist history behind Thanksgiving"[67] was on the liberal website *Salon* in 2018, but by 2020 "Why I'm Not Celebrating Thanksgiving This Year" was in *Vogue*.[68] The Fourth of July will be on the chopping block at some point too. A July 2021 piece in *USA Today* was originally titled, "4th of July: What to do if you're not feeling proud to be American," and was later changed to: "Are You Ambivalent about Celebrating July 4? You're Not Alone."[69] These leftist ideals are ripping through American history, and it is the Left who is doing the pushing.

Totalitarianism only works if there is a single ruling party. To get people to join, membership has to come with benefits. Among those benefits is the ability to lord your status over others. It's OK, preferable even, if there are different rules for different people. Membership has its privileges, as the old American Express commercial goes. In September of 2020, Alexandria Ocasio-Cortez said that following a Biden win in November, "I need folks to realize that there's no going back to brunch. We have a whole new world to build."[70] By saying there's no going back to brunch, Ocasio-Cortez signals that no time can be taken off from fighting for the leftist cause, but she, herself, lives a lavish life of luxury. The picture of her at the Met Gala, where a ticket costs over $30,000, in which she wore a dress that had "tax the rich" printed on the back and was unmasked despite all the servants around her wearing masks, did more to illustrate the privileges of the elite than anything could.[71] You're not going back to brunch, but she is.

The fight for our children is a fight against this exact collectivism. Your child is your child. Totalitarians will always try to sever that tie.

A September 2021 CNBC piece worried that kids had spent the pandemic at home with conspiracy-theorist parents and that schools would have to un-brainwash them: "It's bad enough that kids are exposed to dangerous untruths across their favorite social media apps like Facebook, YouTube and TikTok. An equally large problem is that, while stuck at home during the pandemic, many students had their days of virtual schooling interrupted by screaming parents, who themselves had fallen deep into the internet's darkest rabbit holes."[72] The article bemoans the increased influence of parents, as if schools and parents have some sort of shared custody over these children and the parents had somehow managed to inflict more of their ideas on their children during their pandemic time together.

As President Joe Biden said in late April 2022, "They're all our children. They're not somebody else's children. They're like yours [the teacher's] when they're in the classroom."[73] But that's simply untrue. My children have had some terrific teachers, but my children still belong to me—not to their teachers and not to society at large.

Parents have to start drawing a sharp line when it comes to their kids. Our children belong to us. The home is where we teach our children to stand up for themselves and learn they don't have to hide their true beliefs. There are a lot of jokes about "safe spaces," a term that hit the popular lexicon when colleges began providing rooms with Play-Doh and crayons where students, the majority young adults, could hide from controversial opinions.

But a real safe space is somewhere that kids can feel free to be themselves, to get things wrong and learn from mistakes.

Your kids must be able to question the ideas they've heard out in the world, and you must be ready to vocalize your principles. Kids don't pick up values by osmosis; we have to impart values. They're being assaulted by a culture that verbalizes a lot of different, often contradictory, beliefs. It will be impossible to counter that barrage of propagandistic information with limited rebuttal or by thinking that your children will simply pick up what you believe by being near you. They have to hear you articulate what matters most.

They also have to see you fight.

Take courage: wins are not impossible, even in the bluest of American areas. In 2017, 1,600 parents signed a petition in Palo Alto, California, voicing their disapproval of a sex education class that included lessons for middle-school students on "hooking up" and "sex toys."[74] This is not some red town. The "birthplace of Silicon Valley," Palo Alto has five times as many Democrats as Republicans. The school board heard the complaints of the parents and still decided not to make any changes to the curriculum whatsoever. There was an agenda to push, and they pushed it.

But the parents didn't give up. In February of 2022, three ultra-Left members of the San Francisco all-Democrat school board were recalled in a landslide election in a rebuke over the school-renaming fiasco. According to the Associated Press, "Parents in the politically liberal city launched the recall effort in January 2021 out of frustration over the slow reopening of district schools, while the board pursued the renaming of 44 school sites and the elimination of competitive admissions at the elite Lowell High School."[75] Closed schools, woke renaming, and a destruction of merit: even liberal parents in this far-Left city had had enough.

Parents have to treat wokeism being forced on their children similarly to how they might treat a religion being dictated to them. The options are to remove the child from the place where wokeness is being prescribed—not an easy thing to do when wokeness has taken over so much of our culture—or to make their home life a deprogramming effort.

My mother told me that, in the Soviet Union, her parents would not dare contradict what she had learned in school. They had to reinforce things they knew to be untrue, or they would be in danger. Worse, their child would be in danger. They parroted what would keep the family safe. We're in a dangerous moment today in America, but we have not reached dire times like these yet. Speaking up might get you nasty Facebook messages or, more seriously, a call to your boss. But it's a necessity now to protect your children and say what you know to be true.

The home is the last line of defense. In totalitarian societies, parents have to pretend to believe the lies that kids are taught at school, lest they make themselves or their children a target. In a free country, you don't have to do that. You can and should explain to children that life isn't black and white and that America's history is complicated, just like any other country's history. You can and should reassert the morals that matter in your family. You can and should teach your child to be himself or herself and not be coerced into other people's opinions.

Whose kid is this? In the home, you provide the answer: mine.

2

WOKENESS IN THE TIME OF PANDEMIC

The tentacles of wokeness have gripped onto everything, and the COVID-19 pandemic only sped up the politicization and enforced sameness. Schools being closed during COVID was an egregious example of the wokest groupthink.

In March 2020, when COVID-19 first hit American shores, schools began to close their doors. On March 5, 2020, the Northshore School District in Washington State was the first to move to remote learning. On March 12, Ohio became the first state to close schools statewide. Other states quickly followed.

In New York City, already the epicenter of the pandemic, Mayor Bill de Blasio was reticent to close schools. The hapless mayor, known for showing up late for his news conferences and for his general incompetence, did, however, have a pulse on the societal importance of public schools. New York City schools are a point of many services for families in the five boroughs, and the mayor understood this acutely. Many poor children have breakfast and lunch at school, and after-school programs allow parents to work after the school day ends. Schools provide a backbone for society and a safety net for children.

On March 13, the mayor said that closing down schools should clear "a very high bar" and warned that if they "shut down the school system, you might not see it for the rest of the school year, you might not see the beginning of the new school year," which he said would weigh on him "heavily."[1] He was right. It turned out that closing down the school system and then reopening it again would be a giant challenge. *Politico* reported, "He resisted calls to close schools as he fretted about the displacement of more than 1 million students—in particular, those relying on free meals and other social services. One former aide vented over the weekend that his posture stemmed from his resentment toward wealthy people, who were particularly vocal in their criticism" likely because they were hearing from friends abroad about the measures taken in other countries.[2]

Two days later, on Sunday evening, March 15, in anticipation of a dangerous pandemic hitting the city, Mayor de Blasio made the call to close America's largest education system. And then on Monday, March 16, he took his chauffeured car to his favorite gym in Park Slope, Brooklyn, eleven miles from his Gracie Mansion mayoral home, a perfect encapsulation of the way grown-ups found a way to continue living their lives during the COVID-19 era, but children's lives were to be paused indefinitely.

In May of 2020, New York's then-Governor Andrew Cuomo released a four-phase plan for reopening the state. In the very last phase, dead last on the list, were schools.[3] His defenders would say that the placement made sense because it would be months before the start of the next school year. But it was clear to those of us watching that this wasn't about time; rather, it was about priority. Schools simply didn't matter. Children simply didn't matter.

For a minute there, it even seemed like the governor was ready to make physical schooling a thing of the past. In that same month, Cuomo announced the state would be partnering with Microsoft founder Bill Gates to "reimagine education" and floated the idea that maybe remote school was the future. As reported in the *Washington Post*, Cuomo said, "The old model of everybody goes and sits in the classroom, and the teacher is in front of that classroom and teaches that class, and you do that all across the city, all across the state, all these buildings, all these physical classrooms—why, with all the technology you have?"[4] As Valerie Strauss noted in the *Washington Post* at the time of this announcement, "The Bill & Melinda Gates Foundation has spent billions of dollars on education reform projects it has conceded did not work as hoped."[5] It turns out kids need actual interaction, in actual classrooms, in order to learn.

While Cuomo was busy reimagining education without actual schools, the governor had also held off on making the decision as to whether day camps could open for the summer of 2020. Camps in neighboring states, like Connecticut, had already outlined guidance on summer camps but Governor Cuomo refused to. When New York Rep. Elise Stefanik sent Cuomo a letter pushing for that guidance, he responded with an entirely nonsensical comment about funding. "What you can say to Rep. Elise Stefanik and all of our great Washington representatives, we could provide rental assistance for people who can't pay rent, we could provide child care for essential workers now. You know what it takes? Money. Funding. Money."[6] But it didn't take money to open camps at all. It took will. The governor simply didn't have it where children were concerned.

The practical concerns—and mental health—of children and their parents simply were not considered. How was the economy to reopen if there was no childcare in the form of summer camp? It was an obvious question, but no one in the media was asking it. Governor Cuomo was COVID's conquering hero. He had been a steady voice early in the pandemic, giving daily briefings in a calm, reassuring manner. But much of it was a very good facade. He made many terrible mistakes in his handling of the COVID crisis and was a foe to anyone wanting normalcy for kids.

Cuomo's media coverage was all soft-focus. Who was he dating? Would he run for president? It was the perfect storm of a Left-leaning media celebrating and covering for a Left-leaning politician. No one would step out of line.

It would be another month before his highness Governor Cuomo would reopen playgrounds for kids. Parks had stayed open the entire pandemic. Beaches had reopened on Memorial Day weekend. But

kids had to wait until mid-June to see their playgrounds again because they weren't "safe."

Yet, after George Floyd was killed by a police officer in Minneapolis,
Minnesota, and protests spread throughout the country, all of the
pandemic rules set for society were simply discarded. Did we need to
stay indoors? Did we need to mask? Did we need to socially distance?
It appeared not. Worse still, medical experts assured us that we did
still need to do these things—unless we were protesting. By the
middle of June, large protests were taking place nightly in many cities.
Parents watched in horror and anger as the idea of their children returning to school that fall seemed impossible, yet massive protests
were happening every single night. It was wokeness taken to its
natural conclusion, and it didn't need to make sense. Dan Diamond in
Politico wrote, "For months, public health experts have urged Americans to take every precaution to stop the spread of Covid-19—stay at
home, steer clear of friends and extended family, and absolutely avoid
large gatherings. Now some of those experts are broadcasting a new
message: It's time to get out of the house and join the mass protests
against racism."[7]

More than 1,200 health professionals signed a letter indicating that
protesting was important and an exception to the pandemic guidelines.
"However, as public health advocates, we do not condemn these gatherings as risky for COVID-19 transmission. We support them as vital to
the national public health and to the threatened health specifically of
Black people in the United States. We can show that support by facili-
tating safest protesting practices without detracting from demon-
strators' ability to gather and demand change."[8] Not all protests, of
course: "This should not be confused with a permissive stance on all
gatherings, particularly protests against stay-home orders."[9]

It was the moment a lot of people realized that science was not
guiding the pandemic response and decisions were being made on a
wholly political basis. At this point, playgrounds were still closed in
many cities, basketball hoops in parks removed or covered up, and all

other communal activities suspended. Logically, either the pandemic was serious enough that we all remain indoors, with very specific harm being caused to children, or it was not. The woke managed another option where their allies, and only their allies, got an exception.

When the protests died down and it was time to return the kids to school, those same medical professionals were absent from the public conversation. Social justice meant repeating leftist talking points, and leftists did not want schools to open. But at the end of September, after two last-minute delays, New York schools did open.

New York was seen as a national model of school reopening, heralded as a success story by a compliant media: "The New York City public school system, the largest school district in the country, has so far been able to reopen for in-person instruction without a massive outbreak of coronavirus cases. Aside from New York City, the remaining nine of the nation's top 10 school districts started their school years online. New York's preliminary success could potentially serve as a resource for other districts embarking on a return to in-person learning," praised Annie Grayer at CNN.[10] Grayer particularly focused on the testing that was somehow helping the schools stay open. How, exactly, the opt-in testing, which randomly tested 10-20 percent of the students and staff per month, would help was unclear.

They also implemented a routine of sanitizing rooms after someone was quarantined for COVID and, of course, mandatory masking.[11] Mayor de Blasio was very optimistic. "The proof is in the results, and these are amazing results," he said, concluding that this "bodes well for the future of our schools and our ability to fight and overcome this disease."[12] What it actually showed was that New York's seasonal COVID-19 spike wouldn't happen for another two months. But that was unclear in September of 2020 when New York City public schools opened their doors. They did it! Kids were back in school. Kind of.

Most elementary schools in New York City operated on a hybrid model where kids went to school one to two days one week and two to three days the next. The rest of the time, the kids were home doing remote learning. New York City also provided an all-remote option for people who were too afraid to send their kids in person.

The days that students were home, parents were expected to oversee their remote studies. It's hard to convey just how difficult this was and how thin parents were stretched. Parent boards were filled with growing desperation, as evidenced by posts from parents who admitted to frequently crying stress tears.

In our house we had lists of passwords and schedules for each child. We were doing the best we could, but there were days when my husband and I would be busy with our own work, so the kids' schooling would have to come second. The dining room table was the workstation for our sons. Sometimes Google Classroom worked. Sometimes it didn't. Sometimes Zoom worked. Sometimes it didn't. There was yelling. In between the fairly rare live remote lessons, kids had at-home assignments. Our then-fifth grader didn't have a problem doing them on her own, though the solitude of being alone in her room all day every day certainly took a toll, but our then-second grader and then-kindergartner needed a lot of assistance. There was one day our second grader was told to let us know that the kindergartner had somehow gotten his Physical Education schedule mixed up and had been participating in a P.E. class with fourth graders. I didn't see how it mattered who else was on the screen as he ran laps around the dining room table.

I considered quitting my job. I loved being a columnist at the *New York Post*, but my kids were failing. Women across the country were reporting the same. Female employment dropped. I'd seethe when I saw headlines like "Pandemic Will 'Take Our Women 10 Years Back' in the Workplace" in the *New York Times*[13] or "How the Pandemic Set Back Women's Progress in the Global Workforce" in the *Washington Post*.[14] What did they imagine would happen to women when they indefinitely closed the schools? It wasn't even about childcare. Not really. The kids were failing, and moms weren't going to stand for it.

Only conservative media were pushing for schools to reopen. In February of 2022, *Fortune* reported, "The January jobs report found that

275,000 women left the workforce last month, leaving the women's workplace participation rate at 57%—a rate that pre-pandemic had not been seen since 1988. An entire generation of progress has been erased in two years."[15]

I was writing about the mostly closed schools regularly, and I'd get so much mail from other desperate parents that I felt like I had to keep going. But I also had to focus on saving my kids more immediately. I looked up school districts in Florida. I found a public school called Marsh Pointe Elementary that sounded terrific and could take all three of our kids for in-person learning. In January of 2021, we rented a two-bedroom apartment in Palm Beach Gardens, Florida, an area we'd never even heard of before, and moved our kids down to a state with open schools. It wasn't a forever move. We kept our home in Brooklyn. It was more like a test run and a way to save our children.

I knew that my kids going to part-time school and staring at a screen the rest of the time was untenable. I remembered what we believed about screen time pre-pandemic, which was conveniently pushed to the side when schools closed. A 2018 study by San Diego State University psychologist Jean Twenge and University of Georgia psychology professor W. Keith Campbell published in *Preventative Medicine Reports* found that "even after only one hour of screen time daily, children and teens may begin to have less curiosity, lower self-control, less emotional stability and a greater inability to finish tasks."[16]

In the 2018 book *The Coddling of the American Mind: How Good Intentions and Bad Ideas Are Setting Up a Generation for Failure*, Greg Lukianoff and Jonathan Haidt focus a lot on the dangers of screen time and how it has broken a generation of kids. The rise of anxiety and mental health issues can all be tied to more screen time. That depression and anxiety lead to all kinds of issues, such as "changes in cognition, including a tendency to see the world as more dangerous and hostile than it really is."[17]

This was a perfect storm during a pandemic. By August of 2021, some studies were showing that, globally, "the prevalence of depression and anxiety symptoms during COVID-19 [had] doubled, compared with pre-pandemic estimates, and moderator analyses revealed that prevalence rates were higher when collected later in the pandemic, in older adolescents, and in girls."[18]

The American Academy of Pediatrics suddenly had nothing to say about nonstop screen time. Pre-pandemic, the AAP was pointing out the dangers of screen time. "Correlational studies have shown that 8- to 11-year-olds who exceed screen time recommendations scored lower on cognitive assessments," they noted.[19] Underprivileged kids generally had more screen time than richer kids who had other options for extracurricular activities, and this was certainly something to worry about, according to the AAP. But in December 2020, the AAP told us that screen time was fine, actually. "There's no need to worry about educational screen time during the pandemic if you arrange breaks between assignments, encourage outdoor play whenever safe and limit daily entertainment screen time to two hours a day or less," they wrote, quoting a pediatric ophthalmologist whose advice also included to "blink often" to prevent dry eyes from staring at a screen all day.[20]

In addition to taking away school, many deep blue areas canceled all or most sports. In October 2020 in the *New York Times*, Kurt Streeter pointed out how much was still closed to kids in Los Angeles: "Recreation centers. Gymnasiums. Many outdoor basketball courts are surrounded by fences and locked gates." Streeter spoke to Tom Farrey, Sports and Society Program director at the Aspen Institute, a nonprofit think tank. Streeter writes, "Farrey said that an already ample opportunity gap has widened. Compared with their counterparts in communities like Watts, middle-class and wealthy families are far more likely to have found ways to work around coronavirus restrictions and keep their children playing."[21]

Aspen Institute also conducted a nationwide study on how youth sports were affected during the pandemic, of which Streeter states, "The study showed that nearly 30 percent of youth who were playing sports before the pandemic were not likely to go back without a major intervention. They've lost interest. Likely, some have lost momentum. Others have probably gotten so used to spending time on screens and video games that getting out on a field and running around seems less appealing."[22]

The irony is that obesity is one of the main comorbidity factors for a poor COVID-19 outcome. We stagnated the lives of children, stripped them of exercise and activity, and actually raised their risk profile for the virus with our "mitigation" methods.

Kids stayed out of school even after adults had started going to dinners and concerts again. Stadiums would be filled with maskless people in crowds watching a football game on Sunday, and toddlers would be masked and distanced at daycare on Monday. COVID-19 had exposed that children had their political purposes but could mostly be overlooked. It was deeply disturbing, and it lasted as long as it did because of the leftist woke pressure from people running the teachers unions, their supporters in politics, and their friends in the media.

We needlessly stuck children on a screen for hours every day in the name of safety, and the result was exactly as we might imagine. Virtual school proved worthless and resulted in "significant learning loss,"[23] according to education experts, while the nonstop screen time "led to an increase in mental health issues, as well as behavioral and attention problems," according to studies.[24] Not to mention the negative impact on physical health due to decreased physical activity.

Worse still, the hybrid model actually did little to make attending school safer for children. It was based on the idea that kids needed to be six feet apart in classrooms to lower the risk of contracting COVID, and so only half the class, or less, could attend on any given day. It didn't ever make sense. By July 2020, we knew COVID was spread via aerosols that could hang in the air for long periods of time, so how could it matter if kids sat three feet apart or six?[25] In January of 2021, Former FDA Commissioner Scott Gottlieb, a regular on TV during the COVID era, admitted that six feet was an invented number. "Nobody knows where it came from. Most people assume that . . . the recommendation for keeping six feet apart, comes out of some old studies related to flu, where droplets don't travel more than six feet," Gottlieb told CBS's *Face the Nation* host Margaret Brennan.[26]

But aerosols are different from droplets. Aerosols hang in the air far longer than droplets and are far tinier. By that point the Biden administration had asked the Centers for Disease Control and Prevention (CDC) to reduce the distance allowed between kids in class from six feet to three feet, so that made questioning the official guidelines acceptable. Gottlieb said the change was based on a study the CDC had conducted in fall of 2020.[27] So they knew throughout the 2020-2021 school year that six feet of distance was a pointless metric but waited until the spring of 2021, when it became politically acceptable to say so, to do anything about it.

The hybrid model was another popular but terribly misguided solution. In a hybrid model, when students are kept out of school for multiple days each week, or every other week, a sizable percentage of them are likely to intermingle with other children and adults. This is especially so for younger kids with working parents, as the kids may need to be in daycare, exposing them to another set of social contacts and all of their possible infections. Meanwhile, older kids and adolescents will be inclined to hang out with their peers on their copious "off" days. In many districts, remote learning plans include just a short amount of livestreamed teaching every day, leaving many hours to fill in other ways, again dispersing kids to have many interactions with people when the idea was to keep those interactions limited.

In August of 2020, *Wired* writer David Zweig interviewed epidemiologists who were pointing out that the hybrid model was the most dangerous.[28] William Hanage, an epidemiologist at Harvard's T.H. Chan School of Public Health, stated, "The hybrid model is probably among the worst that we could be putting forward if our goal is to stop the virus getting into schools." Jennifer Nuzzo, an epidemiologist at Johns Hopkins Bloomberg School of Public Health, stated that the hybrid model "only works if students stay home, alone, during all of that time they are out of school," which is, as Zweig put it, "a strangely unrealistic assumption by policymakers."[29] Their argument was simple: if you want to limit children's and teachers' exposure to infection, it's better to have students spend their time within a consistent group of peers. In that case, it would have made far more sense to send the kids to school full-time and have their interactions be limited to each other. Instead, on the days the kids were not in school, they were dispersed throughout the city, having many other interactions. They might be with a babysitter or with a tutor. Some families formed pods on the off days. Others spent their time at their weekend house. Some kids went to stay with extended family so that their parents could work. It was a disaster for kids and for fighting the virus.

But "strangely unrealistic" could describe much of the school system's COVID-19 response.

New Yorkers were so happy for the crumbs. Their kids went to school sometimes. But at least it was something! Middle and high school in-person time was even more limited. Older kids often went to school once a week, if that, and a lot of times the class was "Zoom in a room." In other words, the teacher would be home and the kids would gather in their classroom to watch him or her on a screen.[30] New York schools were barely open, but New Yorkers did not believe they could voice concerns because their kids were at least getting to go part of the time!

In mid-November 2020, the city's COVID-19 case numbers started to go up. New York had suffered terribly at the start of the pandemic, but when the numbers decreased through the summer and stayed low in the fall, politicians celebrated, and New Yorkers were pleased with themselves for having done everything "right."

The deal that Mayor Bill de Blasio had struck with United Federation of Teachers' head Michael Mulgrew was that New York City public schools would close if the positive testing rate in the city hit 3 percent.[31] The number never made any sense. If ninety-eight healthy people for every one hundred decided to test that day, schools stayed open. But if ninety-seven healthy people decided to test for every one hundred, kids would be thrown into chaos and sent home.

When that magic 3 percent number hit, that's exactly what happened. Schools closed. It would be a month, and the COVID case rate would be far higher at that point, before elementary school kids would get back into the classroom, and many months before it would happen for the older cohort. Middle schools didn't return, even to their one-to-two-day-a-week model, until late February.[32]

This was all somehow seen as a win for New York kids. The media, of course, swallowed this line completely. In February of 2021, Peter Szekely at Reuters wrote about New York's successes in a piece titled "New York Mayor Sees High School Classrooms Reopening in Current Academic Year."[33] High schools were open in many places throughout the country, but the idea that they *might*, someday, reopen in New York City was still seen as a success. Elementary schools were open, still on a hybrid model, and middle schools would reopen on their part-time model soon. The assumption was high school could not be far behind. In reality, it would be mid-March by the time high school students got to return for any classroom time at all, and many high school students stayed fully remote.[34]

As late as October 2021, thousands of kids were still unaccounted for in the New York City school system, simply not showing up. Mulgrew put that number at 180,000 lost kids.[35] And yet, writes Szekely, "The mayor touted the city's school re-opening strategy as a national model, noting that the U.S. Centers for Disease Control 'borrowed heavily from the New York City approach' when it issued its guidelines. At schools with in-class learning, the city requires weekly virus testing, masks, distancing, hand-washing, ventilated spaces and contract tracing—all components of the CDC guidelines, de Blasio said."[36] How could a school system that was mostly closed be a model for anyone? It didn't make any sense. Yet the media was compliant in helping New York seem like a success story.

The celebration of New York's extremely meager achievements made even less sense when contrasted with comparable cities. In countries across Europe, major cities had all managed to open schools and keep them open—full-time—some entirely maskless, and their numbers were similar or lower than our rates.[37] There were plenty of examples of what to do domestically too. Yet the states that had managed to open their schools, Florida and Texas most famously, were only highlighted in a negative way. To celebrate their success would mean that kids in blue areas were missing school for no reason at all.

In fact, kids in blue areas *were* missing school for no reason at all, something the media covered up and protected the political leaders from having to face.

There were solutions that could have given kids the opportunity to go to school in person. If public schools wanted to remain closed, all kids should have had the options that the richer set did. Corey DeAngelis, National Director of Research at the American Federation for Children, told me, "The education battles we've seen bubbling up over the past two years—over in-person learning, curriculum, masking, and other COVID mitigation strategies—are all just symptoms of the larger problem: a one-size-fits-all government school system. Forcing millions of kids into a one-size-fits-all school system is destined to fail because families disagree about how they would like their children educated. Families have differing values and preferences, and that's OK. The government school system forces parents into unnecessary conflict, and at the end of the day, many families are left unhappy with the result. The only way out of this mess, out of this never-ending cycle of chaos, is to fund students directly and empower families to choose the education providers that best meet the needs of their children. At the same time, competition would give the government schools stronger incentives to focus on the needs of families and potentially focus less on divisive concepts in the classroom. School choice is the only way forward with freedom as opposed to force."[38]

When we think back to the early COVID days, it's easy to forgive a lot. We didn't know. How could we know?

But we did know. We knew many things that our leadership refused to accept. A lot of it was basic, simple common sense.

In May of 2020, I wrote a column in the *New York Post* urging people to get outdoors for multiple well-proven reasons. "Several studies," I wrote, "including one out of Northwestern University, found a link between Vitamin D and mortality from COVID-19: 'Not only does Vitamin D enhance our innate immune systems, it also prevents our immune systems from becoming dangerously overactive. This means that having healthy levels of Vitamin D could protect patients against severe complications, including death, from COVID-19.'"[39] We also knew, even in May 2020, that outdoor transmission was rare. In the same May 2020 *New York Post* piece I wrote, "Study after study has shown that the coronavirus is far less transmissible outdoors. Jonathan Van-Tam, England's chief medical officer, said recently, 'There is a definite truism across all of the science literature that ventilation is a most critical part of reducing transmission from respiratory viruses.' And a Yale University study in March found that 'winter's cold, dry air makes such viruses a triple threat.'"[40]

We knew. And yet we kept kids off playgrounds and away from their friends even outdoors. We knew, and yet, as late as winter 2022, New York City schools, and those of many other blue cities across the country, continued to force children into masks even outside. Even when it was clear that the flimsy cloth masks[41] (or even the blue medical ones) did little to nothing to slow the spread of COVID, we insisted on keeping kids masked.[42] It was groupthink of the highest order. To be on the Left meant to believe in masking, even long after we knew that they didn't work.

In February of 2022, following the Omicron variant spike, Democratic governors began announcing they would ease masking restrictions. Governors in Connecticut, Delaware, New Jersey, and Oregon announced they would lift mask mandates in schools.[43] School districts would be free to decide for themselves, and it was clear that the most Left-leaning districts would remain masked.

In New York, California, and Illinois, however, the Democratic governors announced they, too, would be lifting mask mandates—other than in schools. At this point, kids in New York City, Los Angeles, San Francisco, and other major blue cities like Portland, Cleveland, New Orleans, and so on were still masking children *outdoors*. This was ten months after Dr. Anthony Fauci said, "The risk when you're outdoors— which we have been saying all along—is extremely low."[44] Kids were the lowest risk population, yet they certainly weren't treated as such. It made no sense.

No exceptions could be made for kids, either. When politicians were caught maskless, again and again, they would say they had recently been eating or drinking. London Breed, the mayor of San Francisco, was caught violating her own indoor masking mandate at a Tony! Toni! Toné! concert.[45] When asked about it, she seemed offended that she would even need to respond. "Everyone was vaccinated," she said. "And it was Tony! Toni! Toné!'s first live performance in decades. Yes, I danced without a mask. Come on, y'all . . . How can you NOT dance?"[46] Yet kids were not allowed to dance maskless in school even if, as Breed described it, they were "feeling the spirit" and not "thinking about a mask."[47]

The "no exceptions for children" rule was especially cruel for kids with special needs. Speech therapy, for example, had to be conducted through masks. Rachel, a mom from West Orange, New Jersey, found out that her son would need speech therapy on the day before his second birthday. Rachel told me how devastated she was knowing that the very next day he would need to be masked in daycare because Governor Phil Murphy implemented indoor masking for kids two and up. Her son also had a hearing issue. "At fifteen months old, he had an ear infection and the doctor said he might have been having them all along without us knowing. He wasn't speaking. For 40-45 hours a week he was in daycare, and he was not hearing or seeing faces." Eventually, her son got ear tubes put in.

Rachel joined together with other parents and called Governor Murphy's Deputy Chief of Staff of Outreach, Deborah Cornavaca. Rachel says that Cornavaca listened to their impassioned pleas on behalf of their children—the way that the masking was actively hurting their development, how difficult it was to conduct speech therapy through masks—and she simply said, "Masks work, and we have to keep the kids safe."[48] Unions had come out strong for child-masking and Cornavaca had previously worked "as a statewide organizing expert at the New Jersey Education Association," a teachers union. Cornavaca could be seen in pictures, maskless, speaking at the 5th Annual Women's Leadership Conference. It was clearly important for her to be understood, unlike small children for whom it was not.[49] No exceptions could be made for children, no matter how many exceptions politicians made for themselves.

Kids were barely an afterthought, if they were a thought at all, until they were politically advantageous. In winter of 2022, states finally moved to unmask kids in schools. It was a political calculation. People were fed up with masking and even more fed up with masking children. The midterm elections were approaching, and Democratic politicians were poised to suffer for their continued refusal to follow anything resembling science.

It helped that Democratic governors in states like California, New York, and New Jersey did it at the same time. They gave each other cover. But it also highlighted how much group dynamics affect policy. Because the Left is "pro-union," and because the teachers unions were against opening schools, parents and the media disregarded all science that said opening schools could be done safely. They sold out their own kids and ours in the name of that conformity.

Parents who wanted schools to open were targeted with such vile hatred that most stayed anonymous. Parents I spoke to for articles at the time asked that I not share their names for fear that, as one mom told me, "someone [would] call my boss and say I want teachers to die."[50] Many were accused of racism, an easy way to invalidate anything they had to say.

Daniela Jampel was an open-schools advocate in New York City and one of the few to advocate for opening schools under her real name. She didn't just get nasty comments online. She told me that Twitter absolutely interfered with her real life. She received veiled threats.

Anonymous people on Twitter would refer to her being pregnant, something she had not shared online, as a way to let her know they knew her offline. She told me, "In Facebook groups and on neighborhood email listservs, I was called a white supremacist, a racist, a bad mom who just wanted her kids out of her house, and someone who didn't care about teachers. I know that these comments were seen by my neighbors, the parents of my kids' classmates, and people I casually knew in my neighborhood."[51] This was a warning sent to others: be quiet or you will be targeted too.

Another open-schools advocate, a lifelong Democrat named Maud Maron, ran for city council in New York City and was targeted because of her support for schools reopening. Maron told me, "When I was scheduled to speak at a rally with [2019 NYC mayoral candidates] Andrew Yang and Kathryn Garcia, a protest group started circulating social media posts referring to our advocacy as 'white supremacy with a hug.' The equity crowd championing closed schools—a policy that disproportionately hurt poor, minority kids—remains one of the most bizarre and cruel twists of the strange COVID bedfellows." By all accounts, the people who marched for equity should have been protesting for underprivileged kids to be in school. They didn't. Maron paints the picture as to why. "I was running for city council at the time, and my opponent sent an email referring to me as an 'anti-mask' radical. There was no nuance to the conversation. It was a 'with us or against us' mentality as they ushered in the most extreme restrictions."[52]

After the death of George Floyd at the hands of police in the summer of 2020, and with the riots that followed, the label "racist" became even more powerful than it had been already. The open-schools advocates were frequently called racists in an attempt to shut down their arguments that kids belonged in schools. As long as racism is the only explanation for everything, every institution is in danger, and public schools are no exception.

Parents weren't just being paranoid when they stayed quiet. There would be real repercussions for people who dared state the obvious.

Jennifer Sey was the brand president for Levi's Jeans—until she became outspoken about opening schools. It was a real-life "The Emperor Has No Clothes" moment. She jeopardized her career by saying what everyone already knew. Writing on the Bari Weiss Substack "Common Sense" in February of 2022, Sey notes that the company had no problem with "politics," but when she spoke out on COVID-sanity, or just the facing of reality of what has contained COVID and what has not, "the calls kept coming. From legal. From HR. From a board member. And finally, from my boss, the CEO of the company. I explained why I felt so strongly about the issue, citing data on the safety of schools and the harms caused by virtual learning. While they didn't try to muzzle me outright, I was told repeatedly to 'think about what I was saying.'" She continues, saying, "Meantime, colleagues posted nonstop about the need to oust Trump in the November election. I also shared my support for Elizabeth Warren in the Democratic primary and my great sadness about the racially instigated murders of Ahmaud Arbery and George Floyd. No one at the company objected to any of that." Sey had been on track to be Levi's next CEO, if only she would have stopped talking about how the COVID regulations were impacting kids. She wouldn't, and the harassment led to her resigning from her position.[53]

It was startling that the idea of children going to school, like they were doing in countries around the world, suddenly became seen as a right-wing cause. Schools had opened in much of Europe in the fall of 2020—including in the UK, France, Ireland, and other places—and they stayed open through spikes.[54] When services were forced to close due to outbreaks, schools were prioritized for reopening before all else.[55] They did not experience any significant increase in cases in schools or in society based on these policies.

Yet in America, good liberals had to oppose kids going to school. Many, of course, put their own kids in open private schools, hired tutors, formed pods with other children, or moved to stay with family or at their weekend home where schools were open. They did what they had to do for their own kids but never fought for the children of their

neighbors, all while spouting the rhetoric of equity. As long as they participated in the pageantry their political side demanded of them and
argued for schools to stay closed, it didn't matter that their kids were
actually going to school.

It wasn't coincidental. If there was one person who did the most to
stand in the schoolhouse door, it was the president of the American Federation of Teachers (ATF), Randi Weingarten. In September of 2020, she
was adamant that schools stayed closed: "If community spread is too high
. . . if you don't have the infrastructure of testing, and if you don't have the
safeguards that prevent the spread of viruses in the school, we believe
that you cannot reopen in person."[56] Other places did not wait to get to
"COVID Zero," or even just a reduction in case numbers, before opening
their schools. The "community spread," or the number of cases circulating, was high in many countries and in many U.S. cities and towns,
which had put kids first and opened schools. States not under Weingarten's influence successfully opened their schools in fall of 2020. It was
only blue cities and suburbs that listened to her and kept schools closed.

Part of this was blatantly political. President Donald Trump wanted
schools to open. In a joint event with First Lady Melania Trump in July
of 2020, the president said again and again that schools should open in
the fall. It seemed like the more Trump wanted it, the more entrenched
the Left became in opposing it.[57]

It made no sense. One of the more obnoxious twists of the COVID-19
era was that around the country, in areas where schools remained
closed, in-person "remote learning centers" popped up. In New York,
Learning Bridges was a program that provided "free child care options
for children from 3-K through 8th grade on days when they [we]re
scheduled for remote learning."[58] The program was run by the same
New York City Department of Education that was invested in keeping
schools closed. The staff members of Learning Bridges were mostly
non-unionized, so when schools closed in November of 2020 over the
made-up 3 percent metric, Learning Bridges remained open. If there
was science involved in these decisions, it was certainly not obvious.[59]

In November of 2020, the NYC Department of Education (DOE) was forced to admit that children with disabilities were not being cared for properly at Learning Bridges: "As a child care program, Learning Bridges has more limited supports than those found in DOE schools . . . We are actively working to identify supports available for our Learning Bridges sites to ensure they can serve as many students with disabilities as possible."[60] Children with special needs were continually tossed aside.

In January of 2021, Joe Biden was sworn in as president, and the political cost of keeping schools closed was beginning to show. Vaccines had started to be rolled out the month before, and Biden had promised to open schools in his first one hundred days. Many people pointed out that these school openings would be at the start of summer break for many regions, and still that goal ended up being too ambitious.

The CDC was set to release school-reopening guidelines in February. It was widely acknowledged they would push for all schools to reopen. Then the lobbying from Weingarten and other union officials began. The American Federation of Teachers Senior Director for Health Issues Kelly Trautner was directly involved. As reported by Jon Levine in the *New York Post*, "The documents show a flurry of activity between CDC Director Dr. Rochelle Walensky, her top advisors and union officials—with Biden brass being looped in at the White House—in the days before the highly-anticipated Feb. 12 announcement on school-reopening guidelines." Carole Johnson, the White House coronavirus testing coordinator, and Will McIntee, an associate director of public engagement at the White House, ran interception between the CDC and Weingarten.[61] In the end, the union won, and the kids, again, lost.

Levine writes, "With the CDC preparing to write that schools could provide in-person instruction regardless of community spread of the virus, Trautner argued for the inclusion of a line reading 'In the event of high community-transmission results from a new variant of SARS-CoV-2, a new update of these guidelines may be necessary.' . . . The AFT also demanded special remote work concessions for teachers 'who have documented high-risk conditions or who are at increased risk for . . . COVID-19,' and that similar arrangements should extend to 'staff who have a household member' with similar risks." Both of these suggestions were included in the text of the final guidance.[62]

That language mattered a lot. As CNN's Jake Tapper would point out to Walensky in a rare contentious interview, 99 percent of American kids lived in areas of "high community-transmission."[63] The CDC's new guidance, if followed, would have had even fewer kids in school than before.

Weingarten's role was to stop kids from going to school, and it was one she took seriously. Schools in blue areas wouldn't reopen even *somewhat* normally until September of 2021. Kids in those areas continued to mask in school, even outdoors through winter of 2022. Normalcy wouldn't be returned to them on Randi Weingarten's watch.

Even in the 2021-2022 school year, schools in blue areas continued to periodically close, and not always due to COVID. The lesson had penetrated: schools are not that important and can close at any time for any reason. The teachers unions could not be questioned. In November 2021, I wrote in the *New York Post,* "Across the country, schools are closing. Sometimes for a day or two. Sometimes for more. In Detroit, schools will close for three Fridays next month 'amid COVID concerns.' Schools in Kenosha went remote during the Kyle Rittenhouse trial. This month, Virginia Beach City Public Schools decided to end school two hours early on seven Wednesdays over the next three months due to fatigued teachers. More than 20 public school districts across the country will be tacking on 'mental health days' to the Thanksgiving break."[64] In Chicago, in January of 2022, the teachers union staged what Democratic Mayor Lori Lightfoot called "an illegal walkout." Schools remained closed for five days.[65] That same month, public schools in Flint, Michigan, one of the poorest cities in America,[66] extended their virtual learning period "indefinitely."[67] If you dared object, you were anti-teacher. The pandemic conformity had spread.

Writing on the *Tablet* magazine website in November of 2021, Alex Gutentag, a teacher of special needs kids in the Bay Area, called the year-plus of online learning "an unforgivable crime" that was "committed against public school children and families." Gutentag added, "And as it unfolded, everyone around me said it was acceptable, necessary, and even good."[68]

It wasn't about safety, but about control. Gutentag had tried to teach her kids but had run into the rigidness that represents our time. She writes, "When it became clear that California public schools would stay closed despite the paucity of evidence that closures were effective, and the far greater amount of evidence that schools could safely reopen, I tried to volunteer to teach kids with severe disabilities in person. But my district and union would not allow it. I emailed other teachers I knew from my union and cited statements from organizations like the American Academy of Pediatrics that were urging schools to reopen."[69] Nothing worked.

Groupthink and intense pressure to stay in line with the opinions of your tribe led to this disaster. In an editorial called "The Conformity Crackup of 2021," the *Wall Street Journal* Editorial Board highlighted the way forced conformity and prohibiting dissent had led to harmful policies: "Two years later we now know that lockdowns at most delay the virus spread. The damage in lost education for children, lost livelihoods for workers and employers, and damage to mental health is obvious for all to see. Even Randi Weingarten, the teachers union chief who did so much to keep schools closed, now claims she wanted to keep them open all along."[70]

In the aftermath of the school closures, people on the Left have started speaking up about how their own political side shut them up. In *The Atlantic* in January of 2022, Angie Schmitt wrote that she had lost faith in her "tribe," as she calls it—the Democratic Party. Her kindergartner had not gone to school in Cleveland, Ohio, through most of 2020. "And when I tried to speak out on social media," she wrote, "I was shouted down and abused, accused of being a Trumper who didn't care if teachers died. On Twitter, mothers who had been enlisted as unpaid essential workers were mocked, often in highly misogynistic terms. I saw multiple versions of 'they're just mad they're missing yoga and brunch.'"[71]

She continued, "Twitter is a cesspool full of unreasonable people. But the kind of moralizing and self-righteousness that I saw there came to characterize lefty COVID discourse to a harmful degree. As reported in this magazine, the parents in deep-blue Somerville, Massachusetts, who advocated for faster school reopenings last spring were derided as 'fucking white parents' in a virtual public meeting. The interests of children and the health of public education were both treated as minor concerns, if these subjects were broached at all."[72]

The harm to some kids will be deep and lasting. Jackie Mader, who covers early childhood education at The Hechinger Report, "a national nonprofit newsroom" focused solely on education, reported how bad the literacy problem was becoming for the children of the pandemic.[73] Mader highlighted that first grade, called "the reading year" by some teachers, is particularly important: "While experts say it's likely these students will catch up in many skills, the stakes are especially high around literacy. Research shows if children are struggling to read at the end of first grade, they are likely to still be struggling as fourth graders." The drop was dramatic: 40 percent of first-grade students were "'well below grade level' in reading in 2020, compared with 27 percent in 2019, according to Amplify Education Inc."[74]

For a society suddenly obsessed with equity, the Left mostly shrugged off the very real inequality that came with shutting down schools. Philip Klein highlighted this disparity in the *National Review* in April of 2021: "The most recent data from the Department of Education's Institute of Educational Sciences show that while 52 percent of white fourth-graders are receiving in-person instruction (which is far too low to begin with), just 32 percent of Hispanic students and 30 percent of black students are receiving in-person instruction."[75]

Some equity.

And, again, the "we didn't know" line won't quite work here either. By June 2020, the management company McKinsey & Company had "created statistical models to estimate the potential impact of school closures on learning."[76] The company found that its models predicted the worst impact on the very students the equity-warriors pretend to care most about: "The average loss in our middle epidemiological scenario is seven months. But black students may fall behind by 10.3 months, Hispanic students by 9.2 months, and low-income students by more than a year. We estimate that this would exacerbate existing achievement gaps by 15 to 20 percent."[77]

It was a direct line from Randi Weingarten to the closed schools for minority students. Writes Klein, "The teachers unions are the strongest in and around large liberal cities, which have been holding out the longest in reopening schools, and those areas tend to have a higher concentration of blacks and Hispanics."[78]

Weingarten was the ringleader, but she wasn't the whole circus. The media helped. Stories were framed to portray schools as far more dangerous than they were. Headlines read, "COVID-19 cases are rising fast. Can schools reopen safely after the holidays?"[79] and "COVID-19 cases rise in children across US as schools begin to open for in-person learning,"[80] linking schools—but not open bars, theaters, restaurants, or sports facilities—to the spread.

Florida in particular bore the brunt of bad coverage. Governor Ron DeSantis was at the forefront of the open-schools conversation. He had prioritized it, and when he received pushback in fall of 2020, he signed an emergency order requiring schools to offer in-person instruction.[81] Schools in Florida had opened, and stayed open, throughout 2020. In January of 2021, Governor DeSantis told me he was proud of keeping schools open during COVID. "I'm most proud of getting our kids back at school," he said.[82] "We knew the data, we knew it was low-risk. We felt we had to hold the line on this. We knew it was the case six to eight months ago. We were able to save the upbringing of hundreds of thousands of kids."[83] This was contrary to what the teachers unions wanted, of course, and the media went out of their way to punish him.

In August of 2021, three teachers, in the same county, died of COVID. The coverage was breathless and mostly wrong, including several pieces which erroneously reported that four teachers died. The news pieces tied the deaths to the mask debate and mostly failed to mention that the teachers were unvaccinated and, most importantly, that school had not yet begun. They had caught COVID on their summer break, and the fact that they were teachers was entirely peripheral to the story.[84] CBS News headlined its piece, "Four Broward County Educators Die from COVID-19 within 24 Hours, as Florida's Battle over Masks in Schools Continues."[85] Anyone dying of COVID is a tragedy, but other unvaccinated people were generally mocked by the same media for failing to get the vaccine. The teacher deaths, because they could be used to hurt Governor DeSantis and stifle debate on masking in schools, were highlighted in an entirely different fashion.

In a March 2022 interview, I asked Governor DeSantis what he remembered about that time. He told me that the media "would take someone who had a poor COVID outcome, who happened to work at a school, and impute that to a classroom environment to drive an agenda. They wanted to raise questions about whether schools should open or not."

Again, this was August 2021, not 2020. Schools had been open for an entire year, but unions continued to push the idea that schools were unsafe. DeSantis told me he "viewed it very clearly from the science perspective that [the safety of schools] wasn't debatable."

DeSantis told me that, in June of 2020, almost all establishment Republicans were opposed to his reopening of Florida. And in summer of 2021, a lot of Republicans "knew I was right on school closures but were full of trepidation on masking." It was a particularly fraught time to speak out against the conventional masking wisdom, but DeSantis knew he was right. The governor told me, "My responsibility is to respect the freedom of Floridians, and if local government is stepping on that, I have to protect them."[86]

How seriously Governor DeSantis took that responsibility deeply resonated with my family. In January of 2022, we moved to south Florida. By that point my children had not been maskless in a classroom in nearly two years. Our older son was constantly getting in trouble for his mask falling below his nose, *outdoors*, during recess. Our younger son was struggling academically because six-year-olds are difficult to understand at the best of times and even more so through a mask. Our daughter, newly in middle school, had to eat lunch outdoors on the ground, even in very cold weather. She preferred that to the silent lunches her school insisted on when the weather dropped below freezing and they had no choice but to move the children inside.

We didn't move to Florida just because of Governor DeSantis. Life is long, and politician terms are short. We moved there because the governor was leading the way with actual science and data and was very openly putting children first, and Floridians were on board with it. Florida was the top destination in both 2020 and 2021 for incoming moves from other states.[87] The number one reason cited for that migration is "family." We moved to save our kids, and so many others did too.

The extreme and illogical response to the COVID-19 pandemic in regard to our schools demonstrates the real repercussions that happen when dissent is shut down and leftist conformity is enforced. We will spend years as a country digging out from what was done to kids during this pandemic. The woke have had a taste of real power, and it's unlikely they won't try to use it again down the road. Already there are discussions about "carbon allowances" with people being limited in their activities to preserve the environment.[88] We have to understand what happened in order to never let them do this to our children ever again. Blind trust in authority, the devaluing of childhood, and so much more can never again be allowed. Parents must be the line of defense for their kids and say no.

3

NO SUBJECT IS SAFE

In 2021, parents all over the country rose up and began speaking out about what they saw happening in their children's schools. It was the Year of the Parent. A coordinated effort to shut them down quickly followed.

In September of 2021, the National School Board Association (NSBA) sent a letter to the Biden administration, which opened with the claim that "America's public schools and its education leaders are under an immediate threat." The claim was that these contentious school board meetings were more than just irate parents expressing their displeasure over what their kids are being taught. "As these acts of malice, violence, and threats against public school officials have increased, the classification of these heinous acts could be the equivalent to the form of domestic terrorism," they wrote. The Association requested that the full weight of the federal government be brought down on these parents who dared question their authority. "As such, NSBA requests a joint expedited review by the U.S. Departments of Justice, Education, and Homeland Security, along with the appropriate training, coordination, investigations, and enforcement mechanisms from the FBI, including any technical assistance necessary from, and state and local coordination with, its National Security Branch and Counterterrorism Division, as well as any other federal agency with relevant jurisdictional authority and oversight."[1]

Had "acts of malice, violence, and threats" increased, though? The letter provided twenty instances of bad behavior at school board meetings. Only one involved violence—hardly proof that the governmental department set up post-9/11 should be getting involved.

The letter, invoking the Gun-Free School Zones Act, the PATRIOT Act, the Matthew Shepard and James Byrd Jr. Hate Crimes Prevention Act, the Violent Interference with Federally Protected Rights Statute, and the Conspiracy Against Rights Statute, was a hysterical plea to save the lives of school board members allegedly under full attack.

They needn't have tried so hard.

The Biden administration immediately sprang into action. On October 4, 2021, Attorney General Merrick Garland sent a memo to the director of the FBI, the director of the Executive Office for U.S. Attorneys, and the Assistant Attorney General alleging "a disturbing spike in harassment, intimidation, and threats of violence against school administrators, board members, teachers, and staff who participate in the vital work of running our nation's public schools" and ordered them to take action.[2]

Activists mostly saw this move as a suppression tactic by the NSBA to shut down speech at the school board meetings. They weren't wrong about the tactic, only about who was ultimately shutting them down.

The Biden administration was in on the crackdown of parents from the start. In an internal memo, the NSBA revealed that they had had discussions with the Biden White House before sending the letter. In an October 5 email, NSBA Secretary-Treasurer Kristi Swett wrote that it was President Biden's Education Secretary Miguel Cardona who had solicited the letter from the group.[3]

Then, on October 13, Cardona tapped National School Boards Association President Viola Garcia to be on the National Assessment Governing Board. Garcia was one of two signatories on the memo. The coordination between the Biden administration and the NSBA was obvious.

Parents saw, many for the first time, how far their own government would go to quiet them. The blatant coordination, and the attempt to shut down the speech of parents concerned about their children's schooling, was startling.

But it would not have been happening if the parents hadn't been winning. Only a month later, Glenn Youngkin, a Republican, won the governorship in Virginia. Another Republican, Jack Ciattarelli, nearly unseated the Democratic governor of New Jersey. Both of these men ran on making schools sane again and returning the power of education to the parents.

Spring of 2021 saw an intense national focus on education that had previously been lacking. Parents who were showing up to school board meetings had a number of grievances. They would passionately argue against critical race theory, or for open schools in the wake of COVID-19, or against gender indoctrination, or to remove masks. They were defending their children against an onslaught.

Because of this focus, California's racist math draft framework, a draft on how math would be taught in schools, got a lot of attention and was ultimately rewritten. It was evidence that so much of the woke push in education could be stopped with attention.

But certainly not all.

In January 2022, the *Daily Wire* published a report by Gabe Kaminsky covering a town in Oregon that had fought and won against the wokesters, only to have their schools ignore them and continue their indoctrination process.[4] Newberg, Oregon, is a right-of-center town. But in 2020, Black Lives Matter flags were hung throughout the school. A group called Newberg Equity in Education (NEEd) was formed and urged the school board to adopt critical race theory in their teachings. Poorly written controversial books like *Stamped* by Ibram X. Kendi became part of the city's library book club.

Parents noticed the politicization of their schools and a decline in test scores and academic performance in general. The school population dropped from "nearly 5,000 students in 2018 to 4,338" in 2021.[5]

In July of 2021, four new school board members were elected specifically to fight the wokeness taking over Newberg's schools. Their first order of business was attempting to strip political messaging from the school. Kaminsky writes, "After years of schools proudly flying the 'progressive flag,' a version of the gay pride flag with shades of black and brown to communicate minority oppression, as well as Black Lives

Matter (BLM) flags, the members voted in August 2021 to ban 'political' flags, signs, and clothing."[6] But this could not be allowed.

The school administration disregarded the directive. The school board members were targeted at their homes and jobs. They received anonymous phone calls. One board member had the gate of his home broken. Another board member was fired from his full-time job. Political action committees (PACs) were formed to recall the board members. Outside money poured in. Nearly $70,000 had been donated to get rid of the elected board members. Actress Rosario Dawson donated money to the recall PAC, as did filmmaker Justin Simien.

Why would woke Hollywood care so much about schools in a town of just over 22,000 people? It is the question of "who do your kids belong to?" The woke do not believe your children should be your own. To them, the collective matters more than the individual. When parents try to fight against nonsense encroaching on their children's education, they are stopped.

Just how woke is your child's classroom?

First, start with the question of how much ideological diversity has existed in our schools. Almost none. In 2015, Verdant Labs released an extensive study on the political affiliations of professions.[7] They used political contribution data to figure out which jobs lean Republican and which lean Democrat. What they found was that teachers were overwhelmingly Democrats. Elementary school teachers were Democrats by an eighty-five to fifteen margin. There were eighty-seven Democrats teaching high school for every thirteen Republicans. School health educators were even more ideologically slanted at ninety-nine to one.

Being a Democrat doesn't mean being woke. But the leftward shift of our schools isn't new; it has been percolating for some time. And it isn't accidental. It begins in teachers' colleges and programs. Future teachers are indoctrinated into leftist thinking and taught to pass it along to their students.

Sol Stern, writing in a 2009 *City Journal*, a magazine produced by the Manhattan Institute, exposed what the New York Teaching Fellows—a program similar to Teach for America that "provides an alternate route to state certification for about 1,700 new teachers" and has them commit to two years of teaching in low-income areas—was teaching our future educators. He writes, "You might expect the required readings for these struggling rookies to contain good practical tips on classroom management, say, or sensible advice on teaching reading to disadvantaged students. Instead, the one book that the fellows had to read in full was *Pedagogy of the Oppressed*, by the Brazilian educator Paulo Freire."[8]

Continues Stern, "To get an idea of the book's priorities, take a look at its footnotes. Freire isn't interested in the Western tradition's leading education thinkers—not Rousseau, not Piaget, not John Dewey, not Horace Mann, not Maria Montessori. He cites a rather different set of figures: Marx, Lenin, Mao, Che Guevara, and Fidel Castro, as well as the radical intellectuals Frantz Fanon, Régis Debray, Herbert Marcuse, Jean-Paul Sartre, Louis Althusser, and Georg Lukács. And no wonder, since Freire's main idea is that the central contradiction of every society is between the 'oppressors' and the 'oppressed' and that revolution should resolve their conflict."[9] The concept is called "critical pedagogy," and so the book is largely about finding power structures and challenging them.

And "critical pedagogy" is an example of a "critical theory." In their book *Cynical Theories: How Activist Scholarship Made Everything about Race, Gender, and Identity—and Why This Harms Everybody*, Helen Pluckrose and James Lindsay describe "critical theory": "A critical theory is chiefly concerned with revealing hidden biases and underexamined assumptions, usually by pointing out what have been termed 'problematics,' which are ways in which society and the systems that it operates upon are going."[10] The educational model Freire supports would have teachers rely on this "critical pedagogy" to instruct students on their oppression and thus help them be free.

In the spring of 2020, schools were pressured to "do something" to make education more equitable. "Equity" had become the leftist buzzword, replacing the earlier "equality" which is now hopelessly outdated. The idea of equity isn't terrible. It requires schools to give each child what they need to succeed instead of giving all children the same education. In practice, though, what the teachers did instead was turn to the victimization lessons of critical race theory with which they were already familiar.

A November 2021 article in *City Journal* by Daniel Buck and James Furey explains how "critical pedagogy" evolved and spread. "Critical race theory flows from the more general philosophy of education called 'critical pedagogy,' which, in brief, seeks to leverage every math class, English lesson, history unit, elective, and scientific concept as a means to inculcate a political goal: the overthrow of Enlightenment-based, classically liberal principles—including the scientific method, objective reasoning, evidence-based argument, and so on."[11]

Before CRT, the educational buzzword was "multiculturalism."

"One does not see charts indicating tremendous improvement in reading or math skills through multiculturalism," writes Jay Schalin in *The Politicization of University Schools of Education*, taking an extensive look at what is being taught at teachers' colleges.[12] This 2019 deep dive into what the teachers were being taught, by the James G. Martin Center for Academic Renewal Policy Institute, found a lockstep among the schools in the pedagogy they use. Schalin writes, "To discover ideological patterns in the education school curriculum, we reviewed syllabi—the detailed descriptions of a course's content usually presented to students on the first day of a class—from three highly ranked public schools of education. These are the University of Wisconsin at Madison, the University of North Carolina at Chapel Hill, and the University of Michigan."[13] Sometimes the books used were not transparently pushing CRT. "For instance, the biography of Ladson-Billings—the most assigned author at both UNC's and Wisconsin's education schools—at the National Academy of Education says that she 'investigates Critical Race Theory applications to education.' In other words, she figures out how to insert CRT into the curriculum."[14]

The authors of these books play a myriad of roles in our education system and are widely respected in the establishment. Schalin writes,

"These educators serve as advisors to top public officials, as officers of leading education associations, and as trustees of state higher education systems. They serve on the editorial boards of leading organizations, and as department heads. They receive top awards for writing and teaching, have founded or head influential education centers and institutes, and their opinions are widely sought in the media. They are not a fringe element, seeking converts around the edges of academia. They are the education establishment."[15]

As early as 2018, British comedian Tracey Ullman had a viral video with a satirical skit called "Overly-Woke Support Group."[16] In it, the actors shared how difficult life was becoming for them because they saw everything through a woke lens. Ullman said, "All of the young people in this room are ruining their lives by being overly virtuous." Their nonstop virtue-signaling had rendered them unbearable. The group used all the right buzzwords: "representation," "microaggression," "subconscious bias," "denying agency," "problematic," and so on. Ullman called it a "slippery slope" and lamented, "one minute you're carrying a reusable water bottle, fine, and the next minute you're arguing that water is racist." At that, a member of the group gasps and asks, "Oh my God, is water racist?"

It's all a joke, of course, until 2021 when a very serious argument erupts over whether or not math is racist. This isn't a fringe idea limited to *Socialist Weekly* magazine. It's permeating all kinds of "mainstream" spaces. In the *Washington Post* in December 2021, in an article titled "Racism in Our Curriculums Isn't Limited to History. It's in Math, Too," Theodore Kim, an associate professor of computer science at Yale University, argued that math was indeed imbued with racism.[17] His evidence was that the Greek scholar Euclid has a theorem named after him while the scholar responsible for Chinese Remainder Theorem remains unremembered. Maybe the 300AD Chinese mathematician Sun Tzu indeed should have the theorem named after him. But Kim makes the leap that Tzu doesn't get the correct credit because, you guessed it, America is racist. He ties it to anti-Asian violence in the United States in the nineteenth century. The conclusion makes no sense. The allegedly racist mathematician L.E. Dickson, who discovered Sun Tzu's work, could have claimed the credit for himself or stripped away the Chinese origins of the theorem altogether. But as long as racism is the only explanation for everything even marginally wrong with the world, every institution, subject, and course of study is in danger.

The Left, having set ablaze our college campuses with their woke indoctrination, is now targeting children in grades K-12. In May of 2021, California rolled out a draft framework for teaching mathematics, using a manual called "A Pathway to Equitable Math Instruction: Dismantling Racism in Mathematics Instruction."[18] The framework instructed educators not to group children by ability or to refer to gifted children as "gifted." The framework also dropped algebra for eighth graders and calculus for high school students. Merit is racist, you see. The idea is that we have to "decolonize math"[19] because math is a tool used to oppress and marginalize people of color.[20]

It's not just race-related insanity either. Christopher Dubbs is an assistant professor in the Department of Mathematics at East Stroudsburg University in Michigan. In a 2016 paper, this teacher of future mathematics teachers argues that "mathematics education researchers are continuing to marginalize the experiences of queer youth and the only resolution is to center the queer student experience in the mathematics context."[21] Professor Dubbs concludes, "I challenge the mathematics education research community to push against the borders of mathematics education research by centering the experience of queer students in their current research while simultaneously advocating that more mathematics education researchers must adopt a queer theoretical stance to accomplish this centering, not only in the mathematics context, but within the overall education system."[22]

The fact is: math is math. Math doesn't care if you're black or gay or anything else. But teachers already can't say so, and they're being pushed to take ever more fringe positions on how to educate children. But public schools are in jeopardy of replacing math with abject nonsense.

Private schools face an even tougher situation. As Aaron Sibarium reported in the *Washington Free Beacon* in July of 2021, private schools are increasingly woke—because they have to be. The National Association of Independent Schools, "which sets accreditation standards for a group of more than 1,600 American private schools, including the country's most elite and rarefied secondary schools," has gone fully woke.[23] Sibarium writes, "The association keeps a list of 'approved accreditors' and outlines 'principles of good practice' it expects them to enforce, including the promotion of 'diversity, inclusion, equity, and justice' through 'cross-cultural competency.' If schools do not comply with these standards, they risk losing their accreditation and the perks that come with it, including access to the association's marketing tools."[24]

CRT is not a peripheral subject taught by one or two teachers in the big liberal cities. It's a method of teaching that is being spread throughout the entire country. Teachers attend these liberal education programs, learn critical pedagogy, and disperse throughout the country to teach it in our schools. By the time new teachers get to the classroom, they've been fully indoctrinated into these methods. They will look for the oppressor and the oppressed in every child. They will judge them on their accident-of-birth features and their place in the "structures of power and oppression," as they call it, and expect them to do the same.

Because the vast majority of teachers and administrators hold progressive beliefs, those beliefs make their way into classrooms in covert ways as well. From the comments and lesson planning of individual teachers to the institutionalization of progressivism in textbooks and core curricula, schools have become brainwashing centers. In many places, academic subjects are a far second to woke propaganda.

While this pedagogy had been growing and spreading for a long time, 2020 was the year parents became acutely aware that something was taking over the curricula at their children's schools. The realization was directly tied to the fact that for the better part of 2020 and 2021, many children were home and learning remotely. Suddenly, parents could hear what their kids were being told, and many didn't like it at all.

Christopher Rufo is a Senior Fellow at the Manhattan Institute and is widely considered the person who brought the evidence of critical race theory to the masses. Rufo was able to obtain internal documents and videos from corporations and schools pushing what Rufo calls "racialist indoctrination."

I asked Rufo how he first noticed that CRT was taking hold in schools. "Critical race theory started weaving its way into large, urban school districts in the early 2000s," he said, "then steadily expanded through departments of 'diversity, equity, and inclusion' in the 2010s. But after the death of George Floyd in 2020, there was an explosion: suddenly, critical race theory was everywhere. Because I had done the original reporting on critical race theory in the federal government, right-leaning parents across the country started leaking my documents. At first, I received tips from a few dozen school districts, then, after I began my reporting series, more than 1,000 school districts in nearly every state—red, blue, purple. It dawned on me: this is the new, dominant ideological orientation of American education."

Rufo told me, "Critical race theory teaches children to see themselves and each other as inherently 'oppressors' or 'oppressed.' It traffics in the ugly emotions of guilt, shame, and resentment, which dooms students of all racial backgrounds to a life of pessimism and despair. It's antithetical to excellence, achievement, hard work, and individual potential. It destroys successful merit-based programs in American school districts, rips families apart on the basis of race, and promotes an insidious narrative that America is a fundamentally evil country. Luckily, most Americans oppose this hateful ideology—and it's time for them to vocally oppose it in their communities."[25]

There's an ongoing debate about whether all race-based learning is actually CRT. Sometimes it's not. The Left loves pointing to race-based education and noting that any one specific lesson is not CRT. It's true that not every backward, racist idea pushed on children will be CRT. Some of it will just be general woke nonsense with no critical theory woven in at all.

Ibram X. Kendi is an author, humanities professor, and the founding director of the Boston University Center for Antiracist Research. Widely considered one of the "preeminent scholars of critical race theory," he has become the woke Left's favorite CRT sherpa.[26] He guides white people into believing they are racist, everyone they know is racist, and everything is about racism. Kendi has played a major role in forcing the conformity around CRT in our culture. You can't simply be "not racist" now; you must be "anti-racist." As I wrote for *The Spectator* in October 2020, Kendi "demands a shift in language . . . to a new way of using words. If you call yourself 'not racist' then you likely are racist. The new term is 'antiracist' and only a racist wouldn't understand that."[27] The specific language matters very much, not to root out racists but to show who is in the preferred group.

In the *New York Observer*, in August of 2016, Michael Malice observed the importance of language and of keeping up with the most current terminology as a signaling method: "What non-PC people often don't understand is the role that language policing provides for progressives. Using jargon is one of the quickest and easiest ways to demonstrate that a person is who they are presenting themselves to be. Conversely, saying the wrong thing is immediate proof that we are dealing with someone who doesn't belong."[28] Malice continues, "It costs nothing for someone to adopt the correct term in their speech. So as a 'proper' term becomes popularized and pervasive, it inevitably loses its function of distinguishing 'good' people from those who are simply trying to pass."[29] The constantly changing language reinforces conformist thinking and makes sure to punish anyone who deviates from the acceptable leftist norm in any way.

This emphasis on correct terminology is now being pushed as part of school curricula. The book *Stamped* by Kendi and Jason Reynolds is being used in middle schools throughout the country. There's even a junior edition of the book by Sonja Cherry-Paul being used in elementary schools. In June of 2021, one of the top public schools in New York City, the Anderson School for the Gifted and Talented, began using these books. As I wrote in the *New York Post* at the time, "The children's version of *Stamped* calls math 'a racist weapon' and portrays Abraham Lincoln as a villain. The prose is comically bad. A typical line: 'This is a present book. Not like a birthday present book, but like an everyday present book. Or maybe just an everyday book.' It only gets worse from there. Is *Stamped* CRT, technically speaking? Maybe not. But why is this book being forced on kids at a school where academic achievement is allegedly taken seriously?"[30] Anderson is one of only five stand-alone gifted and talented schools in New York City.

It helps that Ibram X. Kendi is part of a class of race hucksters which has been profiting off the idea that schools aren't doing "enough" for equity. His way is the right way, his language the only kind allowed. His TED talk was on the idea that it's not possible to not be racist, that you must be "anti-racist," his term.[31] And who doesn't want to be anti-racist? His solution is for schools to buy many copies of his books and to hire him to give talks to teachers and administrators on how they can bring his "anti-racist" education to the kids of their school. Fairfax County Public Schools in Virginia, for example, paid him $20,000 for a one-hour Zoom call with their staff.[32] Charlotte-Mecklenburg Schools in North Carolina paid Kendi his $25,000 fee and $420 to buy twenty-eight copies of his book *How to Be an Antiracist.*[33]

Kendi is just one of the people banking on schools paying up to make sure everyone knows they're not racist. It's a system ripe for con artists. Montgomery County Public Schools in Maryland paid $450,000 to The Mid-Atlantic Equity Consortium to conduct an "anti-racism audit."[34] That's money that could have been spent on actual education services for kids. It seems like a scam because it is. In April of 2021, the *New York Post* broke a story about BLM's co-founder Patrisse Khan-Cullors "snagging four high-end homes for $3.2 million in the US alone."[35] Since then, many news organizations have investigated the abject lack of transparency from the organization, including a story by Sean Campbell in *New York Magazine* titled "The BLM Mystery: Where Did the Money Go?"[36] A January 31, 2022, letter from California's Department of Justice warned the organization if "directors, trustees, officers and return pre-parers" failed to submit annual reports, they would be "personally liable for payment of all penalties, interest and other costs incurred to restore exempt status."[37] The grift is obvious, and yet somehow this organization is idolized and gets to dictate what kids are taught in schools.

The Left paradoxically argues CRT is not used in schools; they also argue it's good that it *is* used in schools. (If it's not used in schools, how could it be good that it is used in school?) Carmen Black and Christy Olezeski, both professors of psychiatry at Yale School of Medicine, are on the side of "CRT in schools is good." Writing in *Newsweek* in February 2022, they describe themselves thus: "Dr. Black is an African American woman specializing in medical antiracism and Dr. Olezeski is a bisexual woman specializing in transgender healthcare."[38] In the piece, they lament that schools don't have enough money to spend on the CRT boondoggle and some professional development budgets are limited so teachers haven't received proper training.

Similarly, the idea that CRT isn't taught in schools would be a surprise to the largest teachers union in the country. The National Education Association (NEA) adopted New Business Item 39 in July of 2021, which reads, "It is reasonable and appropriate for curriculum to be informed by academic frameworks for understanding and interpreting the impact of the past on current society, including critical race theory." Not only that, the NEA specified they would provide "an already-created, in-depth, study that critiques empire, white supremacy, anti-Blackness, anti-Indigeneity, racism, patriarchy, cisheteropatriarchy, capitalism, ableism, anthropocentrism, and other forms of power and oppression at the intersections of our society."[39] They also stated that they "oppose attempts to ban critical race theory and/or The 1619 Project."[40]

The 1619 Project is a widely debunked project by Nikole Hannah-Jones at the *New York Times* that rewrites American history and which historians say is riddled with factual errors.[41] The 1619 Project is named for the year the first ships arrived carrying slaves from Africa. The idea is to reframe 1619 as America's birth year. In addition to the many factual problems historians have identified in The 1619 Project, the idea of starting America's founding story on a date other than its founding is antithetical to the study of history. And yet The Project is making its way into curricula around the country.

Often, the more politicization in a school, and the more a school is influenced by these far-Left forces, the worse it performs. Take Centennial School for Expeditionary Learning, a public elementary school in Denver, Colorado, that participated in "Black Lives Matter at school." Kindergartners and first graders were taught using BLM organization principles like "disruption of Western nuclear family dynamics."[42] Centennial School for Expeditionary Learning is, of course, a failing school. Only 29 percent of the school was proficient in English, 24 percent in math, and a dismal 10 percent gets a passing grade in science according to their 2019 Colorado Measures of Academic Success, the state's standardized assessment that measures proficiency in core subjects.[43] Every moment spent on woke education is a moment not spent on academics.

But at least they succeed in equity? Not really. According to Great Schools, a website that tracks information about schools across the country, Centennial School for Expeditionary Learning scores a 1/10 for equity: "Underserved students at this school may be falling far behind other students in the state, and this school may have large achievement gaps."[44]

This isn't the first time in history that schools became indoctrination factories and saw a plummet in actual education. In his book *Hitler Youth*, Michael H. Kater laid out how schools in Nazi Germany became indoctrination centers—with predictable academic results: "By 1937 it had become obvious that the mounting politicization of the teachers combined with the growing neglect in school matters in favor of HJ [a German abbreviation for Hitler Youth] service by many students was leading to a dilution of conventional pedagogical standards; students were learning less."[45]

It isn't a coincidence. Every minute a school spends on indoctrination, whether to teach kids how to be racists in 1937 or teach them how to be "anti-racists" in the 2020s, is a minute not spent on reading, math, science, and other subjects. No amount of nonsense equity education can take the place of actual academic instruction, and no amount of rejiggering the standards will help. Obviously, the poor academic results were some of the lesser problems with Hitler Youth, but it remains indicative of the way indoctrination elbows out academics in the classroom.

In response to the argument that parents don't want CRT used in schools, some leftist activists paint the picture that these parents, who are racists of course, don't want history taught in the classroom. This is absurd. CRT interferes with all learning, including history. Kids develop a very shallow understanding of history, with winners and losers, good guys and bad guys. Math is no longer black and white, but history somehow is. There's no depth or complexity since little questioning of anything is allowed.

In a widely shared piece from *The Atlantic* called "When the Culture War Comes for the Kids," writer George Packer traverses this evolution. Packer was, before wokeness took over, impressed with his son's civics class: "Every year, instead of taking tests, students at the school presented a 'museum' of their subject of study, a combination of writing and craftwork on a particular topic. Parents came in, wandered through the classrooms, read, admired, and asked questions of students, who stood beside their projects. These days, called 'shares,' were my very best experiences at the school. Some of the work was astoundingly good, all of it showed thought and effort, and the coming-together of parents and kids felt like the realization of everything the school aspired to be."[46]

But then wokeness hit: "The fifth-grade share, our son's last, was different. That year's curriculum included the Holocaust, Reconstruction, and Jim Crow. The focus was on 'upstanders'—individuals who had refused to be bystanders to evil and had raised their voices. It was an education in activism, and with no grounding in civics, activism just meant speaking out. At the year-end share, the fifth graders presented dioramas on all the hard issues of the moment—sexual harassment, LGBTQ rights, gun violence. Our son made a plastic-bag factory whose smokestack spouted endangered animals. Compared with previous years, the writing was minimal and the students, when questioned, had little to say. They hadn't been encouraged to research their topics, make intellectual discoveries, answer potential counterarguments. The dioramas consisted of cardboard, clay, and slogans."[47] The repetitive and narrow thinking that wokeness demands ultimately leads to this kind of boring work. No one is allowed to go outside the lines.

For a long time, Americans believed these kinds of loopy ideas and programming sessions were the province of coastal elites. Sure, the kids in New York City or San Francisco would be subject to woke brainwashing, but the red states were safe. What parents found over the past few years is that the rot goes far deeper than a few blue cities.

Take the example of Alvin Lui, who moved to Indiana from the San Francisco Bay area in California to escape wokeism. Lui told me, "While there were several factors, chief among them is that we didn't want to raise our young daughter in the toxic and unhealthy climate that has ruined California. We love the culture, family values, and fiscal responsibility of a city like Carmel, Indiana." What Lui quickly realized was that Carmel was following California's same woke path. "Unfortunately when we got to Indiana we saw many of the same seeds that had already [been] deeply planted that ruined our old home. It wasn't immediately obvious to anyone who wasn't [from] where we were from. Many native Hoosiers had no idea what was coming for their way of life. The majority are kind hearted and the leftist ideology takes advantage of that."

Lui started a nonprofit organization called Unify Carmel, which was among the first groups in the country to bring up to their school boards that shockingly explicit books were in their school libraries. After discovering the books, Lui says, "We read the sexually explicit and gender-propaganda books during open comments at a school board meeting." The video of that school board meeting "really shocked a lot of people in our community because many parents are simply asleep at the wheel."[48]

The Carmel Clay Schools had a $2 million shortfall because of declining enrollment, even as the population of Carmel has increased.[49] Parents wanted their kids out of the woke schools.

Lui adds, "A great majority of people in Carmel still cannot see the devastating downstream impact to a community of children that is raised under this ideology. Many still think 'it's just about teaching kindness' or 'to not be racist.' The work we've done has certainly awakened many parents up who otherwise wouldn't realize what is happening until it's too late."[50]

The woke indoctrination is happening everywhere. Inez Stepman, a senior policy analyst at the Independent Women's Forum and an expert in education policy, told me red states ignore what is happening at their peril. "Many conservatives in red states tend to think of radical lessons, including critical race theory and gender ideology, as a blue state problem. Unfortunately, many of the forces that make schools increasingly Left-leaning are national, and they certainly do affect schools in red states and districts. Both major teachers unions, for example, have embraced woke ideology. Teachers' trainings are drenched in it. The districts have large DEI bureaucracies. And the whole system is staffed from top to bottom by people trained in our universities—particularly our schools of education, which are to the Left even of the rest of campus—which has ensured that most of them have imbibed the ideology of the academy."[51]

The teachers then disperse through the country, armed with the leftist training they've received. The organization Parents Defending Education (disclosure: I sit on their board) collects incident reports from across the country. A clickable "IndoctriNation Map" shows various instances of woke indoctrination across the country. In Tennessee, teachers in Hamilton County underwent training on "white privilege." Lessons included teachings like "people of color cannot be racist because they lack the institutional power to adversely affect white lives." In Missouri, teachers at Cherokee Middle School were forced into a "diversity training program" where they placed themselves on an "oppression matrix" depending on their race, gender, and sexual preferences. They learned, among other things, about "covert white supremacy" that includes things like "education funding from property tax" and "colorblindness."[52] Again, only a very specific way of looking at race, where some people are oppressors and some are oppressed, is tolerated.

Part of that view is a critical exploration of "whiteness" as a continuing theme. "Whiteness" is a stand-in for everything bad in society. We're simply not born to spend all of our time thinking about our accidental identity and how it has shaped our lives. But the woke narrative demands it.

For example, Grant High School in Portland, Oregon, asked kids to recount racial trauma and watch a video called "How Does Whiteness Impact You?"[53] One of the "working definitions" of the term "whiteness" is defined as "characteristics and experiences associated with being white, and it is connected to the belief that white people are the standard in society." They also discussed "white fragility" and "white saviorism." An associated term they explored is "white tears," which "appear in response to confrontation regarding race, shifting focus to and victimizing the white experience." The teaching explained that "this weaponization occurs against Black men and women in particular" and cited the example of Kyle Rittenhouse, who was acquitted of shooting three men in Kenosha, Wisconsin, during the 2020 riots, "crying during his homicide trial." In this situation, Kyle "expected comfort and accommodation from others."[54] The fact that a young man might have been actually upset that he killed two people was never considered. Rittenhouse is white, as were his victims, so no grace could be offered to him. The idea that anyone white is automatically bad, even an enemy, permeates woke thought.

No one is more obsessed with whiteness than those who profess to be challenging that whiteness. There's no discussion about the negative effect on kids of telling them they're either an oppressor or oppressed, the country they live in sucks, and their parents are probably racist.

It's not just older kids, either. This kind of woke indoctrination extends to elementary and even preschool students. In January of 2022, education groups in North Carolina, including Education First Alliance, No Left Turn in Education, and NC Citizens for Constitutional Rights, successfully beat back a proposal that would have taught disabled pre-schoolers statewide to "deconstruct whiteness."[55]

Part of how this became so widespread is that it's often cloaked in very different language. For example, on the *Tablet* magazine website in January of 2021, Emily Benedek wrote about California's "ethnic studies" mandate, signed into law in 2016 by then-Governor Jerry Brown.[56] "Ethnic studies" is a typical example of how leftist indoctrination takes hold in the K-12 classroom. What parent doesn't want their children learning about the world and different countries and ethnicities? In our household, we love learning about different countries and cultures. But this is very much not that.

Benedek quotes one mom, Elina Kaplan, a self-described lifelong Democrat, who was initially excited about the mandate: "In one sample lesson, she saw that a list of historic U.S. social movements—ones like Black Lives Matter, #MeToo, Criminal Justice Reform—also included the Boycott, Divestment, and Sanctions Movement for Palestine (BDS), described as a 'global social movement that currently aims to establish freedom for Palestinians living under apartheid conditions.' Kaplan wondered why a foreign movement, whose target was another country, would be mischaracterized as a domestic social movement, and she was shocked that in a curriculum that would be taught to millions of students, BDS's primary goal—the elimination of Israel—was not mentioned. Kaplan also saw that the 1948 Israel War of Independence was only referred to as the 'Nakba'—'catastrophe' in Arabic—and Arabic verses included in the sample lessons were insulting and provocative to Jews." As this story shows, a lot of indoctrination is about what's included and what is left out. Kaplan "was further surprised to discover that a list of 154 influential people of color did not include Dr. Martin Luther King Jr., John Lewis, or Supreme Court Justice Thurgood Marshall, though it included many violent revolutionaries. There was even a flattering description of Pol Pot, the communist leader of Cambodia's

Khmer Rouge, who was responsible for the murder of a quarter of the Cambodian population during the 1970s."[57] This was not the mandate Kaplan had in mind.

"Ethnic studies" often becomes an examination of grievances and blame, steeped in critical race theory. In his book *Race to the Bottom: Uncovering the Secret Forces Destroying American Public Education*, *Daily Wire* reporter Luke Rosiak broke the story of Tracy Castro-Gill, the ethnic studies program manager at Seattle Public Schools, under whose leadership some Seattle schools replaced part of their math curriculum with "math ethnic studies."[58] Castro-Gill, who self-describes as a "radical atheist" and "far-Left anarchist," identified herself as "Xicana," a "gender-neutral" term for Latin-American,[59] although her own father told Rosiak she was white. She created a fantasy world of an immigrant childhood that led her to drugs and gangs, stories her family denies. Rosiak writes, "In spring 2018, the math ethnic studies program was piloted in six schools. The school board had approved the pilot program to decrease the achievement gap." Yet it is unclear how a curriculum heavy on "ethnic studies" and light on actual "math" was going to eliminate "opportunity gaps." Even if one believes that math has been stolen by the West from other cultures, as the framework for this course suggests, does that mean we should turn math class into a history class that explores this? And how would that help black students perform better in math?

Rosiak details the school board's approval of the pilot program to decrease the achievement gap, in their writing: "1. We affirm our belief that the integration and addition of ethnic studies into the education of Seattle Public Schools' students can have a positive impact on eliminating opportunity gaps. 2. We direct that the Superintendent incorporate ethnic studies . . . as a high-leverage gap eliminating strategy."

Castro-Gill's "math ethnic studies" had predictable results. Rosiak reports, "At one pilot school, John Muir Elementary, black achievement had been rising steadily every year, but all those gains and more were wiped out, with the black passing rate dropping from 28% to under 18% the next school year. At another pilot school, 69% white and with only seven black students, the white students' pass rates also plunged, from 60% to 36%."[60] Castro-Gill said this was fine. In fact, she brushed this off, justifying it by arguing that "closing 'Achievement/Opportunity' gaps is a Western way of thinking about education . . . We should never 'close' that gap because it provides space for reflection and growth."[61] Once it became clear that woke teaching would not produce good academic results, those results ceased to be the goal.

Ironically, as Robby Soave revealed in an investigation for *Reason* magazine in January of 2022, ethnic studies classes, which are typically intended for "privileged white students to learn about other cultures," are also required for minority students. The irony gets worse. Soave's investigation centered on a high school teacher in Salinas, California, Kali Fontanilla, who teaches Hispanic students learning English as a second language and "noticed that many of her students were failing one of their other classes: ethnic studies." Fontanilla, who is black of Jamaican descent, decided to learn more about the course and was shocked by what she found. "This was like extreme Left brainwashing of these kids," she said. "Critical race theory all throughout the lessons, from start to finish. The whole thing . . . The teacher had the kids all learn about the four I's of oppression," Fontanilla continued. Soave explained, "The four I's were institutional, internalized, ideological, and interpersonal oppression. And then there was a whole presentation on critical race theory and they actually had the students analyze the school through critical race theory."[62]

Soave points out that "Salinas has a majority Mexican population; all of Fontanilla's students were Hispanic and were learning English as a second language." The kids took privilege quizzes and were asked to "rank themselves based on their marginalized status or lack thereof."[63] Fontanilla says about half the class was failing. When all the time is spent on wokeness and not academics, this is the obvious result.

It's not just "equity" or "privilege" that is on the brainwashing menu at schools. Gender identity issues are on the docket as well. This kind of woke teaching puts identity over everything. You're not an individual.

It also isn't consistent: the race you're born into decides everything, but your gender can change at any time.

The woke narrative demands that we spend all of our time thinking about our accidental (and malleable) identities and how they have shaped our lives. In his book, *Madness of Crowds*, Douglas Murray writes, "Identity politics is where minority groups are encouraged to simultaneously atomize, organize and pronounce. The least attractive-sounding of this trinity is the concept of 'intersectionality.' This is the invitation to spend the rest of our lives attempting to work out each and every identity and vulnerability claim in ourselves and others and then organize along whichever system of justice emerges from the perpetually moving hierarchy which we uncover."[64]

Murray continues, "Intersectionality has broken out from the social science departments of the liberal arts colleges from which it originated."[65] It moved from social science departments to other departments, then to media, corporate offices, accreditation bodies, and publishing houses. It was inevitable it would infect our high schools, middle schools, and even grade schools.

All of this can only go on in schools if a certain degree of secrecy is maintained. In Oshkosh, Wisconsin, the director of pupil services sent a memo to all staff members that they are "no longer required to seek parental consent prior to honoring student requests to be called by their preferred name and/or pronouns."[66] A Leon County, Florida, middle school developed a "gender support plan" for a child and noted it should be kept secret from the child's parents.[67] It seems to be less about support and more about indoctrination. We used to understand that keeping secrets from a child's parents was crossing a very serious line, yet schools now do it as a matter of course if children proclaim themselves transgender.

In response to the uptick in gender ideology being taught in schools, Florida's Governor DeSantis signed the Parental Rights in Education bill into law in March of 2022. The law, pejoratively called the "Don't Say Gay" bill despite not having the word "gay" in the law whatsoever, made clear that this type of gender ideology could not be taught in kindergarten to third grade.[68] Many critics of the law said that this type of teaching was not happening in those grades anyway. But parents know that's untrue.

A mom in Staten Island, a fairly conservative part of New York City, told me her second grader's class read a book about whether an avocado is a fruit or a vegetable and told the kids they can be anything they want to be as well. While in the past this kind of conversation may lead to a child imagining themselves as an astronaut or a firefighter, in our current era, this led directly to what gender the child identifies with and how he or she wishes to be perceived by the class. Thus, a seven-year-old is being conditioned to the idea that his or her birth gender might be temporary and can be switched up at any time.

In April of 2022, Christopher Rufo broke the story that the Evanston/Skokie School District in Illinois would be adopting a radical curriculum for pre-K to third grade where kids would be taught to "break the gender binary."[69] Attaching pictures of the content, Rufo tweeted, "The kindergartners read books that affirm transgender conversions, look at photographs of boys in dresses, and perform a rainbow dance. At the end of the lesson, the students are encouraged to share their own gender identities with the class. 'Your identity is for you to decide!'"[70] First graders learn gender is completely malleable: "In first grade, the teacher encourages students to experiment with gender pronouns such as 'she, tree, they, he, her, him, them, ze, zir, [and] hir.' The students read gender scripts and the teacher reminds them: 'Whatever pronouns you pick today, you can always change.'"[71]

Then the kids move on to middle school, an even more secretive experience. Abigail Shrier, author of the 2020 book *Irreversible Damage*, broke the story that at the "October [2021] conference of California's largest teachers union, California Teachers Association (CTA) . . . two middle school teachers from Spreckels, California instructed educators statewide on how to establish middle school LGBTQ clubs, recruit students, and hold meetings, all while concealing these clubs and their membership from the students' parents. The teachers even told their audience that they had monitored students' Google searches and chat histories to determine which students might be receptive to in-person invitations to join their LGBTQ clubs."[72] Shrier notes that she "also received access to a trove of webinars put out by the CTA in which other teachers outlined similar strategies for the recruitment of even elementary school kids to LGBTQ clubs and the deliberate concealment of these clubs from the children's parents."[73] The secrecy is a big part of the indoctrination process. Parents will, understandably, buck at their kids being targeted in this way, so schools keep all of this from them.

Rufo refers to these people as "political predators," a term he uses "for describing teachers who indoctrinate their students and treat the public school system as a recruiting ground for their private ideologies."[74] Deliberately cutting parents out of what is happening in the school building is a hallmark of this modern indoctrination method.

. After publishing her story on the covert indoctrination of middle school students, Shrier notes she "received communications from parents showing [her] their email exchanges with the school in which they complained about these teachers' activism; some of these email exchanges went back several years."[75] The pandemic brought the lessons home to parents, and many were exposed, some for the first time, to the ideas being presented to their children daily.

While they might have been surprised that their kids were being taught this gobbledygook, parents were mostly familiar with what it was. Peggy Noonan, in the *Wall Street Journal* in November of 2021, writes, "When parents heard indoctrination during the kids' Zoom classes, they'd heard it before. They knew it from work, from endless human-resources antiracism and gender-bias sessions. They didn't know the kids were getting it too, and didn't like it."[76]

Covertness is a large part of the wokeism march. In January of 2022, NBC News reported that parents who had fought CRT education were looking for transparency from their schools and this was somehow a bad thing: "Lawmakers in at least 12 states have introduced legislation to require schools to post lists of all of their teaching materials online, including books, articles and videos. The governors of Arizona, Florida and Iowa, who have previously raised concerns about how teachers discuss racism's impact on politics and society, called for curriculum transparency laws in speeches to their legislatures this month."[77]

There's absolutely nothing controversial about parents wanting to know ahead of time what their kids will be learning in school, but the way the story was reported made it seem like there was something new or contentious about parents being involved in their kids' schooling. The report stated: "But teachers, their unions and free speech advocates say the proposals would excessively scrutinize daily classwork and would lead teachers to pre-emptively pull potentially contentious materials to avoid drawing criticism. Parents and legislators have already started campaigns to remove books dealing with race and gender, citing passages they find obscene, after they found out that the books were available in school libraries and classrooms."[78]

Rufo told me, "Parents must fight for information. Critical race theory can only survive in the shadows, manipulating children through subtle techniques, while keeping parents in the dark. Parents should demand to see the curriculum, attend class as an observer, and ask their state legislators to pass mandatory curriculum transparency legislation, which requires school districts to post all teaching materials online for parents to review. And trust your instincts: if something feels wrong, it's likely that it is wrong. The critical race pedagogists use euphemisms to cloak their ideology in the soft language of 'diversity' and 'compassion,' but in reality, it's an abusive neo-Marxist theory that seeks the total deconstruction of the United States."[79]

Florida Governor Ron DeSantis made mention of curriculum transparency legislation in his State of the State speech in January 2022: "Florida has enacted a Parents' Bill of Rights, and we reject the notion that parents shouldn't have a say in what their kids learn in school. Indeed, Florida law should provide parents with the right to review the curriculum used in their children's schools. We should provide parents with recourse so that state standards are enforced, such as Florida's pro-hibition on infusing subjects with critical race theory in our classrooms . . . Our tax dollars should not be used to teach our kids to hate our country or to hate each other."[80]

The American Civil Liberties Union (ACLU) tweeted out the NBC News article with the comment, "Curriculum transparency bills are just thinly veiled attempts at chilling teachers and students from learning and talking about race and gender in schools."[81]

Of course, the ACLU is a perfect example of an institution which has collapsed under the weight of wokeness. Once a civil liberties organi-zation so committed to their cause that they defended actual neo-Nazis who wanted to march in Skokie, Illinois, the ACLU now sends fund-raising emails for projects such as "reparations advocacy," "permanent child tax credit," and "increased broadband access."[82] A 2021 docu-mentary about former ACLU National Executive Director Ira Glasser highlights what the ACLU once represented and what it does now. From a review of the film for *Tablet* magazine by Jamie Kirchick, Glasser, a true blue liberal, says the organization has become wholly politicized: "'My successor, and the board of directors that have supported him, have basically tried to transform the organization from a politically neutral, nonpartisan civil liberties organization into a progressive liberal orga-nization,' Glasser says about Anthony Romero, an ex-Ford Foundation executive who continues to serve as the ACLU's executive director."[83] Kirchick notes, "In 2018, the ACLU spent over $1 million on advertise-ments likening Supreme Court Justice nominee Brett Kavanaugh to Bill Cosby and Harvey Weinstein, essentially accusing him of crimes for which he was never tried or convicted."[84] So much for civil liberties.

And so much for fighting opacity in education. In 2013, the ACLU was on the side of transparency, arguing that parents had a right to see what sex education curriculum would be used to teach their kids. "The days of back door decision making are over. Compliance with the open meetings law is meant to secure the opportunity of parents, students, and community members to have a meaningful impact on the development of policy. We are all well served when decisions on the appointment of sex education advisory committee members is subject to public scrutiny, rather than the result of the presentation of a narrow range of interests," said Staci Pratt, legal director of the ACLU of Nevada.[85]

In 2018, the ACLU conducted an "Open Records Act investigation" to look into the curricula at Kentucky's 173 school districts to discover if they were covertly teaching the Bible.[86]

But now that kind of transparency is bad since it will inevitably uncover leftist teachings that the ACLU believes should be allowed to stand. The ACLU should be a force for parents who think neither teaching the Bible nor teaching woke activism should be permitted in school. That they're not is evidence of how far they've fallen.

However, fighting back, or even simply asking questions, can lead to negative repercussions for children. For example, Jeff Myers has kids in elementary and middle schools in Beaverton School District in Oregon, the same schools *he* attended. He told me, "The principal rolled out a '21-day social justice challenge' starting on January 3rd, and when I requested the lesson plans and materials, I was met with a lot of resistance. During the process, the principal decided on her own to have my daughter removed from class during these lessons. She did so without my knowledge or approval. I didn't find out until later in the week."[87] Separating a child from her classmates, drawing attention to her, and making clear there is an in-group and an out-group are features of forced conformity. You don't want to be like her, so do what we say.

Many black parents we've spoken to have many concerns with the racialized way their kids are being taught. Quisha King, who is black and a spokesperson for the Moms for Liberty group, got involved after her daughter taped an incident in class that appalled King: "The teacher told them that some books have racial themes. But instead of talking academically, she started talking to the kids in their different identity groups. 'As an African American child . . .' 'As an LGBT child . . .' All demographics except 'white.'" King says, "The kids started arguing like they're in the oppression Olympics. Kids were trying to best each other on who is more oppressed. The teacher is encouraging it and asking leading questions. It was my first realization that woke theology was in the schools."[88]

Don't be tempted to think it couldn't happen anywhere. The spreading of the woke philosophy is insidious, and it sometimes won't be clear your school is in the grips of it until it's too late.

Many activists like King recommend that parents start with involvement at the school board level. Attend the meetings, support candidates, and take seriously the local elections, as they have the biggest effect on what happens inside your child's school. Support candidates who want school choice. Push for curriculum transparency. That one should be easy, and you can assume that a school district with nothing to hide will not have a problem with telling you what they teach.

Electing candidates who will pass laws to fight wokeness in schools works too. The DeSantis Parental Rights in Education law is very popular. According to a Public Opinion Strategies poll taken in March 2022, "When Americans are presented with the actual language of the new Florida law, it wins support by more than a two to one margin," sixty-one to twenty-six. Even among Democrats, it's fifty-five to twenty-nine.[89]

School choice has to go hand in hand with taking the fight to the school boards. Stepman, the senior policy analyst at the Independent Women's Forum and an expert in education policy, told me, "It will require actual realignment of incentives and tying people's salaries to what parents want. The only policy that provides that leverage is universal school choice."[90] King told me, "I would say over the last year and a half, I've learned that although attending school board meetings is necessary, it seems to fall on deaf ears unless there are significant policy changes at the state and federal level where you can bring legal action. At this point my recommendation to parents would be to get your kids out of these indoctrination camps as soon as possible."[91] Pulling your children out of woke public schools may be the only option.

People opposed to left-wing ideology have to fight to remake the institutions which have been gripped by this woke extremism. But individual families have to make the decisions that best fit their lives. If the fight is possible to win—if your district is even a fifty-fifty or sixty-forty split between the woke and the not—then mount that fight and try to save your child's school. However, if you live in a school district where you are vastly outnumbered and have no allies, fleeing it might be the best option for your family.

Fighting takes time. Rebuilding institutions takes time. And childhood is short. No one will fault parents for doing what has to be done for their own children.

A win is a happy, healthy child who is not forced to parrot the opinions of indoctrinators. A win is a family who is free.

PART II

INSTITUTIONS IN TROUBLE

If you look at the polling on how many Americans identify as "woke," it's a minority of Americans. In the summer of 2021, *The Hill* reported, "Thirty-two percent of registered voters in the July 8-9 survey said they see themselves as woke to the extent that they understand the term. Twenty-three percent of respondents said they do not identify as woke while 13 percent said they are unsure. Thirty-one percent of voters said they don't know what the term 'woke' means."[1]

The Hill defined "woke" as someone who is "aware of social issues such as racial prejudice and discrimination."[2] The reality, we know, is much more complex—and much more ominous. The reality is that conformist, woke ideology is taking over our institutions, and this takeover of every aspect of our lives, from medical and mental healthcare to our media and entertainment, touches every single American—those who buy into the ideology and the many of us who don't.

With wokeism setting standards for our workplaces in healthcare, education, banking, and more, we aren't just subject to mind-numbing workshops from HR on inclusion and diversity commercials on television. The woke takeover of our institutions is a mechanism to instill these beliefs into our children, indoctrinating them not only in their schools but also as they read and watch for pleasure.

As is the case in schools, when the highest priority for any given industry is jumping through adequate political hoops, the highest priority is, therefore, *not* excellence. What does this look like in entertainment, for example? It negatively impacts the quality of the books, movies, and television because a political agenda eclipses artistic merit. If writers are more concerned with checking off diversity boxes and treading too carefully with anything that could be perceived as offensive, their minds aren't where they should be: the writing. And when woke indoctrination rules in medical schools and healthcare practice, providing the best medical education and care possible is no longer the most important part of the job. That has terrifying ramifications for our health and welfare, especially for that of our children since the field of pediatrics is dominated more than almost any other medical field by progressive politics.

4

WHEN MICKEY AND SCHOLASTIC WENT WOKE

In the spring of 2022, Florida Governor Ron DeSantis signed into law the bill that pushed the Disney Corporation into the culture wars.

HB 1557, the Parental Rights in Education bill, which his detractors quickly coined the "Don't Say Gay" bill, doesn't ever mention homo- or heterosexuality.[3] The legislative text of the House version of the bill reads, "Classroom instruction by school personnel or third parties on sexual orientation or gender identity may not occur in kindergarten through grade 3 or in a manner that is not age-appropriate or developmentally appropriate for students in accordance with state standards."[4] It does not ban specific words or even casual discussion of gender issues. But it does remove gender and sexual orientation issues from the formal curriculum for five-, six-, and seven-year-olds and mandates that instruction for older children is age and developmentally appropriate.

When DeSantis signed the "Don't Say Gay" bill into law, The Walt Disney Company issued a statement vowing to help repeal the controversial legislation. "Florida's HB 1557, also known as the 'Don't Say Gay' bill, should never have passed and should never have been signed into law," the statement reads.[5] "Our goal as a company is for this law to be repealed by the legislature or struck down in the courts, and we remain committed to supporting the national and state organizations working to achieve that. We are dedicated to standing up for the rights and safety of LGBTQ+ members of the Disney family, as well as the LGBTQ+ community in Florida and across the country."[6]

Disney, we soon learned, had decided to go all-in on radical gender ideology. In a leaked video released by the anti-CRT activist and journalist Christopher Rufo, Executive Producer for Disney Television Animation Latoya Raveneau proudly explains in an all-hands staff meeting: "In my little pocket of Proud Family Disney TVA, the show-runners were super welcoming . . . to my not-at-all-secret gay agenda."[7] She says that she no longer has to be afraid, for example, to "have these two characters kiss in the background," and she adds, "I was just, wherever I could, adding queerness . . . and no one was trying to stop me."[8]

Karey Burke, president of Disney's General Entertainment Content, pledged to drastically alter the makeup of its characters, with at least 50 percent being LGBTQ or racial minorities by the end of 2022.[9]

Writing for *Quillette* in March of 2022, an "Imagineer" at Disney blew the whistle, sharing, "The last couple years have brought COVID, lock-downs, the summer of 2020, and the doctrines of critical theory and its various permutations to the Disney corporation. Ibram X. Kendi was a featured speaker in the 'Reimagine Tomorrow' series, an internal Disney effort to promote Diversity, Equity, and Inclusion (DEI) initiatives within the corporation. . . . The DEI department within the company expanded by an astonishing 633 percent in 2019–21, at the same time that nearly every other department was contracting by 25–75 percent. Most surprising of all was the addition, in April 2021, of a FIFTH key—Inclusion—to the traditional Four Keys used in training."[10]

How does the most wholesome, family-friendly entertainment company, beloved for multiple generations, go completely off the rails? Disney is the cautionary tale of what happens when a creative company is entirely based out of California and spends the majority of its time not on content, but DEI.

While in the midst of researching and writing this chapter, I (Bethany) took a trip with my five kids to the library. We were there to meet with friends, and my then-eight-year-old wandered off to the children's graphic novel shelves to pick out a few new books. I waved my daughter off with my library card to let her check out whatever she had picked out. I threw the bag in my trunk and forgot to take it out for a week. Incidentally, over the course of that time, I spoke with several parents about their crusades to clean up the books in their school libraries—books that were written for children that exposed them to inappropriate ideas about sexuality, gender, and race. Two mothers specifically mentioned the same book to me, *The Breakaways*. The first time I heard about the book, I wrote down its name. The second time, however, the mother told me about how the book, a graphic novel about girl soccer players, contained a sexual scene between two of the young girls at a sleepover. My mind flashed back to that day in the library, with my daughter mentioning one of the books she had picked out in the graphic novel section that she was the most excited about: it was about soccer players, just like her! I looked in my trunk and confirmed it: the book two different mothers had warned me about was sitting in my own trunk, picked out by my young daughter at our local library just a week prior. It went right into the return pile, thankfully unread.

How does this happen? How does a graphic novel written for and marketed to children end up including a scene about a sexual encounter between two young girls at a sleepover? How does that scene get approved by editors, by a publisher, and then, by librarians? There are a number of steps and "lines of defense" between an author's idea and that author's work that ended up printed and in circulation in a library system. Was this a mistake? Or is it part of something more widespread and sinister?

If you've read this far, you already know the answer to that question.

Indoctrinating a society by indoctrinating its children is nothing new; it's the oldest play in the propagandist playbook, as you read in chapter one. Before television and movies, children's literature served as the primary vehicle for child propaganda. Writing for *Atlas Obscura* in 2017, Anika Burgess examined Soviet children's literature, quoting Andrea Immel, curator of the Cotsen Children's Library at Princeton University, who says, "reformers or radicals believed that the key to a

better future was to provide children with books communicating su-
perior values" and that "one of the best ways to turn the tide was to
bring up children differently."[11]

In the modern era, we're watching a similar effort aimed at indoctrinating children via literature, albeit sponsored not by a state but instead
by an ideologically captured corporate elite and supported by a market
that has been infiltrated to incentivize woke ideology over more traditional fare. Now, even children's librarians have fallen prey to the woke
agenda, and they're inflicting it on kids.

Once upon a time, libraries didn't take political positions or stances;
they just existed to provide every possible literary perspective to patrons.
They would stock books that were not just your standard children's
classics, but also material from the Left and the Right and maintained a
neutral stance on that content. Those days are over, and the end came
right from the top of the profession. One librarian remarked to me, "I'm
a librarian in my late 50s, and I barely recognize my profession anymore.
I think the most egregious example of this trend is the 2021 American
Library Association (ALA) 'Resolution to Condemn White Supremacy
and Fascism as Antithetical to Library Work,' which was adopted by the
ALA Council. It proposes that the profession forsakes one of its core
values—neutrality—and directs a sub-committee to come up with new
language to replace it." What are the core values of the ALA? It isn't exposing patrons to challenging ideas and quality literature, or providing
a vital public service. It's a certain kind of activism. "However," my
source continued, "a close reading of the document shows that none of
the five sources that it cites in the opening paragraph actually support
the proposition that neutrality buttresses or enables 'white supremacy.'
In fact, one of the articles (by Em Claire Knowles, a member of the ALA's
Black Caucus) actually defends neutrality. Myself and some of my colleagues are appalled that the Council could have adopted something this
shoddily researched and argued."[12] The fact that such shoddy work will
be accepted and adopted as readily as serious scholarship exposes the
pressure institutions feel to conform, and the fear of the consequences

of falling outside the lines. Wokeness metastasizes through sheer force. The seeming ridiculousness of its arguments is no safeguard against its intrusion into academic spaces.

Nor do woke warriors even try to hide their agenda. In the spring of 2022, a self-proclaimed lesbian Marxist, Emily Drabinski, was elected president of the ALA. In her vision for the ALA that led to her election, Drabinski wrote, "The consequences of decades of unchecked climate change, class war, white supremacy, and imperialism have led us here. If we want a world that includes public goods like the library, we must organize our collective power and wield it."[13] Mombian, a site for lesbian moms, highlighted more of Drabinski's background: "Her scholarship has included work on applying queer theory to library cataloging and library spaces, including a 2014 paper in which she critiqued how gender is identified in library cataloging rules, and a 2008 paper in which she explored some implications of a Florida county's negative response to a library Pride exhibit."[14] The ALA went into this with eyes wide open.

At its last in-person conference before the onset of the COVID-19 pandemic, the ALA devoted a full third of its programming to woke content, according to the journalist Joy Pullman. Writing about the event for *The Federalist* in July of 2019, Pullman explained that the conference "featured more than 100 workshops with an 'equity, diversity, and inclusion' theme," addressing both race and gender/sexuality.[15] She writes, "That included workshops with these titles (some shortened): 'Creating Queer-Inclusive Elementary School Library Programming,' 'Developing an Online Face for a Lesbian Pulp Fiction Collection,' and 'Telling Stories, Expanding Boundaries: Drag Queen Storytimes in Libraries,' . . . 'A Child's Room to Choose: Encouraging Gender Identity and Expression in School and Public Libraries,' and 'Are You Going to Tell My Parents?: The Minor's Right to Privacy in the Library.'" One of the slides informed attendees that "talking with kids about race is essential work that we should all be engaging in. We live in a country built on white supremacy. White supremacy is the operating system in the U.S. We are here to push against systemic, institutional, and individual racism."[16] This is the goal of the group responsible for choosing which books are available to children in libraries across the country.

These priorities also inform the ALA's selection of award winners. In a column in early 2022 for the *Wall Street Journal* about the announcement of the most recent ALA award-winning books, Meghan Cox Gurdon explained that selections demonstrate "a determined effort to shape the culture. People in the industry say as much. There's been gushing, for instance, that Kyle Lukoff's novel 'Too Bright to See,' about a trans middle-school child with they/them pronouns, won a Newbery Honor. . . . It's something parents may want to keep in mind when they see an ALA medallion."[17]

One of the primary policy focuses of the ALA involves "fighting censorship," as they see it, at least. The ALA compiles lists of "banned" books that they "celebrate" in honor of "the freedom to read."[18] These books are ones that patrons have filed some sort of an objection to. Looking at the titles on these lists over the years is quite revealing. In 2013, the most commonly opposed book on the ALA list was a popular graphic novel series called *Captain Underpants*, which is filled with "offensive language." My sons love them. While they aren't what I love my kids to read, they are only mildly objectionable.

Between 2013 and the present, however, the content of the top ten most challenged books list took a dark turn. For three years running (2018, 2019, and 2020), *George* by Alex Gino took the top spot. In 2018, the ALA explained the most common reason for objections to *George* was "because it was believed to encourage children to clear browser history and change their bodies using hormones, and for mentioning 'dirty magazines,' describing male anatomy, 'creating confusion,' and including a transgender character."[19]

Here's an excerpt from *George*, just to get an idea of what many parents objected to:

> George stopped. It was such a short little question, but she couldn't make her mouth form the sounds.

Mom, what if I'm a girl?

George had seen an interview on television a few months ago with a beautiful woman named Tina. She had golden-brown skin, thick hair with blond highlights, and long, sparkling fingernails. The interviewer said that Tina had been born a boy, then asked her whether she'd had the surgery. The woman replied that she was a transgender woman and that what she had between her legs was nobody's business but hers and her boyfriend's.

So George knew it could be done. A boy could become a girl. She had since read on the internet you could take girl hormones that would change your body, and you could get a bunch of different surgeries if you wanted them and had the money. This was called transitioning. You could even start before you were eighteen with pills called androgen blockers that stopped the boy hormones already inside you from turning your body into a man's. But for that, you needed your parents' permission.[20]

This is a book marketed for ages eight to twelve. It was the winner of the Stonewall Book Award, Lambda Literary Award, E.B. White Read Aloud Honor, and a best book of the year for *Booklist, School Library Journal,* and *Kirkus Reviews.* It also won a New York Public Library Notable Book Award. This is what librarians are recommending kids be reading, and attempts to shield children from content like it is viewed by librarians as "book banning." *Captain Underpants* is downright wholesome in comparison to this.

Oh, and in case a story about a fourth grader scouring the internet for advice on prescription hormones and sex-change surgery wasn't dizzying enough, the title of *George* isn't even *George* anymore; it's *Melissa. The Guardian* reported in November 2021—six years after *George* was initially published—that "Gino and publisher Scholastic said they made a mistake in titling it with a name 'the main character does not like or want to use for herself' . . . Now Scholastic and Gino are officially changing the title of the book from *George* to *Melissa* 'to respect Melissa

[George's preferred name when he begins identifying as a girl] and all trans people', said the author."[21] Nothing is ever woke enough.

Other books the ALA defended on its challenged books list included *Beyond Magenta: Transgender Teens Speak Out* by Susan Kuklin, *Stamped: Racism, Antiracism, and You* by Ibram X. Kendi and Jason Reynolds, and *Something Happened in Our Town: A Child's Story About Racial Injustice* by Marianne Celano, Marietta Collins, and Ann Hazzard, and illustrated by Jennifer Zivoin. The top six "banned" books of 2020 were, in reality, woke books that patrons objected to for their depictions of sexuality, anti-police sentiment, and overall political divisiveness. In 2019, the top six spots were similar in makeup, with eight of the top ten "censored" books the ALA mentioned objected to by parents because of their woke or non-age-appropriate content.[22] For parents who want to be able to go into the kids' section without having to prescreen every picture book their kid picks up, librarians across the country are basically telling them, "Tough luck. We know what's best when it comes to the content your kids should be reading."

Librarians ought to be (and used to be) guardians and fighters for freedom of literary expression. Not so. Librarians today are fierce defenders of the ability to expose children and teens to sexually explicit content. Those books will not be "censored." But when a book or author doesn't tow the party line, librarians engage in their own form of censorship. For example, a librarian in Indiana (not exactly a progressive stronghold) told me, "A [fellow] librarian . . . didn't think we should be doing Harry Potter programs because [J.K. Rowling] is a TERF." TERF, or trans-exclusionary radical feminist, is a term used by the Left against actual feminists like Rowling who defend the definition of womanhood and the safety of women in women's spaces. Norwegian libraries have gone so far as to cancel Potter events over the controversy.[23]

It's not just modern literary heroes who dare to deviate from the woke orthodoxy on gender that are targeted by woke library professionals. Acclaimed classics are under attack as well. In the summer of 2018, the Association for Library Service for Children (ALSC), a division of the ALA, voted to strip Laura Ingalls Wilder's name from its lifetime achievement award for children's literature. On their website, the ALSC explained, "This decision was made in consideration of the fact that Wilder's legacy, as represented by her body of work, includes expressions of stereotypical attitudes inconsistent with ALSC's core values of inclusiveness, integrity and respect, and responsiveness."[24]

Next, they came for *The Cat in the Hat.* In 2019, Colorado Public Radio reported, "This week, millions of students and teachers are taking part in Read Across America, a national literacy program celebrated annually around the birthday of Theodor Geisel, better known as Dr. Seuss. . . . But some of Seuss's classics have been criticized for the way they portray people of color and the author's personal legacy has also come into question. In light of this, the National Education Association rebranded the event in 2017, backing away from Seuss books and Seuss-themed activities. Its website now highlights works by and about people of color."[25]

Tragically, the decision to remove several Dr. Seuss books from circulation in the spring of 2021 was undertaken by the very people in charge of upholding Seuss's legacy. Six Dr. Seuss books—including *And to Think That I Saw It on Mulberry Street* and *If I Ran the Zoo*—were canceled because of "racist and insensitive imagery" according to Dr. Seuss Enterprises, the company that preserves and protects the author's legacy. Dr. Seuss Enterprises, in a statement that was given on the author's birthday, told the Associated Press, "These books portray people in ways that are hurtful and wrong."[26] The statement also remarked: "Ceasing sales of these books is only part of our commitment and our broader plan to ensure Dr. Seuss Enterprises' catalog represents and supports all communities and families."[27] Instead of excising a few marginally eyebrow-raising illustrations, they threw out entire classics completely, essentially throwing out the baby with the bathwater because of select illustrations that suddenly, after decades of printing, were characterized as racist. While Seuss's widow, Audrey Geisel, founded Dr. Seuss Enterprises in 1993, it is now run by a CEO unrelated to the family and who treats it as a business and brand instead of as a personal mission. Thus, it is not Seuss's family or kin defending his legacy who are making these decisions; it is simply unrelated people. In a truly dystopian move, the books weren't just taken off the publishing schedule; they disappeared from circulation on used books reseller websites, and existing copies were removed from Amazon. In a telling twist, before they were removed from circulation completely, sales went through the roof, with Americans realizing that access to these classics would soon become limited.

American librarians are talking out of two sides of their mouths: they are decrying the "censorship" of books that are wholly inappropriate for children while at the same time engaging in actual censorship against classic writers like Jane Austen, Dr. Seuss, and Laura Ingalls Wilder.

Seuss isn't the only author to have their literary legacy betrayed by those who should be responsible for guarding and honoring it. In April of 2021, exhibits at the Jane Austen Museum were being revamped as staff "re-evaluated" Jane Austen's place in relation to "Regency-era slavery" in the wake of Black Lives Matter protests.[28] Also in the spring of 2021, John Daniel Davidson reported for *The Federalist* that The Tolkien Society annual conference would focus on "Tolkien and Diversity."[29] Davidson writes, "Papers to be presented include, 'Gondor in Transition: A Brief Introduction to Transgender Realities in The Lord of the Rings,' 'The Lossoth: Indigeneity, Identity, and Antiracism,' and 'Something Mighty Queer': Destabilizing Cishetero Amatonormativity in the Works of Tolkien."[30]

There are no classic books safe from the mob's pitchforks. In a survey about summer book lists in 2022, the *School Library Journal* (SLJ) asked K–12 librarians and teachers to identify titles they would suggest removing. The SLJ wrote, "*To Kill a Mockingbird* and *The Great Gatsby* were the top books people wanted cut from lists, while favorite titles to add included the graphic novel *New Kid* by Jerry Craft and the novel *The Hate U Give* by Angie Thomas. Instead of historical fiction, some respondents suggested science fiction and manga."[31] The SLJ quoted one teacher saying, "Students cannot relate to some [older books] anymore. I understand that classics should be appreciated, but I think it's time to allow books published from the 2000s to be given a fair shake."[32] Daniel Buck, the editor of the education watchdog website Chalkboard Review, remarked about the list, "They'll tell you this is about diversifying curriculum. It's not. It's about getting rid of any commitment to excellence, aesthetic beauty, or canons."[33] Buck continued, "The irony. The list of books they want to remove would make a brilliant high school curriculum."[34] This is the future that the woke want: an erasure of the past, of all classics, replacing them with books about radical gender ideology, from toddlers to adults.

Librarians and teachers exert a huge influence on what children—and adults—read. One librarian told me, "I have a co-librarian who also orders books. If I wasn't there, we would have no biographies on Donald Trump. I had to push to order some several years into his presidency. Yet, the second Biden won, she ordered several books on both Biden and Harris. I won't even tell you how many Obama books we have (at least ten). This is how the message is being pushed—through super unbalanced collection development."

The power of librarians, library associations, and the top review companies not only impacts what appears on library shelves but also what content makes its way through the publishing process itself. From the perspective of publishers, the financial incentive is to continue to publish books on progressive figures and ideas because librarians are guaranteed to order these books to stock their shelves in local libraries, school libraries, and classrooms across the country. Appeasing the tastes of progressive librarians is financially advantageous for publishing companies, which are already ideologically inclined toward woke content from the outset. A librarian told me, "Collection purchasing decisions [are] heavily encouraged to skew Left/woke and suppress conservative viewpoints."[35] Think about the market dynamics at play: one conservative parent only buys one copy of a book, but a woke school librarian could be responsible for purchasing a dozen or more, all with funds from taxpayers for libraries and school libraries. For example, at my local library in Montgomery County, Maryland, the entire system owns eighty-five copies of the board book *Antiracist Baby* by Ibram X. Kendi and thirty-nine copies of the book in paperback form. When publishers are faced with book proposals, they know they can sell more copies of woke books in bulk to libraries than more neutral or—gasp—conservative books to individual families.

At large publishing companies, the woke worldview is the default, and those involved in the process, from editors to executives, are only too happy to conform to the wishes of librarian organizations like the ALA. For conservative children's books like mine (I edit a series of children's biographical books called *Heroes of Liberty*), *The Tuttle Twins*, and various children's titles by Fox News personalities like *Freddy the Frogcaster* by Janice Dean, there is a large and captive audience of conservative parents looking for "safe" content for kids. But in order to publish these titles, they need a famous name and a conservative imprint (like Dean at Regnery Books) or must self-publish with their own publishing house (like *Heroes of Liberty* and *The Tuttle Twins* have done).

I spoke with one editor at a large publishing house, Susan, who works exclusively on their children's books, about how the obsession over equity, diversity, and other woke buzzwords impacts her work. She told me about how, on the most basic level, it's eating hours and hours of her work weeks with nonstop meetings. She explained, "We have biweekly meetings to discuss the initiatives we're going to take to make our publishing programs more woke and activist oriented." Another goal of these meetings is to align the publishing house's hiring to make its employee base more woke.

She noticed the shift occurring about a decade ago: "There was always an interest in publishing a diversity of voices and perspectives. [But] ten years ago, that meant something wholly different. I think there was always a desire to be inclusive and help children from all backgrounds to see themselves in books they have access to. [But], whereas [once] the real impetus was to find great books, meaningful books and not really put the color of the author's skin at the fore, now the question of race and sexual orientation and gender and all those woke buzzwords feels like it's more important than finding great literature. I've never been told that we shouldn't sign up white authors ten years ago; but now it's being said. We've been told: 'we have quotas now.'"[36] She literally means quotas. Susan was told by superiors that she had to publish a certain number of authors of different "minority" groups, from racial to sexual, every year. The books had to touch on or revolve around these themes as well.

I heard from a number of authors about how these quotas and fixations on woke storylines impact the quality of the work being published. When publishing houses find themselves more concerned with promoting black, indigenous, and people of color (BIPOC) authors writing about transgender children than they are with publishing literature that will stand the test of time, the end product isn't going to be nearly to the level of the books in the canon of classic literature. When the top priority of a writer, agent, or editor is producing woke content instead of producing art, the quality inevitably suffers. Imagine how many hours of Susan's days are wasted on diversity and activism meetings that would be better spent combing through manuscripts, fine-tuning them, and mentoring talented writers. It's no longer about reading quality literature to children. It's about getting the progressive message out to them so they are indoctrinated.

If we're not seeing books like *Adventures of Huckleberry Finn* or *The Chronicles of Narnia* being published by major publishing houses, what kind of literature *is* being churned out? How bad could it be, you might wonder. Buckle up.

Recently at a local library, a friend spotted a new book on display in the picture-book section (for ages four to eight years old) called *How Mamas Love Their Babies* by Juniper Fitzgerald, a radical feminist who tweets frequently about the honor of "sex work." The book flap reads, "Illustrating the myriad ways that mothers provide for their children— piloting airplanes, washing floors, or dancing at a strip club—this book is the first to depict a sex-worker parent. It provides an expanded notion of working mothers and challenges the idea that only some jobs result in good parenting. We're reminded that, while every mama's work looks different, every mama works to make their baby's world better."[37] Kids know that all different kinds of jobs exist; that's not the purpose of this book. This book wants to send kids a message that validates and legitimizes sex workers.

Also written for children between four and eight, *Julián Is a Mermaid* won the Stonewall Children's and Young Adult Literature Award. The ALA explains, "The Stonewall Book Awards are presented to English-language books that have exceptional merit relating to the LGBTQIA+ experience."[38] A 2018 picture book with over 3,700 reviews and an average rating of 4.9 stars on Amazon, and deemed a "Teachers' pick" on the site, *Julián Is a Mermaid* depicts a young boy dressing in drag as a mermaid. In their review, the website Gothamist gushed, "This beautiful book is one of the very few picture books about a gender non-conforming child. Yet it feels like a celebration of all children who want to do things differently than the parental figures in their lives—and a love letter to the grownups who deeply understand them."[39] Imagine the message this sends to kids: being "gender non-conforming" is something to celebrate. And the message to parents: the only way to "deeply understand" a child is to accept all of their imaginings when it comes to gender.

In fact, Scholastic, one of the largest publishing houses for children's literature, has an entire featured section on their website devoted to "LGBTQIA+" topics. Among those books is *George*, the top ALA "censored" book several years running mentioned earlier in the chapter. Other books featured in the same section for middle and high school students: *Drag Teen*, a novel by Jeffery Self, and the graphic novel series *Heartstopper* by Alice Oseman, optioned by Netflix for the screen. These graphic novels, with story lines about psych wards, homophobia, eating disorders, and self-harm, are marketed to young teens and older adolescents, which is often inappropriate in itself. But because they look like comic books, they can also find their way into shelves accessible for younger children as well.

Plus for middle and high schoolers, the content gets increasingly sexually graphic. In Virginia, Fairfax County Public Schools celebrated a victory at the end of 2021: they would reintroduce books with porno-graphic material after a fight by members of the parent community to get them removed, explaining the move was the district "reaffirming their ongoing commitment to provide diverse reading materials that reflect the student population."[40] One of those books, *Gender Queer* by Maia Kobabe, features illustrated scenes of sexual acts like blow jobs and text with conversations about sex involving minors. It's not just pushing the envelope; it's straight pornographic content.

It's not enough to indoctrinate kids with sexually charged content; the other main focus is on making kids hyperaware of race, often through a critical race theory (CRT) lens. Colin Kaepernick's new chil-dren's book about race, also from Scholastic, while surprisingly inof-fensive overall, boasts a page recommending other black trailblazers and heroes who "inspire, create, lead and change the world" with black nationalists pictured like Malcom X, famed anti-Semite and author Toni Morrison, and Olympic athletes holding up the black power sign at the medals ceremony.[41] Scholastic also added Che Guevara and Fidel Castro, two radical violent communist revolutionaries, to their "Who Was?" biography series, which, according to Scholastic, exists to "tell the incredible stories of trailblazers, legends, innovators, and creators."[42] To place figures like these alongside Abraham Lincoln and Neil Armstrong, equating the two groups, normalizes the dangerous ideas of these individuals, putting them on equal footing with actual heroes. In no world could one compare Castro with Lincoln, except apparently in the Scholastic universe.

The situation with Scholastic is made even more disturbing be-cause Scholastic enjoys an unusual position of access to American school children through its effective monopoly on school book fairs. In 2019, Joy Pullman reported on the contents of the Scholastic Book Fair catalog for *The Federalist*, writing, "Inside, we find a novel about a middle-school girl who is cast as Romeo in the school production of *Romeo and Juliet* and finds herself attracted to the also-female lead playing Juliet. Is it possible to be bisexual in middle school, the catalog copy breathlessly asks?"[43] Another title, from the author of the highly controversial *George (Melissa),* is called, *You Don't Know Everything, Jilly P!,* and defined by the author as a heartwarming tale about bigotry. Pullman continues, "Then there is the also gender-bending 'The Witch Boy,' by Molly Ostertag. It's also aimed at children ages eight to 12."[44] These are the books Scholastic chose to sell to American schoolchildren.

Scholastic is far from the only offender, as every other major publisher publishes similar titles touching on these race and gender themes; they're just the only American publishing company with unfettered access to schools via book fairs.

Publishing companies are further incentivized to publish woke content because these books tend to get better reviews, which are crucial for garnering bestseller status. This process is also skewed toward books which promote a certain ideology. A private school librarian alerted me to a new picture book called *Bright Star.* She told me, "[There are] beautiful illustrations but the concept is strange. It's basically about how the construction of the border wall is destroying the ecology of that area and hurting the migrants who are stuck on the border. This is meant to be read to very young children and is considered a contender for the Caldecott [Award]."[45] Positive reviews and placement on suggested book lists lead to awards, which are directly linked to sales.

Kiri Jorgensen is the publisher and senior editor at Chicken Scratch Books and talked to me about how her company, which was created to provide a safe alternative for parents looking for quality modern children's literature, confirmed this causality. She told me, "One list I use in my presentations is the [Publisher's Weekly] '2021 Best Books for a Summer Read' and if you go through the dozen books they're listing, it's pretty eye-opening; the books they say are the best books of the year and the books that are going to win the awards and the books that are being highlighted. Most of them bring in some sort of environmental issue or sexuality or racism. Most of the books bring in all of those agendas. . . . It shows what they're emphasizing, it shows what they're promoting. And those will be the books that win the awards for the year; therefore, the libraries and schools will pick them up because they're award-winners. It's all a big conglomerate of them working together to get these agendas into the minds of our kids."[46]

A librarian explained to me how powerful these lists and awards can be: "Most school librarians are super pressed for time because they both teach and run the library. Imagine a public children's librarian single handedly doing four story times a day, and doing circulation, and ordering books, and managing the physical space, doing book repairs, etc. Many books are ordered based on the starred reviews in Booklist, School Library Journal, Horn Book, etc. And the industry in general is currently very biased, so those woke books get the starred reviews and then end up on the shelves."[47]

The 2021 Newbery Medal award winner, *When You Trap a Tiger*, is a good example of how the process rewards and incentivizes progressive content; its status as a Newbery book meant a massive bump in sales. But woven into the story about a Korean-American girl hearing stories from her grandmother is a subplot involving a sister with a crush on a girl at school. There are countless examples of more subvert propaganda making its way into modern children's media in books and movies.

Josh, a young adult and adult author published by a major publishing company, explained how this kind of subplot has become so common. He told me, "If you're a young author, agents are telling them, 'If only you had a gay or trans character in this book, maybe we could sell this.' They're messing with the art in order to shoe-horn these characters in."[48]

I spoke to a number of previously published and aspiring authors, and all of them related a similar tale: They were finding themselves increasingly shut out of the industry unless they were willing to conform to the woke narrative and include its themes in their work.

Christine, a middle-grade author with books published by a Big Five publisher and whose work appears on shelves in Barnes & Noble, told me, "I don't want to use hyperbole; I'm a person of faith and there is an enemy prowling. He is in the middle grade books."[49] As the mother of a daughter who is currently racing through middle-grade books, I can attest to the shocking content that publishers and librarians find to be acceptable for children in second grade and up. It's not just sexualized content like we saw in *The Breakaways*; it's the unimaginative drivel that is published by an industry terrified of falling afoul of "sensitivity" screeners.

It's a catch-22. Authors must include diverse characters, but then they're blasted for not portraying them the "right" way. The *New York Times* reported, "Children's book publishers have grown increasingly cautious when acquiring books that deal with charged subjects such as race, gender, sexuality and disability. Many publishers and authors now hire 'sensitivity readers' who vet books and identify harmful stereotypes."[50] Christine gave one example, "I have a character who was African American, and everything I had her do my editor [chided me] 'That's stereotypical!' . . . if she had any flaws at all. But if we can't write flawed characters, we're going to get a lot of boring and shallow books. They're so prescriptive. We're not allowed to let characters mess up, except the white one." For another book, she was told she couldn't have non-white bullies in her book about middle-school-aged kids.

This hews pretty closely to propaganda rules under Mao and Stalin— that's why they had culture ministers. For example, in Russia, you couldn't depict a house on fire in art or literature, because it suggested that their fire prevention institutions weren't capable of getting that put out. The proletariat had to be pure and good with no flaws.

Christine went on, saying, "What you're allowed to write about is so small. If you try to write outside of your experiences in any small way, you just really can't win. Unless you're going in with a very strong agenda, then you can win. And that's why they're the books being pushed on kids. If you look at what's selling for middle grades, it's super agenda-driven. You're between a rock and a hard place; it's a hard time to be a middle grade author who's just trying to create hope-filled content and not woke content."

Christine continued by explaining how the entire process is stacked against her and traditional and wholesome stories in favor of an extremist woke agenda. She told me, "Every time I get a book deal, it feels like a miracle. First I pitch ideas to my agent. [Once], I pitched an idea that was not my life experience but I have extensive experience learning about; one of the fun things about being a writer is writing about new things you have to learn about. But if it's outside of your experience, you're told you better watch out and be careful. [We're told to] send the list of 'sensitivity readers' you're going to use. I can't spend a lot of time on a book my agent doesn't feel confident about . . . But it's very important to me to not just have books about white characters, they aren't realistic. But every note on my books from editors (who are white themselves) is critiquing the non-white character portrayal."[51] The problem isn't just Christine's editors; it's the entire industry.

So how do they want race portrayed? The review of the 2020 winner of the coveted Kirkus Award in the children's category, *I Am Every Good Thing* by Derrick Barnes, gives a good window into the kind of content and narrative that those at Kirkus (and other reviewers) are most interested in. The review calls the book a "celebration of Black excellence . . . [that] provides a tool for building Black resilience."[52] The artwork depicts "black boys of every shade of brown playing, celebrating, achieving, aspiring, and loving. Through every stroke readers will see that Black boys are 'worthy / to be loved.'"[53] This is the kind of content the children's book publishing industry craves: hyper-focused on race and displaying only positive characteristics.

Now, I'm all for books portraying racially diverse characters. Historically there have not been enough books about black characters in children's literature; books like Ezra Jack Keats's *The Snowy Day* and *Whistle for Willie* were the exception, not the rule. But with classic books like Keats's, the emphasis wasn't on a character's race; it was instead focused on the character's adventures and stories. They showed children of all races that a black child could be the main character in a children's book, but they didn't set race as the focal point of the boy's identity. Writing in *Commentary* magazine in February 2022, Abe Greenwald said it best: "Being told that you are destined to be only your race, never an individual, cuts against the American creed."[54] This is exactly what we're doing when we publish children's literature obsessed with race to the exclusion of everything else. We strip black children of the ability to see themselves as anything but their race, and we strip children of other races of seeing their black friends as individuals.

Today, thanks to the woke censors, black characters can only be portrayed in one way, victims, and their race must be the focus of the story. Deviate from this script, and everyone involved with the project is put at risk. If any part of a book's content doesn't pass the ambiguous woke litmus test of any random person online, an online mob can form, jeopardizing the whole project.

Unfortunately, the woke mob comes for authors frequently and often claims scalps. Such was the case with a young adult novel called *Blood Heir* by Amélie Wen Zhao, which involved slavery as part of the fantasy plot. Alexandra Alter reported in the *New York Times* that "on her website, she described how 'Blood Heir,' which takes place in a fictional Cyrilian empire where a group of powerful people called Affinites are feared and enslaved, drew on real-world issues, including 'the demonization of the Other and this experience of not belonging.'" She even paid lip service to the anti-Trump orthodoxies required of the day, writing on her website, "As a foreigner in Trump's America, I've been called names and faced unpleasant remarks—and as a non-citizen, I've felt like I have no voice—which is why I've channeled my anger, my frustration, and my need for action into the most powerful weapon I have: my words."[55] It wasn't enough. A mob composed mostly of people who had not read the unreleased book accused Zhao of being racially insensitive in her depiction of slavery. The firestorm led Zhao to pull the book before it was even published, a book that was part of a three-book package sold to Delacorte Press for more than $500,000.

Blood Heir is far from the only children's book to have met its doom at the hands of the woke mob. In its article on the demise of Zhao's book, the *New York Times* reported, "In 2016, a picture book titled *A Birthday Cake for George Washington* was withdrawn from stores after critics complained that it glossed over the horrors of slavery. A similar scandal engulfed the 2015 picture book *A Fine Dessert*, which depicted an enslaved mother and daughter hiding in a cupboard and cheerfully licking a bowl of batter clean. . . . In 2017, Laura Moriarty's dystopian novel, *American Heart*, was savaged, months before its release, by readers who said Ms. Moriarty had peddled a 'white savior narrative' in her depiction of a future America where Muslims are placed in internment camps. Harlequin Teen delayed publication of Keira Drake's fantasy novel, *The Continent*, after readers blasted it as 'racist trash,' 'retrograde' and 'offensive.'"[56]

Rachel Rooney, a (formerly) successful children's poet, is another cautionary tale. Josephine Bartosch with *UnHerd* reported on the "trans publishing purge" and profiled Rooney who, "with nine books and several prizes to her name—her debut collection, *The Language of Cat*, was long-listed for the Carnegie Medal."[57] But her career came to a screeching halt "following what she describes as 'two and a half years of intensive bullying for doing nothing more than telling the truth': namely, that there's something deeply concerning about the prevailing orthodoxy around gender identity."[58]

According to Bartosch, Rooney began to "gently question whether our understanding of gender identity has become warped" because she "felt compelled to investigate why so many autistic teenagers were identifying as the opposite sex." Rooney explains why curiosity had been sparked: "I was once a gender non-conforming autistic child . . . I know how it is to be uncomfortable in your own skin, to hate what society tells you it is to be female." She actually wanted to support children like herself who felt uncomfortable with their bodies—while challenging the increasingly trendy, "simplistic idea" that such children had been "born in the wrong body." Rooney ironically laments, "I had always been progressive, even 'woke'."[59]

None of this mattered to the woke police. Bartosch continues, "While JK Rowling might be too famous to cancel, those with heterodox views in the foothills of literary fame have two choices: keep quiet or leave." When Rooney dared begin to question the woke orthodoxy on gender identity, she became a pariah in the industry. Bartosch reports, "Rooney received an urgent call from her agent to inform her that the publisher of her children's books was unhappy with her outspoken questioning of gender identity." Rooney relates, "I was told that my stance could be considered offensive and that people had been complaining. Two independent bookshops had refused to stock my latest picture book, *The Problem with Problems*, even though it was entirely unrelated to gender ideology."[60] For a children's book author to buck the trend of total and complete acceptance of the woke perception of gender, it's career-ending.

What can parents and concerned residents do about the woke takeover of the publishing industry and library system? Given that a great deal of the shift in kids' literature is driven by publicly funded institutions like schools and libraries, one librarian suggested, "Patrons need to use the online purchase suggestion forms that most libraries have and start asking for titles! I had already been trying to figure [out] a way to get your books into our libraries before today, but it is difficult to justify ordering from lists of different companies without a specific patron request or without surrounding libraries doing the same."[61] Moderates and conservatives should also vote with their wallets and support smaller publishers in a David and Goliath fight against the massive power that Scholastic (with its in-school book fairs) and other large publishers wield.

How can a parent identify appropriate reading material? Parents in America have come to think of any reading as good, thinking, "as long as they're reading." But we know that just like all food isn't equally nutritious, all books aren't equally beneficial. Some books are good quality, some are junk food, and some are straight poison. After a parent realizes this, how are they supposed to tell the difference?

There are a number of resources in the homeschooling community (lists from AmblesideOnline, Read-Aloud Revival, or The Good and the Beautiful) or from literacy experts in books like *Read-Aloud Revival* or *The Enchanted Hour*. All of these resources provide examples of quality reading material. After my experience when I let my daughter check out *The Breakaways*, I always recommend that parents look books up on Amazon and check the one-star reviews. Had I done so with *Breakaways*, I would have been alerted to parents sounding the alarm on the hidden sexual content. I had a similar experience after my daughter read the book series *Ivy & Bean*; she came to me to tell me that she didn't think it was appropriate how the characters were talking, and my daughter decried their poor manners and bad attitudes. I looked up the negative reviews on Amazon and patted her on the back; she was correct, with parents commenting about the same concerns. It's not realistic to expect parents, especially those of many kids and/or voracious readers, to screen every book. But having a suggested reading list and then screening the rest through one-star reviews can go a long way toward making sure that kids are reading appropriate content.

The next battleground parents have to address is television, even content marketed for children of an extremely tender age. At the start of Pride Month in June 2021, Nickelodeon shared a video on its official YouTube page for the show marketed for preschoolers called "Blue's Clues and You!" that featured an animated Pride parade led by American drag queen and activist Nina West.[62] But that wasn't enough. Viewers noticed the inclusion of a beaver with "top scars" (the scars from a surgical procedure known as "top surgery," in which biological females have their breasts removed).[63] This beaver appears during a portion of the video that features a family with transgender members. In addition to carrying the standard pride flag, members of this family wear bracelets and skirts and hold balloons with the colors of the transgender flag (light blue, pink, and white).

And then there's the cross-dressing, nonbinary Muppet. (Gosh, I never thought I'd be writing those words.) In the summer of 2021, the Disney Junior series *Muppet Babies* for children four years old and up featured one of its characters, Gonzo, dressing up in a ballgown and transforming into "Gonzo-rella." CNN applauded the plot, explaining, "Gonzo doesn't formally come out in the episode as nonbinary. But Gonzo's dream of donning a beautiful gown isn't played for laughs -- their desire is sincere, as is their fear that their friends won't accept them. Miss Piggy even uses 'they' and 'them' pronouns to refer to 'Gonzo-rella.'"[64]

And for older kids, it's much of the same on television. Take Cartoon Network's *Steven Universe*. CNN reported, "The cast is full of characters who are nonbinary, LGBTQ or otherwise challenge the gender binary through their gender expression." However, reporter Scottie Andrew gushes that *Steven Universe* "doesn't do subtle hints or winks to a character's identity or sexuality, and it doesn't deal in crude jokes designed to go over kids' heads. Characters aren't always labeled as nonbinary, queer or trans on the show. They simply are who they are." According to the show's creator, Rebecca Sugar, the show intends to "scramble all the gender tropes" in the hope that children will learn to "love the parts of [themselves they] see in that character."[65]

Steven Universe is one of a growing number of shows labeled PG that is aimed at redefining traditional gender roles for children. *Insider* reported a dramatic increase industry-wide in the number of characters in kids' cartoons occupying different places on the "gender spectrum." According to the analysis by *Insider*, there was a "222% increase from 2017 to 2019 in the number of LGBTQ characters confirmed in new series or [announced] by showrunners of series that had ended."[66] Another difference is the way the characters are presented. "Historically," says *Insider*, "that inclusion has been illustrated through subtextual representation, leaving viewers to extract what they will—or won't—from coded characters and storylines. But in the past decade, small-screen animation has undergone a noticeable shift. Representation in children's cartoons in particular has increased in frequency, nuance, and overtness."[67] The representation is no longer "discrete" and now overtly promotes the woke agenda regarding gender and sexuality.

You might expect the rating system to provide some guidance, but this is not often the case. For example, a popular Netflix show, *She-Ra and the Princesses of Power*—which boasts an official rating of TV-Y7-FV, indicating that it is technically most appropriate for children ages seven and up and contains some fantasy violence—has both central and secondary lesbian romances. This makes the show ill-suited for young kids unless the parent wants to have "the talk" with them young.

Another trend is taking beloved classics and twisting them to promote the woke agenda. In the summer of 2020, my friend Elisha Krauss wrote about a disastrous Netflix corruption of one such classic for *The Federalist*: "Betrayal, internet shaming, eating disorders, menstruation sculptures, feminism, gay dads, divorced families, transgender issues, and Tinder. Nope, this isn't the second season of Netflix's 'The Politician,' it's season one of the 'kid-friendly' show 'The Baby-Sitters Club.'"[68] Based on the popular book series of the same name, the show is rated TV-G and marketed for tweens.

Our research assistant, Neera Deshpande, commented, "I think the really pernicious thing about how Netflix does those shows is that they take these innocent concepts and characters (Archie! Sabrina!), often in high school settings, but then because there is no censorship (as there would be with, say, standard cable TV), there is gratuitous sex and violence and straight up indoctrination. It's almost a false marketing [situation]. You expect one thing with revivals, and suddenly you have 16-year-old girls watching unrealistic sex scenes that are way more explicit than they've ever been before on television."[69] With the advent of streaming, activist showrunners can indoctrinate unsuspecting audiences more easily on streaming than they ever could on broadcast.

But while broadcast TV has more constraints on content than streaming, it also has more commercials, which means that on broadcast TV, it's not just the content of the shows that needs to be monitored for propaganda, but the commercials too. In December of 2020, *The Daily*

Signal reported that Cartoon Network had created an "anti-racist" ad erroneously "claiming Thomas Edison didn't invent the lightbulb, and that the credit should instead go to black inventor Lewis Howard Latimer."[70] It goes on to claim that "all history is whitewashed and that systemic racism is inherent in the education system," and as of the publishing of *The Daily Signal* article, the ad is the pinned tweet on Cartoon Network's Twitter feed.[71]

Similarly, Nickelodeon aired a racially charged commercial highlighting scenes of Black Lives Matter protests with the stated goal of "equity and equality for all." The advertisement encouraged viewers—children—to become part of the "change," the "solution."[72] One child in the advertisement explained, "I want to live in a world where my future children can grow up and enjoy their innocence."[73] At the time of this writing, it appeared Nickelodeon was planning to do the same with Pride, listing an open casting call (with agents and all) "seeking Los Angeles based families with at least one child 4-8 years old who can speak about their connection to LGBTQIA+ Pride and the LGBTQIA+ community."[74] The call information included a commitment "to diverse, inclusive casting . . . without regard to disability, race, age, national origin, ethnic origin or any other protected grounds under applicable law." It donned a large rainbow flag square in the middle, with lots of decorative flare.

On PBS, which is funded by taxpayer dollars, even shows for preschoolers like *Arthur* have poisonous Easter eggs hidden within. In the summer of 2020, Ben Kew with *Breitbart* reported on a particularly political episode: "The segment began with a conversation between the protagonist Arthur the aardvark and his best friend, Buster the rabbit, in which the pair make obvious reference to the distressing video of George Floyd in police custody (though they don't mention Floyd by name)."[75] The dialogue was as follows:

"Did you see that video?" Arthur asks Buster.

"Yeah, I just watched it. It was awful! I can't believe someone would be hurt like that, just because they're black."

"Buster, it happens everywhere!" Arthur responds. "I was talking to Mrs. MacGrady the other day and she said there's a really long history of black people not being treated fairly in this country."

"It has to stop!" Buster exclaims.

Kew continues, saying, "The pair are later joined by their school lunch lady Mrs. MacGrady, who explains how racism is 'like a disease' that is 'gonna get worse' without further action. 'Yes, I saw [the video] too. And let me tell you, it made my blood boil,' she says." Mrs. Mac-Grady adds that "it's not enough to say, 'I'm not racist, it's not my problem.'" Kew explains, "This is not the first time that *Arthur* has employed progressive propaganda. Last May, the show featured the gay wedding of the protagonist's primary school teacher Mr. Ratburn."[76] Parents and kids place a great deal of trust in these kinds of shows, carried on a taxpayer-funded network. They trust in these writers and creators to provide their children with wholesome, unobjectionable content, and that trust is entirely misplaced.

Just like with books, paying attention to one-star reviews online and looking up potential shows and movies on Common Sense Media are important steps for parents wishing to keep tabs on what their children are watching. The assumption with any new show has to be that there will be objectionable content; and even shows we grew up on like *The Muppet Show* and *Blue's Clues* can't necessarily be trusted.

This is the state of children's entertainment today. Kids are exposed to sexuality and nonbinary gender norms in *Muppet Babies* and told that they're racist starting in baby board books. But there is some content that's a bridge too far for these woke elites. What is triggering enough to elicit a warning label or editing? *Lady and the Tramp, Home Alone, Peter Pan,* and *Dumbo.*

Back in 2019, Disney+ placed a warning in the description of films so that viewers were made aware of any controversial or outdated scenes before watching some of Disney's older, classic content, such as Disney's *Dumbo* and *Lady and the Tramp.* After it added warning labels,

Disney+ took the extra step to block some films like *Peter Pan, Dumbo, Lady and the Tramp,* and others for those viewers watching on children's profiles. They weren't totally removed, but now they can only be viewed by a user from an adult profile, not a child's. Following the 2020 election, a seconds-long cameo with Donald Trump was removed from the 1992 classic film *Home Alone 2.* The authoritarians, the book burners, the censors, are now the woke. God forbid we allow children to be exposed to "outdated" content peripherally related to race or a humorous depiction of a former president filmed two decades before his election.

For those of you keeping score at home: *Peter Pan, Dumbo,* and *Lady and the Tramp* are out. Gender-bending Muppets are in.

The censoring of libraries and streaming services makes clearer than ever the vital importance of owning physical media. Owning the physical copies of books and video media is expensive and takes up space, but as we've observed, when even Dr. Seuss and *Dumbo* aren't safe, there are truly no limits on what could "disappear" from "polite society" next.

There's a lot to be said for vintage when it comes to books and movies: The titles you loved as a kid are fun and safe to share with your kids. The most objectionable parts of films like *Richie Rich* seem almost quaint now, such as Richie's mother complimenting her husband's butt. Those were simpler times, and on rainy Sundays, it's better, easier, and more fun to take a trip down memory lane than to turn on live TV and watch what's currently airing on Nickelodeon or Cartoon Network.

Any form of media produced in the last ten years by a mainstream studio or publishing company should be considered suspect, guilty until proven innocent. It's not enough to look at reviews; it's imperative to look at the negative reviews first, in hopes of catching questionable content. It's always been safe to assume that internet-based content might contain inappropriate material, but parents have to also be on alert for everything, even books on the shelves of local libraries and the latest Disney or PBS offering. Even content that is billed as family-friendly or produced for children is now questionable—including, unfortunately, companies parents have memories of from their own childhoods. Children's media is now agenda-driven, with the intention of sending moral messages to readers and viewers. Those moral messages always existed in children's entertainment; but the creators' sense of morals has shifted significantly. No longer is the moral of the story just about sharing or being kind; now it is moral to practice radical acceptance of every racial and sexual theory of the day. Whereas the moral once was that we were color-blind with our friendships, now children are taught to be hyperconscious of race. Whereas the idea of introducing sex and sexuality to a young child was unthinkable, it's now commonplace to see Pride Month programming, and other content related to sexuality throughout the year.

5

THE PERIL OF WOKE MEDICINE

"I would never speak on the record about any of this because I'm terrified of losing my livelihood. I have a family that relies on my income. This is a career I've spent decades building from high school to medical school to the present. I'm terrified to speak out on the record because if I have an unpopular opinion and a 'wrong' opinion according to the conventional perspective of the day, that's it."

Almost every single expert I spoke to in this chapter echoed these remarks from Alexandra, a pediatrician working in a hospital in the Washington, DC, area. She was so nervous about speaking about how politics—more specifically, woke and progressive politics—had seeped into her work providing healthcare for children that she wouldn't even put a word in writing between the two of us.

Alexandra told me she had "never thought about how political the profession was until the last several years."[1] Several pediatricians echoed this observation, telling me they only noticed how politicized their profession had become in recent years, but especially during the COVID pandemic.

Throughout the mental and physical health establishment, there has been a takeover of woke ideology, from schools to training programs to workplaces. In many situations, it's possible for parents to opt out of how woke ideology is trying to creep into their children's lives; however, in the field of healthcare, it is impossible. We need doctors, psychiatrists, nurses, and therapists; we need them to be trustworthy in their ideology (not indoctrinating our children) but also just downright *competent*, and the prioritization of woke ideology comes at a cost: their ability to improve our health. Starting in medical school and working as a pediatrician, adhering to woke orthodoxy has become a distraction from what should be the only objective of medical providers: professional excellence. Medical schools, professional conferences, and even professional organizations shape the way care is provided, and when wokeness infects these institutions, at best, the quality of instruction and care is impacted, and at worst, patients are endangered.

Pediatrics is among the three most Left-leaning medical specialties, along with psychiatry and epidemiology according to a 2016 study. We find younger doctors are more liberal, which explains a great deal of how a global pandemic became so political as to erode patient care and health policy.[2] Research on this topic shows certain specialty areas to be overwhelmingly Democratic leaning. For example, 67 percent of general surgeons and 65 percent of anesthesiologists are Republican while only 32 percent of pediatricians and 24 percent of psychiatrists are. The results, while somewhat surprising, are still somewhat expected considering what we know of the field.

The first indications that the American Academy of Pediatrics (AAP), the most influential professional association in American pediatrics, wouldn't be doing their duty advocating for American children and their parents during COVID came in the summer of 2020, as school districts across the country debated their reopening plans. President Donald Trump had spoken out forcefully in favor of reopening in-person learning nationwide, and when Trump came out in favor of *anything*, that was the cue for anyone on the Left to advocate for exactly the opposite. That's what the politics of the day demanded of progressives. And so, that's exactly what the AAP did.

On July 10, 2020, Fox News reported, "The American Academy of Pediatrics joined teachers unions on Friday in calling threats from President Trump to withhold federal funding for schools that don't fully reopen this fall amid the coronavirus pandemic a 'misguided approach,' warning it would 'threaten the health' of students and teachers."[3] Just two weeks prior, the AAP had insisted policymakers "should start with a goal of having students physically present in school."[4] NPR reported, "The Trump administration this week repeatedly cited the AAP in pressuring school leaders to reopen. Dr. Sally Goza, the association's president, appeared at a White House roundtable with President Trump."[5] What changed? NPR explains, "The previous guidance was criticized for saying little about the safety of educators and other school personnel." The new statement called "for putting educators as well as other stakeholders at the center of decision-making."[6] Given the choice between students and their parents or teachers unions, the AAP sided with the latter. In so doing, the AAP doomed millions of American kids, mostly students in Left-leaning states and districts, to suffer through isolating and inferior remote learning for yet another school year.

Wrap your mind around that. The AAP had two roads in front of it in the summer of 2020. One: encouraging in-person learning because they knew it was best for America's children. The second: promoting public policy based on politics and the feelings of adults. The American Academy of Pediatrics chose to prioritize the feelings of adults over the well-being of children.

The AAP wasn't just content to side with teachers unions against American kids; by the following year, toward the end of summer 2021, it actively lied to parents about the effects of COVID-mitigation policies on child development in order to match the political narrative of the day. Specifically, they dramatically changed their tune about the importance of face time for infants.

Before this shift, the AAP had promoted a fact sheet titled "Face Time and Emotional Health," which was often distributed to new parents to educate them on infant development. The sheet read, "By the time babies are 6 to 8 weeks old, they may smile back when they see a face. These 'social smiles' are both fun and important. Make time for 'face time'! That means taking time to smile at your baby's face and to return a smile whenever your baby smiles . . . If your child learns early in life that he can easily get your attention by smiling or cooing or being happy, he will keep it up. But if you do not make time for face time, he may give up on smiling and try more fussing, crying and screaming to get the attention he needs."[7] Curiously, at the same time that the AAP began downplaying the importance of seeing faces, this fact sheet disappeared. But the internet is forever, and sleuths were able to dig up its contents, which you read above.

Instead, the AAP backpedaled to assure parents that masks were not a problem. On HealthyChildren.org, a parent-facing advice site, the AAP explained, "A year and a half into the COVID-19 pandemic and no solid end in sight, some families wonder whether continuous use of face masks by daycare providers, preschool teachers, and other adults may negatively affect their child's speech and language development. While this is a natural concern, there is no known evidence that use of face masks interferes with speech and language development or social communication. Plus, children can still get plenty of face time at home with mask-free family members."[8] Whereas the AAP—and common sense—once acknowledged the vital importance of seeing faces for child development, that undeniable truth was shelved for the sake of a narrative: that masks would help us claw out of the pandemic, and that there were absolutely no downsides whatsoever to their use.

In Europe and elsewhere in the world where policies are based upon the recommendations of the World Health Organization (WHO), the situation has been quite different. The WHO recommendation reads, "In general, children aged 5 years and under should not be required to wear masks. This advice is based on the safety and overall interest of the child and the capacity to appropriately use a mask with minimal assistance."[9] In contrast, the CDC and the AAP contended, without citing evidence for their divergent view, "Face masks can be safely worn by all children 2 years of age and older, including the vast majority of children with underlying health conditions, with rare exception."[10]

These recommendations ignore the negative impact masking has on language skills. Dr. Kristen Walsh, a pediatrician and early childhood champion for AAP in New Jersey for a decade, told me, "I am concerned that in this country, our pandemic mitigation measures for children have done, and continue to do, more harm than good. The U.S. has one of the strictest mask policies for young children in the world; if not the most strict! Prior to the pandemic, much of my advocacy work focused on early literacy and infant mental health, so I know how important it is for infants and young children to be able to see faces. Similarly, it is crucial for early literacy that students be able to see their teachers' faces, and vice versa. This is why many European countries are not mandating masks in schools for anyone under 12 and also don't recommend them for staff while teaching." Furthermore, she says evidence does not show that remaining unmasked in schools is dangerous: "In countries where they have had open schools without masking young children throughout the pandemic, they are not seeing excess student/child or teacher mortality—in many places, just the opposite, as attending school in person seemed to be protective."

For Dr. Walsh and others, it is near impossible to find a scientific basis for the American approach. Walsh told me, "I find it surreal that we are now in a place where the AAP seems to be trying to downplay the importance of seeing faces for babies and small children, in order to double down on a masking recommendation that, to me, is very hard to defend based on evidence. In all honesty, every day feels like I'm stuck in some sort of alternate reality or bad dream regarding the way we are treating children during this pandemic. I do feel that our pandemic response was heavily politicized, which really hampered our ability to have evidence-based responses that changed as our knowledge increased. Other Western nations seem to have done a much better job of pivoting with new knowledge than we have."[11] In short, she believes that politics drove the illogical masking policies that caused immeasurable harm to child development.

What makes "the science" so different across an ocean? We don't know; the CDC has never explained why their recommendations related to COVID differ so drastically from every other health agency anywhere else in the world. This is a question Rep. Jason Smith (R-AR) and Sen. Mike Lee (R-UT), among other congressional leaders, asked the CDC in a letter sent from their offices to the health agency. They requested an answer in May; they received it in August. The eventual response from the CDC? "In circumstances where the public faces an emerging threat, but where scientific evidence is limited, CDC adopts a conservative approach in making recommendations affecting the health and well-being of all Americans."[12] At the point this letter from the CDC was sent, we were a year and a half into the pandemic and had ready access to the data: we knew what risk COVID posed to children (to a healthy child, almost zero); we knew the efficacy of the vaccines at-risk adults had already received (high); and we knew the likelihood of spread from children to adults (minimal). The CDC went rogue, adopting recommendations that they refused to justify or explain, and hid behind absolutist and pompous assertions that their position was unquestionable and irrefutable. How dare Americans question them?

Another concern about the AAP amid the COVID pandemic expressed by every single pediatrician I spoke with was the threat of losing their medical licenses for spreading "misinformation." On July 29, 2021, the Federation of State Medical Boards issued a statement that read, "Physicians who generate and spread COVID-19 vaccine misinformation or disinformation are risking disciplinary action by state medical boards, including the suspension or revocation of their medical license. Due to their specialized knowledge and training, licensed physicians possess a high degree of public trust and therefore . . . must share information that is factual, scientifically grounded and consensus-driven for the betterment of public health."[13] Physicians asked and received no answer if they dared question: Who decides what is misinformation? What constitutes misinformation? What kind of process can one expect if they are accused of dissemination of 'misinformation'? Doctors around the country had their entire livelihoods threatened and could receive no reassurances about how they might stay within the good graces of the medical powers that be.

The result? A further stifling of free conversation and debate around COVID-mitigation policies and vaccines.

This has terrifying consequences for medical care. Alexandra, the hospitalist pediatrician in Washington, DC, explained why relying on official statements is a bad idea, especially when dealing with novel diseases: "By the time any official position guidelines or statements [are released], they are generally already outdated. There's a reason why people go to academic centers when [they're] really sick or [they] have a confusing diagnosis . . . You need state of the art things, and those aren't in the position statements." Leaving doctors with little to work with is not a sign that the medical boards and the CDC put the health of the nation's public over their own political agendas. Alexandra continues, "There's this idea that if this isn't something that the FDA, CDC or AAP hasn't put out in their position statement, [it must be] misinformation or wrong, when really those position statements are five or sometimes even ten years old—though obviously COVID moves faster. So it's really the . . . academic centers who are pushing the envelopes, the people in the new data in journal articles and studies . . . that's what informs good medical care. This idea that we only can rely on official guidelines as truth . . . What is truth? There is no truth. So to me, that's scary." When doctors are having to lower the bar for medical standards because of political agendas and orders from higher authorities, "we don't allow the people who are on the cutting edge of things to come out and to say things that may turn out to be totally wrong, or to raise issues or spark debate."[14] The fact that eighteen months into the pandemic the AAP and CDC were still recommending masking two-year-olds for eight hours a day because we had "limited data" on the "emerging threat" is evidence of Alexandra's concerns about what the stifling of free and open debate can do to medical care.

Debate is also stifled when it comes to issues of equity. The trend today is to emphasize anti-racism in healthcare to the degree that actual medicine takes a back seat.

In the short term, this stifling of debate during COVID was amplified because of the mediums through which the health community was forced to communicate during the pandemic. Online conversations on listservs and physician Facebook groups became dominated by the most paranoid and progressive voices; all other viewpoints were shut down or bullied into silence. Anyone with a cursory understanding of online political debate has witnessed how this dynamic takes shape. And unfortunately, these online debates are not just a Facebook fight between your college roommate from sophomore year and your colleague three jobs ago, but instead, between doctors who can impact health policy and healthcare.

One of the only pediatricians publicly addressing the issue of wokeness invading medicine is Dr. Erica Li, a member of the Foundation Against Intolerance and Racism (FAIR). FAIR's mission statement explains, "Increasingly, American institutions—colleges and universities, businesses, government, the media and even our children's schools— are enforcing a cynical and intolerant orthodoxy. This orthodoxy requires us to identify ourselves and each other based on immutable characteristics like skin color, gender and sexual orientation. It pits us against one another, and diminishes what it means to be human."[15] FAIR in Medicine, a sister organization, addresses these same issues within the medical field, and Dr. Li's focus is on pediatrics. She appeared in a video produced by the group about wokeism within the AAP's continuing education coursework.[16]

In a course titled "Fighting Racism to Advance Child Health" she explained, "In the course, I learned that in some training, pediatric resident doctors were divided into different groups based on their own skin color; there was a group for black doctors and a separate one for . . . white doctors. The presenter said, 'For our black, indigenous, and people of color groups, the work was around healing from trauma, reflection, and creating space to have discussions in a safer space without having to take care of the emotions of white people. The white group talked about topics like white fragility, power, privilege, and allyship.'"

For doctors of color, the messages of unavoidable victimhood were promulgated, and white doctors were bullied and reminded that they were irredeemable due to their race.

Unsurprisingly, this led to division and conflict. Dr. Li went on to explain, "Colleagues began telling me what was happening in their medical training programs. For example, residents in one psychiatry program were refusing to see patients suffering from psychosis who said racist words, directly violating well-established medical ethics. At another program, a medical student forced several deans to chant the phrase 'I'm a racist' in public. I also learned that the AAP had invited Ibram X. Kendi to give an address at the AAP's annual national conference. Dr. Kendi is a best-selling author and self-described antiracist who explicitly advocates *for* discrimination based on race. He has publicly criticized white people who have adopted black children, claiming that their motivation to do so is not to extend love to children in need of a family, but to use the children as props to hide their racism."[17] His inclusion at the AAP's conference is a troubling signal; that his ideas are endorsed by the leadership of the organization and should be disseminated to pediatricians nationwide.

Dr. Li shared another video available for continuing education for pediatricians called, "Fighting Racism to Advance Child Health Equity." The course description explains, "Structural racism, implicit bias, diversity, inclusion, and cultural humility are all concepts taking center stage in the medical community as we strive to end racism and improve health equity. This video series will explore what these concepts mean for pediatricians in our practices, institutions, and communities, and how we can advance child health equity by applying an anti-racist lens to the systems shaping health and medicine."[18] This doesn't sound so bad, you might say, but the content devolved into CRT propaganda by the second half of the four-hour course. The problem with this kind of messaging is that activism is prioritized over health, even during a pandemic.

Dr. Li explained how the course became progressively more extreme, telling me "the more juicy woke stuff is in the second half. I think they are strategic about trying to sound more reasonable [at the beginning]. That is how brainwashing works. It starts out as pretty reasonable and then it gives you incremental bits of crazy. Then at the very end, it becomes pretty crazy."[19] And she's right. The last part of the four-part course, given by Dr. Rhea Boyd, is the most eye-popping. She tells her fellow doctors, "Protest is a powerful and vital public health intervention."[20] At the same time, she decries protests against lockdowns early in the pandemic filled with predominantly "white crowds." This was a recurring theme during the pandemic; protest is vital for public health, but only certain kinds of protest by certain kinds of people.

Boyd's plan for abolishing racism involves "four core principles," which are: "truth, reconciliation and reparations; wealth distribution; robust Safety Net Systems; and expansion of public goods." Basically, we need to redistribute wealth (which includes divesting from police forces nationwide in order to invest those resources in anti-racist programs), universalize everything, and abolish racism through, and only through, the lens of anti-racists like Dr. Boyd.[21] And, just to remind you, this is the concluding lesson of a course for pediatricians on providing healthcare to children.

The course is packed full of CRT talking points, and it's not just a one-off deviation the AAP made from their core mission. Instead, the AAP is riddled with CRT, and it has reoriented their mission away from providing for the healthcare needs of children toward preaching woke politics.

In early 2021, the AAP announced its "Equity Agenda" that "guides the Academy's efforts to achieve health equity and actualize our goals to become an equitable, diverse, and inclusive organization."[22] A great deal of the messaging from the Equity Agenda sounds similar to that of the continuing education courses the organization provided to pediatricians. The AAP explains their goal: "advancing racial equity with an emphasis on addressing anti-Black racism in year one."[23] Dr. Li echoed the concerns of several other pediatricians around the AAP's release of the Equity Agenda. "They talk a lot about prioritizing diversity rather than ensuring competency in recruitment of child healthcare workers," she said. "It doesn't say instead of [ensuring competency] but there's only one thing that can be a top priority. If your top priority is diversity, then by definition it is not competence."[24]

In the context of our conversation, Dr. Li was concerned about medical school recruitment, but the idea that there can only be one top priority, and that a focus on politics is corrosive to the overall mission of an organization, played out during a controversy over a national medical panel run through the Pediatric Academic Societies (PAS), co-hosted by the AAP, in May of 2021. The session was scheduled to focus on caring for babies born severely prematurely, on discussing best practices in the delivery room, and on managing cardiac care and caring for immature lungs.[25] But an activist doctor, Dr. Erica Kaye, noticed that the panel was lacking any female voices and lamented this on Twitter, noting "more than 70% of the pediatricians are women."[26] She went on to question why there was also "not a single Black physician to speak on a topic that disproportionately affects Black women."[27] So what did the PAS do? They groveled at the feet of a social media mob, telling Dr. Kaye, "Thank you, Erica. PAS acknowledges and apologizes for this error. This session has been canceled. It does not align with our values and our commitment to no manels [a panel comprised of just men] and to a diverse and inclusive program. We must—and will—do better."[28] Another activist, Rhea Liang, celebrated, tweeting, "Advocacy works. The meeting has been cancelled."[29] Given the choice between offering a panel about how to best provide medical care to the most vulnerable newborns and appearing sufficiently diverse, the latter was more important—you can't have "too many white men" in any one place, even when their expertise could mean the difference between life and death for the 380,000 babies born prematurely every year in the U.S.[30]

This has terrifying implications for medical care and research. What happens next time the PAS, AAP, or another similar organization is planning a panel of experts? They won't be looking for the very best in the field; they'll be looking to check off boxes. "Do we have enough women? Do we have enough black presenters? What about Hispanic or Native American? Can we find a transgender doctor also?" This kind of thinking about identity instead of expertise has real consequences for the future of medical innovation and care.

Fred, a pediatrician in a deep-blue coastal city, bemoaned the situation. "The AAP has been a disappointment; how insanely left-wing they are in terms of topics," he told me in a private interview. "There's so much activism and not a lot of science. I hate to think of the human capital and money that goes into all of this stuff; what I see is non-actionable, non-medical virtue signaling." He said that for the last four or five years, he's been "tuning out each issue of *Pediatrics* because there was so much that didn't feel actionable or medical; it felt much more [like] activism." In order to "stay current," he looks at the table of contents and will "pick out the one or two worthwhile articles."[31]

The illogical nature of wokespeak of academic papers like "Racial Disparities in Pediatric Type 1 Diabetes: Yet Another Consequence of Structural Racism"[32] and "Implicit Weight Bias in Children Age 9 to 11 Years"[33] mirrors wider discussions on these kinds of issues and shuts down important conversations about healthcare. Regarding the dangers of messaging surrounding "fatphobia" seeping into medicine, Fred explained, "We're seeing an increase in diabetes and obesity. We want to tell them that they need to fix that. But we're also telling them 'you're OK this way,' and pediatricians are saying that too."

This kind of messaging from medical professionals terrified of being offensive to patients doesn't just impact healthcare outcomes in the short term but also changes how children and teenagers optimize their behavior for their own health. Instead of trying to make healthy choices through diet and exercise, Fred explained, "They will try to find *everything* external to blame for a person's or group's bad health outcome, while conspicuously avoiding *internal* causes: choices, culture, personality traits, and so on."[34]

A further consequence of increasingly politicized research is that pediatricians like Fred tune out material disseminated for professional development. Where is the energy from these groups being spent? Not on medical advancement, but on sounding the right tone on diversity, equity, and inclusion. Is that what you want medical experts spending their energy on? Is that the best use of our resources? None of these questions are being asked.

The AAP isn't the only medical association interfacing with children obsessed with woke talking points, either. In an open letter on his blog, Dr. Richard Bosshardt explained why he was resigning his membership with the American College of Surgeons (ACS): "Recently, the ACS has taken a turn I find disturbing. I first noted this in a lecture given before the College by Dr. Joan Reede . . . titled 'Diversity, Excellence, and Inclusion' in medicine and, more specifically, surgery, even though she is not a surgeon. The text of the lecture made no mention of excellence. She checked off multiple progressive boxes in her lecture—diversity, inclusion, equity, biases of various sorts, microaggressions—as problems in surgery training and in the ACS. What was notably absent was balancing this with traditional surgical values of excellence, hard work, and meritocracy." Bosshardt says that many recent "lectures and articles coming out of the College" have promoted "progressive ideology" and "focused on issues of diversity, equity, and social justice." He continues, "All are laudable goals, but they have become poisoned with ideological meaning and taken primacy over other considerations, such as excellence, professionalism, competence, and compassion, which should be the overarching priorities in something like surgical practice."

Success in obtaining a residency position in any surgical specialty depends more on one's performance in medical school, recommendations from one's professors, and demonstrated dedication, such as taking a year to do research (as my daughter did to obtain an excellent residency in dermatology), than on gender, race, ethnicity, or some other identity. With medical school classes now 50% or more female and wide diversity in racial and ethnic composition, it is disingenuous to claim that our residencies and our College lack diversity or inclusiveness. Moreover, anyone who meets the requirements of Fellowship is welcome.[35]

Are these kinds of policies ensuring that the best and the brightest doctors pass through the halls of medical schools and then into offices and hospitals around the country? That should be the one and only goal of medical training: the output of professionals who exude competence. That's not what we're getting, and the situation is deteriorating with every successive graduating class.

In his open letter resignation, Dr. Bosshardt continued:

The last straw came when I reviewed the recommendations of the College's task force on racism in surgery, among which was adding anti-racism to the College's existing values. My College is now considering embracing Critical Race Theory (CRT), which posits all of human history as little more than the never-ending oppression of non-whites by whites and views literally everything through a racist lens. There is wide disagreement regarding this even among those of color and many find CRT abhorrent. According to CRT, it is not enough to declare oneself not a racist; one has to specifically support anti-racism, a construct of CRT. Why? Because whites are so endemically racist they no longer see this in themselves. Whites cannot even enter in the discussion of racism because they lack self-awareness of their own racism and must be re-educated to recognize their unconscious racist tendencies. The College has proposed such re-education programs already.

In addition to its new anti-racism stance, the College has embraced the concept of microaggressions, which can be literally anything- a comment, a word, a facial expression, even an almost imperceptible twitch or gesture- that makes someone of a different race, ethnicity, gender, or ideological position uncomfortable. Nuance, context, and perspective are irrelevant. There are no accidents or unintentional actions. Microaggressions are to be interpreted in the worst possible way. I was incredulous when I read that the College was planning 'safe spaces' for young surgeons.[36]

When your child suffers from a condition requiring the expertise of a surgeon, the knowledge that the person holding the knife in the operating room was trained in this kind of environment is terrifying. Instead of spending their energy perfecting their training and skills, that surgeon is working to make sure he or she appears adequately woke for his or her peers and professors, lest he or she commits a microaggression.

The infestation of this ideology into the inner workings—and priorities—of medical professional organizations isn't the exception. It's the norm. In late 2021, the American Medical Association (AMA) released "Advancing Health Equity: A Guide to Language, Narrative and Concepts" as part of a multi-year project called the "Organizational Strategic Plan to Embed Racial Justice and Advance Health Equity." They explain that "fulfilling the AMA's mission to promote the art and science of medicine and the betterment of public health requires an unwavering commitment to equity and a comprehensive strategy for embedding racial and social justice within our organization and domains of influence." The document calls for doctors to change their language to insert progressive politics into everything, even statements of fact. For instance, instead of saying, "Low-income people have the highest level of coronary artery disease in the United States," members are encouraged to say, "People underpaid and forced into poverty as a result of banking policies, real estate developers gentrifying neighborhoods, and corporations weakening the power of labor movements, among others, have the highest level of coronary artery disease in the United States."[37] Everything must be modified to fit woke orthodoxy.

This is the medical equivalent of the bigotry of low expectations—only it has consequences not just for academics, but for health as well. There are reasons why low-income Americans are less healthy, but instead of focusing on the behaviors, attitudes, and environments that contribute to adverse health outcomes, the woke response is to say that low-income people are forced into this situation, and as a result, are powerless to escape it. This isn't helping the health outcomes of those in low-income areas; it's worsening them. This is most clear in the case of obesity; we need to be honest about negative health outcomes for those who are overweight and obese instead of dancing around excuses for excessive weight, for fear of being labeled "fat phobic."

As bad as the situation is among physical health professionals, it's that much worse among their counterparts in mental health. Mental health professionals are just as woke, but their "science" is more subjective. The invasion of woke ideology in psychology and psychiatry has direct impacts on how mental health professionals counsel their patients and, as a result, has a direct impact on patient outcomes.

Even before COVID, the topic of worsening pediatric mental health was one of the most pressing issues facing those concerned with pediatric healthcare and health policy, but in May of 2021, we got a window into just how dire the situation had become as we transitioned into a post-pandemic world. The American Psychiatric Association (APA) explained, "More than half of adults (53%) with children under 18 in their household say they are concerned about the mental state of their children and almost half (48%) say the pandemic has caused mental health problems for one or more of their children, including minor problems for 29% and major problems for 19%."[38] The APA reports that "nearly half (49%) of parents surveyed who have children under 18 say their child has received help from a mental health professional since the start of the pandemic." The demand for pediatric mental health counseling has increased, but the supply has not, as evidenced by the APA's finding that "more than one in five parents have had trouble scheduling appointments for their child with a mental health professional."[39] This is a crisis caused in part by the woke response to the pandemic.

Similarly, the AAP declared that the pediatric mental health crisis had reached a tipping point in October 2021. And based on the numbers, they're right that the crisis is real. In a statement in *U.S. News & World Report,* the AAP stated, "Between March and October 2020, the percentage of emergency department visits for children with mental health emergencies rose by 24% among children aged 5 to 11 and by 31% among children aged 12 to 17 . . . And there were 50% more suspected suicide attempt-related emergency room visits among girls aged 12 to 17 in early 2021 than in early 2019."[40] They explained, "As health professionals, we have witnessed soaring rates of mental health challenges among children, adolescents, and their families over the course of the COVID-19 pandemic."[41]

Do you think either organization considered the cost of closed schools, the use of masks for nine hours a day on children aged two and up, the toll of constant fearmongering about a virus with statistically a zero chance of killing a healthy child? No. Instead, the AAP put the blame elsewhere: "Children and families across our country have experienced enormous adversity and disruption. The inequities that result from structural racism have contributed to disproportionate impacts on children from communities of color."[42]

One would think that the APA's focus would be on the betterment of mental health post-pandemic. You would be mistaken. Just a few months later, in late October of 2021, the APA announced what it had been busying itself with: "The APA Task Force on Strategies to Eradicate Racism, Discrimination, and Hate and its five-member Apology Advisory Subcommittee" drafted an apology to communities of color based on extensive surveys and research.[43] They also announced resolutions "to develop a long-term plan" to dismantle "systemic racism" and to "advance health equity in psychology."[44] The APA doesn't just support the other professional organizations' laser focus on anti-racism and other woke action items, but has developed its own similar action items over the last years, becoming increasingly more radical in their hyper-woke focus.

And race isn't the only area of concern. In August of 2018, the APA released their "Guidelines for Psychological Practice with Boys and

Men," centered around the ideology of masculinity, and suggested that parents and psychologists should think twice before instilling elements of "traditional masculinity" in men and boys.[45] Several months later, *U.S. News & World Report* quoted part of their new guidelines: "Socialization for conforming to traditional masculinity ideology has been shown to limit males' psychological development, constrain their behavior, result in gender role strain and gender role conflict, and negatively influence mental health and physical health."[46] The same article explained, "The latest guidelines linked 'constricted notions of masculinity' to aggression, homophobia and misogyny, saying such notions 'may influence boys to direct a great deal of their energy into disruptive behaviors such as bullying, homosexual taunting, and sexual harassment rather than healthy academic and extracurricular activities.'"[47] Choosing between actually addressing the root causes of mental health challenges of boys and men and playing politics, relying on simplistic excuses centered around "toxic masculinity," the APA chose the latter.

There are plenty of psychologists who aren't members of the APA, but unfortunately, the organization's influence extends past their membership base. One psychologist, who declined to be named and whom I will call Alice, explained how the "APA can go a long way to influence the perceptions of licensing boards. [The] APA is the standard-bearer for everything in psychology. APA credentials graduate school programs and internships, which one absolutely needs in order to survive with insurers and other credentialing bodies. [The] APA also dictates to state psychological associations their priorities, and in all cases, these are Democrat bills and positions."[48]

Writing for Capital Research Center in March of 2019, Harry Kazenoff explains that the APA receives "generous grants to support mental health initiatives"—between $2.25 million and $2.5 million in grants and contracts in both 2016 and 2017, for example—but cautions that "many of the grants suggest a possible political motivation."[49] He writes, "FoundationSearch reports that between 1998-2017 organizations such as the left-wing Annie E. Casey Foundation, the Arcus Foundation, and the W.K. Kellogg Foundation, have contributed $100,000, $120,000, and $355,000, respectively. The Arcus Foundation specified many of its grants to focus on LGBT issues." Furthermore, the APA issues political statements that have nothing to do with psychology: "Since the election of President Trump, the APA expanded its range of issues to include climate change and immigration . . . The APA also opposes President Trump's border wall on the U.S. southern border and advocated for the Dream Act of 2017." As Kazenoff says, "It's unclear what these issues have to do with licensing and educating psychologists."[50]

Going against the APA narrative can have chilling consequences. Alice explained to me, "I was once chastised on our state psychological association's listserv for posting a Medscape article before the ACA [Obamacare] was implemented. It described the way the ACA would impact private practice through its emphasis on pay-for-performance. I was cautioned by state leadership not to share any other information and to leave ACA education to them."

What do conservative psychologists do? Keep their opinions to themselves, lest they run afoul of the APA Ethics Code (even those who aren't even members of it)? The Code states, "Actions that violate the standards of the Ethics Code may also lead to the imposition of sanctions on psychologists or students whether or not they are APA members by bodies other than APA, including state psychological associations, other professional groups, psychology boards, other state or federal agencies, and payors for health services."[51]

Most mental health professionals I spoke with told me they don't see progressive politics seeping into their clinical practice, but one with experience in both the Bay Area and New York serves as a canary in the coal mine for the future of psychological treatment of youth. He told me, "In psychiatry we're trained not to bring our agenda to the table at all, and just give room to people to explore whatever they need to explore. It was always hard; I would meet people who were suspect of the way things have been going towards but not knowing within themselves how to handle it. For example, I was working with a kid, seven years old, terrified that the kids at school would find out his parents supported Trump. That they would make fun of him . . . Another kid that happened to; he did bring it up and didn't realize it was a problem, and he got made fun of."[52]

There are three kinds of parents seeking mental health treatment for their children in this culture: those unaware of the political leanings of the mental health profession who blindly trust their professional judgment, those who understand they are at the mercy of an increasingly woke field (especially as it relates to gender issues—more on that later), and those who are unconsciously feeding their children's mental health crisis. Kyle, the moderate provider who found himself in the lion's dens of liberal California and New York, explained the psychology of the latter, "It's almost like this psychiatric Munchausen-by-proxy, where the parents are exercising their psychological demons through their kids, assigning them these diagnoses and buzzwords that they think to be the case. It sends them down this road that's so, so destructive." He went on, "All the dynamics are at hand. That if my kid has a problem, now I have a thing to fix and to be important and to try to help them the way that maybe I wasn't—especially if I was abused or neglected—and that's the classic dynamic [of Munchausen-by-proxy]."[53] It's this latter group driving the notion that the best way to be a supportive parent to a child facing mental health struggles, especially as they relate to gender, is to buy into the child's pathology.

For as toxic and dangerous as the situation is and could become in clinical practice, it's that much worse in academic settings where mental health and child development is studied and researched. One researcher, Sam, told me that while research on adults tends to focus on race, wokeness is primarily impacting childhood research on gender. Sam expressed his concern, from a developmental standpoint, with teaching children the idea that it's possible to defy biological reality. Furthermore, he said that ignoring biological reality has implications for research where there are biological dispositions toward certain mental illnesses or coping strategies according to the sex of the patient. As grants are written and research is carried out, there are two focuses for scientists: the data and information they are collecting and their need to stay within the confines of The Narrative. When the sole focus isn't on scientific rigor, the science suffers.[54]

But there's another issue at play: if the only research that mainstream institutions allow to be conducted must conform to the accepted reality according to progressives, there will never be any formal understanding as to how this ideology is affecting child development. What negative effects are there for children developmentally and psychologically when there is a hyper focus on race, when they are indoctrinated into the ideology that promotes white privilege and black victimhood, when they are taught that gender is a social construct and that masculinity is toxic? With the inmates running the asylum, we'll never know.

The last few years have shown a substantial deterioration of the line between the political and the professional in the world of physical and mental health, especially for children. The future isn't looking any brighter, unfortunately. Alice, the psychologist I mentioned previously, warned, "There may be no more Dr. Alices in the near future [due to the educational reality in training programs], and children and their parents will be subjected to more radicalization in the therapy room. Truly sobering."[55]

Recently, I was sent a set of admission essay questions that a candidate for medical school must answer in order to be admitted into a program. Medical school applications are all completed through a central website. You are required to submit a generic essay for the first round of applications. If the school believes you might be a match, they'll invite you to complete a second set of essays. This second set is where the schools go woke. The spouse of one applicant explained to me, after walking through the process with his husband, "Some of the schools are less obvious: they ask you to write an essay about how you meet the school's mission statement and values and those statements/ values are all about social justice, etc. It was pretty clear throughout the admissions process that many medical schools expect you to regurgitate woke ideas; there's no way you'll make the cut if you reject the premises of the prompts."[56] Here are a few examples from various universities around the country:

University of Minnesota: "Tell us about a time when you observed, personally experienced, or acted with implicit or explicit bias. Through either situation we are interested in what you learned."[57]

Loyola University: "Social justice in the Jesuit tradition, justice due each person by virtue of their own inherent human dignity, is an essential dimension of education at SSOM. Describe what you have learned about yourself from your concrete social justice experiences. Explain how you plan to sustain your efforts to advocate for current social justice issues as a medical student and as a physician." And another: "Serving underserved and under-resourced communities is an expression of social justice. Describe an impactful experience in working with and for under-resourced communities. Explain what you have learned about yourself through this service OR what has hindered your efforts to serve others in these environments."[58]

University of Kentucky: "Describe a personal activity involving advocacy, social justice, and/or civic engagement that has impacted your personal values about delivering equitable patient care."[59]

There is a political litmus test not only for prospective doctors, but for prospective professors as well. A professor at an Ivy League medical school, Jonathan, compared the mandatory "diversity" consultants in the hiring process to Soviet Commissars. The diversity consultants lengthen and complicate the process, requiring that there be enough "diverse" candidates under consideration before a hire is made. He told me he isn't sure what the effect is on the pool of professors and candidates but that "putting so much emphasis on race or allegiance to a certain set of left-wing ideas ... doesn't belong in a decision on hiring."[60]

In August 2021, the Dean of the School of Medicine at Harvard University, Dr. George Q. Daley, announced a similar initiative from the Harvard Medical School and Harvard School of Dental Medicine for promotions at the school. According to the announcement, "Diversity, Equity and Inclusion (DEI)" work is now a formal component of promotions at one of the most well-respected medical schools in the country.[61]

The classroom is another field fraught with danger for professors. Jonathan described a scenario where a student tried to entrap him into a larger effort by students to identify and blacklist professors who didn't adequately (according to their perception) respond to student communications around race. He had been teaching on Zoom all year during the COVID pandemic when the Black Lives Matter protests erupted following the death of George Floyd. He received an email from a student that said, "I'm white . . . but . . . I'm very concerned about black students being overly stressed over the BLM protests. I'm asking you as an ally to give special accommodation to black students in this class." Jonathan then received an identical email from another student. He wasn't sure what to make of it but sent an email to the entire class (with many screens off over Zoom, he wasn't even sure what race half of his students even were) to let them know that his virtual door was open if anyone needed to come to him with an issue. Then, another student shed light on what was really going on: a group of students had created a spreadsheet to track how every professor handled the BLM email in order to create a blacklist of sorts. They wanted to identify any wrong thinkers in their midst. Jonathan was troubled by the trap laid by students in the medical school and brought it to the school's administration, who did nothing with the information. He told me, "You can't teach in that kind of environment. It's like this Maoist thing where you have to align yourself with the zeitgeist or you'll get canceled. Maybe a struggle session, I don't know what they have in mind. I've been at [this university] for 30 years. I've never seen anything like it before."[62] In order to gain admission to medical schools and in order to teach at them, one must show reverence for the party line or they need not apply—literally.

Woke medical activists understand that their best chance at turning the medical field into an advocacy group is to get them during medical school. Writing for *Scientific American*, Dr. Angira Patel explains that in order to encourage physician advocacy, they have to "start early": "As students begin medical school, we must introduce the theory, practice and modeling of physician advocacy at the same time they are learning basic anatomy and physiology. The Royal College of Physicians and Surgeons of Canada mandates health advocacy as a core competency. Early exposure to examples of how physicians interweave advocacy work into their clinical work may lead to higher likelihood of engaging young trainees. In fact, the medical school where I teach has incorporated a health equity and advocacy curriculum in the first year of medical school. Yet, far more is needed to both train future physicians and stress the urgent importance of advocacy work to existing physicians across disciplines."[63]

This is their blueprint, and they aren't even subtle about it. It's right out in the open: the goal of medical school isn't to produce the best clinicians and diagnosticians and researchers, it's to introduce woke ideology into the medical field. These doctors are expected to be not just healthcare providers but activists.

In a recent issue of Stanford University Medical School's magazine devoted to social justice and race, we learn about how "social justice" is included in the curriculum. Krista Conger writes, "Efforts to rework the medical school curriculum to address racism in health care have been underway at Stanford for several years. But they recently gained more urgency."[64] After the racially charged events of the summer of 2020, Daniel Bernstein, MD, the associate dean for curriculum and scholarship, decided they "needed a deeper and more sustained commitment." Conger continues, "The solution, Bernstein believes, is to incorporate discussions of health inequities and implicit bias into every aspect of teaching. A lesson about hypertension, for example, can include a discussion about the impact of poverty, lack of insurance or poor diet on disease prevalence."[65]

Writing in a now-deleted Twitter thread (accessed November 7, 2021) about how wokeness invaded medical schools, Dr. Brent Williams shared snippets of messages he received from medical students about the oppressive nature of wokeness in their medical education. One message read, "Hey 3rd year medical student. Anatomy labs wasn't mandatory but all the public health/social inequities of health stuff were. I've been harassed less since clinicals started, but I heard it's even worse now from people in years below me." Another message explained, "I'll add to the list of medical students expressing their concerns re: a culture of fear from woke orthodoxy. I'll attach a slide from a lecture in our, 'Structural Competencies' course. A three hour/wk student taught course about being activist physicians. I'm very progressive (worked on Andrew Yang's campaign, etc. . . .) and feel extremely limited in what I can say or do when interacting with the school or fellow classmates." The highly politicized nature of medical schools and the outsized amount of time spent on politics instead of medicine doesn't bode well for the competency of future doctors, let alone for the ideological diversity of the field. Would you rather have a doctor who spent three hours a week on politics, or three hours a week on *actual medicine*?

Nurses face the same challenges. The recently released *American Association of Colleges of Nursing the Essentials: Core Competencies for Professional Nursing Education*[66] calls for "systemic overhaul of the culture of academic nursing" and lists the "barriers to overcome: structural racism, discrimination, systemic inequity, exclusion, and bias, to name a few."[67] Conspicuously absent are long hours, lifting patients, dealing with life or death situations, and just about anything related to medicine.

What happens when a doctor, somehow, miraculously, makes it out of medical school without being fully indoctrinated? Well, it's best if they keep their mouth shut. Writing for the *Philadelphia Inquirer* in August of 2021, Robert Field lays out the land of American medicine: "The days of the stalwart solo physician, hanging out a shingle and seeing patients as he or she sees fit, are rapidly drawing to a close.

Consulting firm Avalere Health reports that almost 70% of physicians in the United States now work as employees of a hospital, health system, or private corporation. That's a 12% increase over just two years ago, and is likely to accelerate after the COVID-19 pandemic."[68]

Because the vast majority of the jobs in the medical field are held by those working for large hospital systems with their own ideological capture from the top, a doctor or nurse could find himself or herself unemployable if he or she speaks out against the commonly held position of those controlling all of the jobs in their field in their geographic area. That's a powerful incentive to keep silent, even for those who don't necessarily believe in the ideas being promoted.

As time marches on and newly educated professionals replace retiring practitioners in the physical and mental health world, woke ideology will almost certainly impact children's healthcare. But what about their physical safety?

Speaking with Vanessa, a registered nurse working with a governmental agency in "infant mental health," was an eye-opening and terrifying experience. Wokeness in her training and practice is ubiquitous; on forms and questionnaires, "parent" has replaced mother and father, "chestfeeding" has replaced breastfeeding, and "Latinx" has replaced Latino. All of these are hindrances as Vanessa tries to interface with a population unaccustomed to this woke terminology, for which there is no easy translation into the native languages spoken by the minority population she serves. While Vanessa is frustrated by the constant politicization of her office, she's also concerned that she's likely the only person in her entire agency who doesn't ascribe to it; she told me she's the only person without her pronouns listed in her email signature.

Vanessa's agency is tasked in part with coaching struggling parents on the brink of coming onto the radar of child protective services. Coming into homes, Vanessa's team members are universally trained to first look at the race of their clients and to assume that any bad behavior on the part of clients of color isn't their fault but the fault of structural racism in society. The bigotry of these low expectations puts the already-endangered children of color even further into harm's way; their parents aren't provided with tools and tough love to clean up their behavior but are instead given an excuse for it.

Journalist Naomi Schaefer Riley recently wrote an entire book, *No Way to Treat a Child,* about how the foster care system, family courts, and racial activists are wrecking young lives.[69] In her book, Riley explains, "These institutions have been co-opted by a radical and, in many ways, nonsensical ideology. In deciding how to treat children who are being abused or severely neglected, they consider factors that are completely unrelated to and often at odds with a child's best interests. The most obvious of these is skin color. Children who have substantiated reports of child abuse and neglect are left in dangerous environments because the system is reluctant to be seen as breaking up black (or Hispanic or Native American) families."[70] These policies all work to protect the feelings of black adults, she says, at the expense of the health and safety of black children.

This is how toxic cycles of abuse and neglect are perpetuated. Those abusing and mistreating black and brown children are given a pass, and these children are raised to believe that they don't possess free will, that they're unable to be better than their parents, that they are doomed to a lifetime of poverty, gang violence, drug abuse, and more. Instead of being raised in a home (be it their own, a foster home, or with an adoptive family) where they are loved, respected, and supported, they are trapped in homes where they are neglected or flat-out abused. The number one risk factor for someone becoming an abuser is having been abused themselves; and when children are raised in these surroundings, the likelihood grows that they'll become abusive or neglectful parents in the future. Children of color, then, are the greatest victims of the racial obsessions of these institutions tasked with protecting children of color.

The total infiltration of our healthcare institutions by woke ideologues is the most worrisome development in the current political moment. With any of the other industries controlled from the top by woke leadership, there's an opt-out option of sorts; there's a way to mitigate the damage on an individual family level.

When a kid's teacher is woke, parents have options. They can develop strategies to deal with navigating the teacher's influence on the child, which could involve activism or switching classes. But when it's the pediatrician who's woke, it's harder to detect their affiliations or how those beliefs might impact care. Even more potentially dangerous and more difficult to detect: How will training be affected by the increased focus on political conformity in the application and education process? In the realm of physical and mental health and government institutions tasked with protecting abused and neglected children, the woke takeover has not just the possibility, but the likelihood of causing severe and long-term damage.

For parents concerned about exposing their child to a new provider, either a pediatrician or mental health professional, recommendations from like-minded friends is a first step at identifying providers who, even if they don't align ideologically, don't allow their political worldview to influence their work. When a family has identified a few possibilities, vetting is critical. Forms are a particularly helpful signal: Do they ask parents to list their children's pronouns? Do they ask if there's a gun in the home? These aren't necessarily disqualifying questions, especially for a mental health professional working with suicidal patients. The presence of a gun in the home is pertinent information. But they are potential signs that the values of the provider may not align with your family's. This is an area where it's critically important to be a proactive self-advocate, asking a potential provider what their standard of care is for hypothetical scenarios like, "What if my child comes into your office and declares himself/herself to be transgender? How would you proceed in that scenario?" This should be one of any number of questions posted to a potential new provider. When we interviewed a potential new pediatrician, we had questions about their procedures regarding sick waiting rooms, vaccine requirements and schedules, weekend hours, philosophy regarding the use of antibiotics,

THE PERIL OF WOKE MEDICINE

and more. A hiring interview of sorts is something more parents should use when choosing a pediatric medical or mental health provider, and asking these questions is important to make sure they are the right one for your family.

The situation in these institutions is unsustainable and dangerous; woke ideology has endangered the health and safety of an entire generation of American children so that adult professionals could adhere to a political trend. It hasn't just impacted training and care; it has and will continue to affect the trust that the American people have in institutions and in these professionals, and rightfully so. In the wake of the COVID pandemic, trust in one of the most highly respected areas—scientists and the medical profession—dipped, with the biggest drops among Republicans. In February of 2022, Pew Research Center reported, "Overall, 29% of U.S. adults say they have a great deal of confidence in medical scientists to act in the best interests of the public, down from 40% who said this in November 2020."[71] It's not hard to understand why: the willingness of everyone, doctors and scientists alike, to fall in lockstep with the prevailing politically driven orthodoxies. We will see the consequences of this reduced trust for a generation; and in the case of pediatrics especially, in plummeting trust in vaccine safety. Reporting on a 1 percent drop in childhood vaccination after the beginning of the pandemic, the *New York Times* said, "Experts attributed to skipped checkups and to a groundswell of resistance to Covid-19 shots spilling into unease about other vaccines."[72] The *Times* went on to explain, "Coverage levels [are] below the target of 95 percent, raising fears that life-threatening childhood illnesses like measles could at some point become more prevalent."[73]

Many parents are tempted by the idea of closing themselves off from the outside world; and in many ways, going "Benedict" or "Galt" (to turn into verbs the Rod Dreher book *The Benedict Option* and the famous Ayn Rand novel *Atlas Shrugged*) is appealing. But until we build an entirely separate civilization, we need institutions that haven't been ideologically captured by radical politics. Americans need to be able to trust in our institutions again, and in order to do that, those institutions have to work to regain that faith. We cannot afford the luxury of shutting out the outside world; we have to stay engaged, stay in the fight, and work to send wokeness to the dustbin of history. We should do it not just for the mental and physical health of our own children, but also that of children around the country for whom there is no voice.

PART III

KIDS AS GUINEA PIGS

We are conducting an unprecedented sociological experiment on our children. Never before have we raised children and told them to ignore very basic biology. We've never told kids, "There is no such thing as a man or a woman," as their brains are forming. Learning how to categorize is a crucial early-learning tool,[1] and the first way young children have learned how to separate human beings is into two camps: men and women. What does that do to the human brain when we tell children as their brains are developing that their inherent drive to categorize in this manner is wrong and incorrect? We're about to find out.

The real human experimentation comes in when that denial of biological reality goes hand in hand with hormone therapy, with unknown long-term side effects on a developing body.

Children have always been exposed to inappropriate content for their age; sexualized content and frightening world events. This moment is unique: while we always understood that the innocence of children should be guarded at all costs, we have now decided as a society that children aren't just unavoidably going to be exposed to sex and fear-inducing news, but that *this is a good thing*. How does this onslaught of sex and fear change the developing brain? We're seeing early indications in the form of drastically declining mental health in children, with sharp rises in depression, anxiety, and more.

6

THE TRANSGENDER CRUSADE

The game of child sacrifice that the Left is playing with children and their well-being is most obvious and most terrifying on the issue of gender identity.

There have always been troubled children and adolescents struggling through puberty, and there have always been adults willing to take advantage of their emotional distress. With gender ideology, parents are beginning to realize the cards are stacked against them and their kids. In previous generations, troubled youth would dabble in substance abuse, cutting, eating disorders—all dangerous and potentially deadly, but also universally recognized as harmful. Now, troubled youth are expressing their distress through gender identity, and unlike other toxic coping mechanisms of the past, adults in positions of power in schools, medical and psychiatric settings, and the media are throwing kindling on the fire. It's like handing a knife to a girl who is cutting and telling her it's a healthy way to express her feelings, or telling a girl struggling with an eating disorder that she does, indeed, look fat in those jeans and should purge to try to lose a few pounds.

As we see the effects of not just the hormones but also the catastrophic physical toll of "gender-affirming surgery," we are getting a fuller picture of what our society has decided it can and should inflict on *our* kids. While young people may recover from their gender dysphoria, the physical and emotional scars of their attempt to change gender will linger. Those who are promoting this pseudo-science lie claim that puberty blockers and their effects are temporary and reversible.

The euphemism "gender-affirming surgery" shields gender extremists from calling it what it actually is: surgical mutilation. Breasts are removed from women, penises and testicles are removed from men, and attempts are made to construct alternative but inoperative genitalia out of the leftover tissue. It leaves bodies battered and broken, susceptible to life-threatening complications and lifelong sexual dysfunction. We are witnessing a mad science experiment taking place in real time, and the lab rats are our children.

The journalist, Abigail Shrier, wrote an entire book about the dangers of transgender activism to kids called *Irreversible Damage*, which was a runaway bestseller when it was published in 2020. Shrier made waves and earned a great deal of attention for her reporting on how the phenomenon of rapid-onset gender dysphoria (ROGD) is gripping an entire generation of teenage girls. In a *Wall Street Journal* op-ed before her book was published, Shrier offered a definition: "ROGD differs from traditional gender dysphoria, a psychological affliction that begins in early childhood and is characterized by a severe and persistent feeling that one was born the wrong sex. ROGD is a social contagion that comes on suddenly in adolescence, afflicting teens who'd never exhibited any confusion about their sex."[2]

In her book, Shrier explains the difference further and why she calls it a "contagion": "Until just a few years ago, gender dysphoria—severe discomfort in one's biological sex—was vanishingly rare. It was typically found in less than .01 percent of the population, emerged in early childhood, and afflicted males almost exclusively. But today whole groups of female friends in colleges, high schools, and even middle schools across the country are coming out as 'transgender.' These are girls who had never experienced any discomfort in their biological sex until they heard a coming-out story from a speaker at a school assembly or discovered the internet community of trans 'influencers.'"[3] Because parents had never heard anything from their children about gender confusion before, they are taken completely off guard by these sudden and dramatic changes: "Unsuspecting parents are awakening to find their daughters in thrall to hip trans YouTube stars and 'gender-affirming' educators and therapists who push life-changing interventions on young girls—including medically unnecessary double mastectomies and puberty blockers that can cause permanent infertility."[4]

The response to the book, which became a bestseller partially because of the controversy it sparked, was intense. All over the literary sphere, from bookstores to Amazon to libraries, *Irreversible Damage* was pulled from shelves after protests, and those who stocked it were forced to repent for their thought crimes: "A top lawyer for the ACLU called for it to be banned. Powerful organizations like GLAAD have lobbied against it and pressured corporations—Target and Amazon, among others—to remove *Irreversible Damage* from their virtual shelves."[5] Shrier was called a transphobe and a bigot. Writing for Bari Weiss' Substack *Common Sense* about the campaign against her work, Shrier gives a response that explains the nuance of her approach: "The book is not about whether trans people exist. They do. And it is not about adults who elect to medically transition genders. As I have stated endlessly in public interviews and in Senate testimony, I fully support medical transition for mature adults and believe that transgender individuals should live openly without fear or stigma. Yet since publication, I have faced fierce opposition—not just to the ideas presented, challenged, or explored—but to the publication of the book itself."[6] Despite the fact that Shrier's book was deeply researched and sensitive, it was labeled as anti-trans for daring to stray from transgender orthodoxy; and for that, it was targeted for cancellation.

It was amid this controversy in 2021 that we were attempting to sell our book project, this book you're holding, to a publisher. We had a top literary agent and enthusiasm among some top editors we pitched the idea to. After half a dozen meetings and enough interested parties, it was decided we'd go to auction in order to generate a bidding war for our project. And then, on the day of the auction, every single interested party pulled out. The reason we were given? Abigail Shrier. No, she's not to blame. But the stifling of her work was. The fear generated by her cancellation was enough to make the bosses at publishing companies want to put the brakes on our book. They simply couldn't risk paying us an advance to commission a project they wouldn't be *allowed* to sell. If they couldn't put it on Amazon or in bookstores, it was dead in the water.

We were asked by one editor if it was possible to move forward on the book without this chapter. We knew it would be impossible. When we approached almost every single source about our project, describing it as an exposé on how wokeness is destroying the American childhood, they pointed first and foremost to the influence of gender ideology. From doctors to psychiatrists to children's book authors to teachers to YouTube and TikTok personalities, we were repeatedly told close variations of the same thing: "In my area of expertise, the impact of wokeness is insidious and often almost imperceptible, but that's not the case when it comes to gender. It's overt and it's aggressive. The issue of gender is where the woke are trying to capture an entire generation." Gender ideology, alongside critical race theory, forms the backbone of the belief system of those who count themselves as "woke."

What is gender dysphoria? Child Mind Institute defines it: "Gender dysphoria is a mental health disorder in which children experience intense emotional distress because they feel that they were born as the wrong gender."[7] Most experts, liberal and conservative alike, agree that this is a real phenomenon that can affect children. However, they differ on how gender dysphoria should be understood and treated. The woke ideology adamantly claims that the only humane way to deal with gender dysphoria is to encourage children to alter their physical bodies to match their internal sense of identity. In her book, *Trans*, editor Helen Joyce explains this ideology succinctly: it's the idea "that people should count as men or women according to how they feel and what they declare, instead of their biology. It's called gender self-identification, and it's the central tenet of a fast-developing belief system which sees everyone as possessing a gender identity that may or may not match the body in which it is housed. When there is a mismatch, the person is 'transgender'—trans for short—and it is the identity, not the body, that should determine how everyone else sees and treats them."[8]

The belief that gender is malleable isn't just some quirky, fringe belief of a few inconsequential radicals (though it once was). It initially took hold in academia and soon spread like a cancer across the woke progressive intelligentsia. It's the new frontier in the fight for gay rights, with no acknowledgement of the drastically different issues at play, nor of how "trans acceptance" often leads to gay erasure. A young gay man is now often told that he is, in fact, a woman. The battle for gay rights was always about acceptance—mainly, the right to marry. For "trans rights" it's a different ball game completely, especially when it comes to minors. "Acceptance" of a transgender child comes with body-altering modifications that can cause lasting damage. That fact is ignored and denied by its proponents. And if you bring up that pesky little fact, you're told you're a bigoted transphobe who wants eight-year-old trans kids to kill themselves.

The idea that a man can become a woman and vice versa—that biology, genetics, and anatomy are irrelevant—is unique to secular modernity. While there have always been cross-dressing individuals throughout history, there has been no historical acceptance of the belief that one can change biological genders prior to the last several decades. Writing for *Public Discourse*, Jane Robbins makes a fascinating and disturbing case for the true origins of transgender feelings prior to our current political moment, citing "another theory that enjoys much more evidentiary support, that explains a great deal of MtF gender dysphoria, and that offers hope for psychological treatment."[9] Referencing the work of an "internationally prominent clinician" with "decades of experience in this area," she explains, "In the early 1990s, Dr. Ray Blanchard coined the term 'autogynephilia' for the condition of a man who demonstrates a 'propensity to be erotically aroused by the thought or image of himself as a woman.'"[10] Today, that understanding has morphed into the idea that it is possible for a male to be born with a female brain, and vice versa, and that children as young as preschool could ferret out their own "true" gender.

How might a child do so?

In popular culture, the most famous transgender youth is a natal male renamed and reborn as a girl, Jazz Jennings, the subject of a *TLC* reality show (2015-present) and children's book of the same name published in 2014, titled *I Am Jazz*. Growing up as a little boy, his favorite activities were "girly" and consisted of dancing, singing, drawing, swimming, and putting on makeup. This behavior prompted his parents to seek medical care, and they were informed their son was actually their daughter, but born in the wrong body. He was transgender, they were told, and his parents embraced this notion.

One irony is that not so long ago we were celebrating the notion that girls can like trucks and dinosaurs and boys can like dolls, but those days are over, apparently. Now we've regressed fifty years and liking dancing and painting one's face with makeup is now indicative of a medical condition in need of treatment.

What does "treatment" look like to radical transgender activists? In the United States, it's unfettered access to cross-sex hormones and surgeries, even for patients still in childhood. Writing for Medscape, Dr. William Malone outlines what this radical kind of treatment looks like in practice: "GnRH analogues (colloquially known as 'puberty blockers') are now available at Tanner stage 2 of puberty—a threshold crossed by females as young as 8-9 years old. Cross-sex hormones and surgeries follow, and mastectomies are now available to children as young as 13. Genital-altering surgeries, as well as the removal of the ovaries, uterus, and testes, can be obtained as soon as a patient turns 18."[11] What makes this even more terrible is that the vast majority of childhood-onset gender dysphoria resolves naturally, "with 61-98% of children reidentifying with their biological sex during puberty."[12] While there are no studies yet to provide comparable data for adolescent-onset gender dysphoria, one can imagine it would not be far different. So what happens to these children who receive irreversible surgery and then realize they actually *weren't* in the wrong body? This is a question the woke do not want you to ask.

In the field of medicine, even in the short time since Shrier's book was released (which is why her book doesn't cover the organizations), a concerted pushback against an activist takeover of the field in the realm of medical care of those presenting with gender dysphoria has formed. The Society for Evidence-Based Gender Medicine's (SEGM) mission is to promote safe, compassionate, ethical and evidence-informed healthcare for children, adolescents, and young adults with gender dysphoria. They see a situation so dire that these like-minded healthcare providers have joined forces to recapture medical care for dysphoric youth from extremists. On their website they explain their concern in light of the high rate of natural resolution for childhood-onset gender dysphoria: "Historically, medical interventions to achieve the appearance of the desired sex were reserved primarily for adults with long histories of dysphoria. . . . However . . . Western Europe, North America, and Australia began to promote the 'gender-affirmative' model of care for youth. Under this model of care, young people presenting with gender dysphoria or asserting a transgender identity are affirmed in their desire to undergo gender transition, and are provided with hormonal and surgical intervention."[13]

The concept of "gender-affirmative" care is a euphemism given for a whole host of interventions, hormones, or surgeries, which come with lifelong side effects. Giving care that is "gender-affirmative" results in children self-diagnosing themselves with gender dysphoria, and then being treated by physicians and surgeons to change their bodies physically and hormonally. SEGM explains, "The 'gender affirmative' model commits young people to lifelong medical treatment with minimal attention to . . . the psycho-social factors contributing to gender dysphoria. This model dismisses the question of whether psychological therapy might help to relieve or resolve gender dysphoria and provides interventions without an adequate examination." Their goal is not radical or dismissive of gender dysphoria in general: "We are asking clinicians and researchers to halt this uncontrolled experimentation on youth and replace it with a supportive framework of research that generates useful evidence about the etiology of gender dysphoria and the benefits and harms of various interventions."[14] In other words, they're simply saying, "We don't know why kids, often with several mental health comorbidities and a history of trauma, are showing up to doctors in droves claiming to be transgender. Before we "affirm" the feelings they've had, sometimes only for a short duration, we need to sit down and discuss with them—and amongst ourselves as clinicians—the risks and the benefits of providing hormones and surgical options." Seems reasonable, but not to the woke police.

What's the rush to "transition" youth before they've even reached puberty? Given how transitory childhood phases can be, why assume that, in the area of gender, children are ready to make decisions that carry lifelong consequences? Couldn't these decisions wait until adulthood? The "problem" with waiting, and why puberty blockers are pushed, is because puberty is the moment when our bodies become clearly and distinctly male or female—young women develop wider hips and breasts, men more distinct jawlines and Adam's apples—so by transitioning before puberty and "blocking" its progress, it's much easier for someone who considers himself or herself to be transgender to cosmetically "pass" as the opposite gender. But what is the cost of such an intervention? It's hardly discussed.

Alexandra, the DC-based hospital pediatrician, had some salient points to make about this. She told me, "I've heard very little discussion regarding how stopping puberty and then putting prepubertal children on cross-sex hormones will affect their future sexuality. I think just discussing this makes people feel creepy, and I've honestly only heard this raised in private comments among physicians. I've not seen it discussed in the mainstream. But insofar as sexuality is a critical component of living a fulfilling life for most adults, we're doing a real disservice by not discussing this. If their sexual organs never mature, and then are masculinized or feminized, will they have any sexual function at all?"[15]

The health consequences for these individuals extend beyond sexual function. Writing for Medscape, Dr. Malone (an endocrinologist) explains the myriad of medical issues that lay ahead for those starting on these hormones: "Puberty blockers have been demonstrated to significantly impair bone health, and it is not clear whether this will result in future osteoporosis. Cross-sex hormones are associated with roughly 3-5 times the risk for heart attacks and strokes, though long-term studies are of insufficient quality for accurate risk assessments. Other risks associated with these endocrine interventions will come to light as the practice continues to scale and as young people spend years and decades on these interventions. The risks to fertility are largely unknown, but it is almost certain that if puberty blockers are given at the early stages of puberty and followed by cross-sex hormones, sterility will result."[16] These children are being consigned to a life of health problems, including higher risk for heart attacks and strokes, as well as impaired bone health and sterility, before they're even old enough to vote.

Just how serious are these health impacts? To some, "impaired bone health" might not sound all that bad. Writing for Kaiser Health News in February of 2017, Christina Jewett explained what that looks like in reality: "For years, Sharissa Derricott, 30, had no idea why her body seemed to be failing. At 21, a surgeon replaced her deteriorated jaw joint. She's been diagnosed with degenerative disc disease and fibromyalgia, a chronic pain condition. Her teeth are shedding enamel and cracking. None of it made sense to her until she discovered a community of women online who describe similar symptoms and have one thing in common: All had taken a drug called Lupron . . . which was approved to shut down puberty in young girls."[17] I'd call that pretty serious.

The most disturbing part of this "treatment" of transgender youth isn't impaired bone and sexual health—it's sterilization. Even those promoting the "gender-affirmative" care model—the use of puberty blockers prior to puberty, followed by cross-sex hormones without any exposure to the natal sex hormone levels they would otherwise experience—acknowledge that this treatment prevents the production of viable sperm or oocytes (eggs) and by all appearances completely eliminates the possibility of future fertility. In short, already-troubled youths are being sterilized by those claiming to help them. In 2012, the World Professional Association for Transgender Health (WPATH), the organization that sets the standards worldwide for transgender medical care, confirmed in its 7th edition of standards, "A special group of individuals are prepubertal or pubertal adolescents who will never develop reproductive function in their natal sex due to blockers or cross gender hormones. At this time there is no technique for preserving function from the gonads of these individuals."[18] Alexandra asked me, "We're essentially sentencing these children to a lifetime of infertility. What child can make a truly informed decision about their future desire to have a child themselves?"[19]

In another universe, the sterilization of troubled youth would spark a five-alarm fire of concern in the media and among experts in the field. Instead, it's barely an afterthought in a crusade to make it slightly easier for a young woman to grow up into an androgynous adult in order to be perceived by strangers as a male.

How easy is it to get these hormones? Across the country, in addition to providing abortion and birth control services, Planned Parenthood provides "gender affirming hormone therapy."[20] According to their Best Practice Guide, Planned Parenthood provides an "informed consent model of transgender care."[21] What does that mean? Without discussing an individual's self-diagnosis with anyone, Planned Parenthood will provide "gender-affirming" care (i.e., powerful hormones and even surgical interventions), without anything resembling a mental health screening. They go on: "We . . . proudly work with our transgender community to lead the way in eliminating barriers to care . . . Informed consent removes the requirement of meeting with a mental health provider or providing a written letter of support from a mental health provider prior to being able to access care. This makes the process of beginning hormone therapy consistent with the process for starting other medications at Planned Parenthood and is in alignment with the WPATH Standards of CARE."[22] Not content with their core mission of providing sexual health counseling, family planning, and abortion, Planned Parenthood is expanding its mission, offering highly potent hormones with little to no barriers to anyone who walks in claiming to suffer from dysphoria.

The WPATH standards of care provide a blueprint of sorts to any practitioner with a transgender patient in their care. As new standards were in the process of being drafted in 2021, alarm bells went off with such intensity that Medscape published a warning that stated, "New draft guidance from the World Professional Association for Transgender Health (WPATH) is raising serious concerns among professionals caring for people with gender dysphoria, prompting claims that WPATH is an organization 'captured by activists.' Experts in adolescent and child psychology, as well as pediatric health, have expressed dismay that the WPATH Standards of Care (SOC) 8 appear to miss some of the most urgent issues in the field of transgender medicine and are considered to express a radical and unreserved leaning towards 'gender-affirmation.'"[23]

Even those who have been intimately involved in working with WPATH are concerned enough about haphazard treatment for transgender-identifying youth. In late November 2021, Dr. Laura Edwards-Leeper, the founding psychologist of the first pediatric transgender clinic in the U.S. and the chair of the Child and Adolescent Committee for WPATH, and Dr. Erica Anderson, a clinical psychologist who is a member of the American Psychological Association committee writing the guidelines for working with transgender individuals, voiced their concerns in the *Washington Post*.[24] Reporting for Bari Weiss' Substack *Common Sense*, Shrier interviewed Anderson about her quest to get her perspective published. Shrier explained, "Earlier this month, Anderson told me she submitted a co-authored op-ed to the *New York Times* warning that many transgender healthcare providers were treating kids recklessly. The *Times* passed, explaining it was 'outside our coverage priorities right now.'"[25] In the piece that was eventually published by the *Washington Post*, the pair wrote, "Now 1.8 percent of people under 18 identify as transgender, double the figure from five years earlier, according to the Trevor Project. A flood of referrals to mental health providers and gender medical clinics, combined with a political climate that sees the treatment of each individual patient as a litmus test of social tolerance, is spurring many providers into sloppy, dangerous care. Often from a place of genuine concern, they are hastily dispensing medicine or recommending medical doctors prescribe it—without following the strict guidelines that govern this treatment."[26]

They continue, clarifying those guidelines, "The standards of care recommend mental health support and comprehensive assessment for all dysphoric youth before starting medical interventions. The process, done conscientiously, can take a few months (when a young person's gender has been persistent and there are no simultaneous mental health issues) or up to several years in complicated cases. But few are trained to do it properly, and some clinicians don't even believe in it, contending without evidence that treating dysphoria medically will resolve other mental health issues." And this is only becoming more common; they write: "We find evidence every single day, from our peers across the country and concerned parents who reach out, that the field has moved from a more nuanced, individualized and developmentally appropriate assessment process to one where every problem looks like a medical one that can be solved quickly with medication or, ultimately, surgery. As a result, we may be harming some of the young people we strive to support—people who may not be prepared for the gender transitions they are being rushed into."[27] The fact that even these experts are sounding the alarm, to largely deaf ears, and that they found themselves unable to do so in other major mainstream publications, is a terrifying wake-up call for those trying to right the ship.

While there is a growing body of concerned clinicians, it's difficult to put a number on how many pediatricians are aware of and worried about the risks to their patients and future patients in the hands of transgender activists. We do, however, have some ability to measure the level of interest and concern. In the last half of 2021, over 80 percent of American Academy of Pediatrics (AAP) members gave feedback on a resolution that appeared before the body about "Addressing Alternatives to the Use of

Hormone Therapies for Gender Dysphoric Youth," which asked the AAP for more debate and discussion of the risks, benefits, and uncertainties inherent in the practice of medically transitioning minors, specifically using hormone therapy.[28] Judging by that statistic, it seems that the vast majority of rank-and-file pediatricians believe there isn't enough debate and consideration being given to such topics.

That concern isn't shared with those at the top of the organization. In August of 2021, on their website, SEGM explained, "Last week, the American Academy of Pediatrics (AAP) rejected SEGM's application to share the latest evidence regarding the practice of pediatric gender transition at AAP's upcoming annual conference in Philadelphia in October 2021. This rejection sends a strong signal that the AAP does not want to see any debate on what constitutes evidence-based care for gender-diverse youth."[29] SEGM applied and paid for an information booth at the conference, which was accepted and then later reversed without explanation.

Medscape reported on the incident: "There is growing concern among many doctors and other healthcare professionals as to whether this is, in fact, the best way to proceed, given that there are a number of irreversible changes associated with treatment. There is also a growing number of 'detransitioners'—mostly young people who transitioned and then changed their minds, and 'detransitioned' back to their birth sex."[30]

On their website, SEGM remarks, "AAP's assertion that 'gender-affirmative' interventions with puberty blockers, cross-sex hormones, and surgeries are the only appropriate treatments for gender dysphoria in minors stands in stark contrast to the much more nuanced approach that has emerged among the leaders in pediatric gender medicine."[31] SEGM concludes, "Because of the low quality of the available evidence and the marked change in the presentation of gender dysphoria in youth in the last several years (many more adolescents with recently emerging transgender identities and significant mental health comorbidities are presenting for care), what constitutes good healthcare for this patient group is far from clear. . . .

The politicization of the field of gender medicine must end, if we care about gender-variant youth and their long-term health."[32] But that doesn't seem likely given recent trends.

Even the president of the United States has decided to get involved. In the spring of 2022, the Biden administration came out in favor of "gender-affirming" care for adults and children alike. The president's spokeswoman, Jen Psaki, explained at a press conference that gender-affirming care was "best practice and potentially lifesaving."[33] President Joe Biden's Justice Department sent a letter to all state attorneys general warning that they could be violating civil rights laws if they keep minors from receiving "gender-affirming care."[34] President Biden released a video message reinforcing the point. "To parents of transgender children," he insisted, "affirming your child's identity is one of the most powerful things you can do to keep them safe and healthy."[35] In many cases, this couldn't be farther from the truth.

One heartbreaking passage from a piece on the Bari Weiss Substack, penned by her sister Suzy Weiss, focused on detransitioners' thoughts in the wake of the Biden administration's declaration. Weiss recounted the story one young woman, Chloe, shared with her: "Before her top surgery, Chloe went to a therapist, then a gender specialist, then a surgeon, who she had two consultations with. She also went to a class put on by her healthcare provider in a building in Oakland with other kids and their parents about top surgery. It was about things like incisions and how to change bandages."[36] Weiss continued, saying, "A few months after she had her breasts removed, she was in class, and the teacher started talking about the psychologist Harry Harlow and his experiment with rhesus monkeys. The experiment showed that the bond between mother and child was much more critical to the development of the child's brain than had been known. 'It occurred to me that I'd never be able to breastfeed my baby,' [Chloe] said. She was 16." Somehow, this had never come up in her consultations.[37]

The ideological capture of the AAP has extended far beyond any plausible claim of benign confusion or even ignorance. In *Trans*, Helen

Joyce explains that the AAP position paper on the "ethical treatment for gender-dysphoric children . . . is so far from evidenced-based that a paper debunking it point by point ran in the *Journal of Sex and Marital Therapy* in 2019."[38] Written by James Cantor, the article lists numerous misrepresentations that Joyce calls "egregious." Cantor writes, "Remarkably, not only did the AAP statement fail to include any of the actual outcomes literature on such cases, but it also misrepresented the contents of its citations, which repeatedly said the very opposite of what the AAP attributed to them." For example, Joyce summarizes, saying, "The AAP statement says that conversion therapy for children has proven 'not only unsuccessful but also deleterious.' But the sources it cites refer to sexual orientation, not gender identity, and therapy for adults, not children." Cantor concludes that the AAP "told neither the truth nor the whole truth . . . committing sins both of commission and of omission, asserting claims easily falsified by anyone caring to do any fact checking at all."[39]

As Joyce quips in her book, "The lack of decent research and misrepresentation of findings mean gender affirmation cannot even be described as a risky experiment on children, since 'experiment' implies someone, somewhere, is tracking outcomes and comparing them with other options." Joyce goes on to explain, "Doctors are usually cautious when treating children, especially when interrupting normal physical development. But very surprisingly, puberty blockers have never been put through clinical trials for use in gender medicine and are not licensed by their manufacturers for this purpose."[40] It's like a horror movie with mad scientists experimenting on hapless victims, only those victims are our children.

Dr. Jeffrey, a physician closely involved with the topic of gender-dysphoric youth, who was unable to speak on the record, told me, "The parallels with the opioid epidemic are astonishing. It's the same sort of deal: You've got a group with a vested interest, you've got weak data, you've got ideological capture. You've got mass psychosis, legions of unthinking clinicians doing what their medical societies are telling them to do." Joyce alludes to this similarity as well. Dr. Jeffrey continues, "The medical societies are captured. They're putting out guidelines that have no scientific basis to support them. And the doctors shrug and say, 'The guidelines say . . . the guidelines say . . . the guidelines say . . .' And so, when you put out bad guidelines that are not based on good data, there is a high likelihood that people will be harmed. That's the whole point of doing medical research. You want good quality data to guide interventions. If you intervene with interventions that carry significant risks, on low-quality research, there's a good chance you're going to hurt people. And now, we're in a game of waiting until a critical mass of people are harmed, where enough people start to take notice who have enough power and influence to shift the direction of things—either through the court system or medical directors at insurance companies or universities—to see the train wreck and start to pull back." What is it going to take to stop this runaway train?

Many wonder why parents allow their children to be experimented on in this manner. Quite simply, they are told that if they don't allow their children to receive this "essential care," they're dooming their children to certain death. Parents are told that this "care" is essential, lest their transgender child commit suicide. Dr. Jeffrey told me, "What's been described to me is a frantic push from the clinicians to 'do something,' with phrases used like: 'Do you want a live son or dead daughter?' Really horrible manipulation like that [because] there's no proof that puberty blockers or cross-sex hormones or surgeries reduce suicide rates in this population."[41]

In other cases, parents aren't aware that their children are considering these options because authorities have no obligation to inform them. In fact, school policies often specify that parents *should not* be informed.

That's exactly what happened to January Littlejohn, an involved stay-at-home mother of three children living in Florida who became an unwitting warrior in the battle against radical gender ideology. Her daughter, then-age thirteen, is one of the children who began self-identifying as male and self-diagnosing herself with gender dysphoria.

January shared with me how she felt her daughter had been targeted and groomed by school officials, who had worked with the child clandestinely to socially transition her while she was on campus. After her daughter decided that she was transgender, three school officials, two of whom January had never even met, talked to her without January's knowledge or consent to develop a six-page gender plan. They talked about how she could go by another name and different pronouns at school, whether or not she wanted her parents brought into the conversation, the gender of the people she could be rooming with on overnight field trips, and what restroom she wanted to use.

The school wasn't going off script; this *was* the script. The Leon County School's Lesbian, Gay, Bisexual, Transgender, Gender Nonconforming and Questioning Support Guide[42] includes these three key points: 1) Parents are not to be informed when their children announce a transgender identity with school personnel. 2) Children are allowed to choose the restroom that matches their gender identity without parental notification. 3) Children have a legally protected right to keep information from their parents regarding their gender identity and the steps taken by the district to affirm that identity.[43]

Littlejohn told a group of parents at Florida Family Policy Council during a speech about her experience in November of 2021, "[This is] driving a very dangerous wedge between children and their parents," and these guidelines "send the message to the child that their parents are the enemy, and that children need to be protected *from* their parents instead of *by* their parents."[44]

The school's efforts were so inflammatory that the Littlejohns filed a federal civil rights lawsuit, still pending in the U.S. District Court for the Northern District of Florida in October of 2021, seeking to "vindicate their fundamental rights to direct the upbringing of their children."[45] The lawsuit names the school superintendent, the assistant superintendent, and the Leon County School Board as defendants.

Like Dr. Jeffrey, Littlejohn believes there are analogs to previous bombshell scandals, comparing the transgender craze to the Big Tobacco scandals of the past, with lying corporations and doctors keeping the dangers of tobacco hidden from the public for years. She told me, "It felt like we were the only ones fighting for the long-term mental and physical health of our child. Everyone was cheering her down this path of self-harm that we knew was the wrong path for our child. She had teachers telling her she was brave for coming out as 'non-binary.' There's so many arms to this issue: social media, schools, the government now that they're trying to solidify gender identity instead of sex into law. It's going to have so many consequences that people don't realize. We're already seeing it in cases where men are erasing women's sports records, the sexual assault in Loudoun County in Virginia. The consequences of what we're doing in the name of tolerance, inclusion, and 'human rights' are going to be immeasurable. Most doctors don't want to touch this. They want to refer out; that's what happened with my pediatrician, even when I sent her all of this information on rapid onset gender dysphoria."

For Littlejohn, going through her daughter's struggle has been eye-opening and has made her question "everything." She told me, "If these medical associations are denying basic biology, then what else are they willing to deny and lie about? How can you trust doctors that are denying very simple truths?"[46]

In her book, *Trans*, Helen Joyce explains how alone parents like the Littlejohns often feel. "There was no one unbiased those parents could turn to for advice, and the stories they and their children read in the media were entirely one-sided," Joyce writes. "These parents say that their attempts to protect their children are actively frustrated by everyone else."[47]

Kay, a young woman I spoke with who "detransitioned" away from self-identifying as transgender, echoed the opinions of Littlejohn, Joyce, and the clinicians with whom I spoke about how this ideology can come to worm its way into a young (and often troubled) person's mind. She was drawn to the content on TikTok, which she described as "a public diary on a transgender journey/timelines. It's romanticized. You see homely and awkward girls turn into more confident (appearing) guys. I could look at these videos and they seem much happier now that they've changed themselves. The testosterone is a steroid that is affecting their mood, but they're reporting feeling happier. The TikTok algorithm keeps feeding them timelines with more and more transgender content. It's a kind of brainwashing; they're inundated day after day." But Kay contends that the hormones and transition weren't curing them of already pre-existing mental illness and confusion. They think the grass is going to be greener on the other side, but Kay has learned the hard way that "you're not going to look like that person, you're going to look like you, even after surgery and hormones."[48]

Quoting another "detransitioner," Joyce shared the story of a young woman named "Helena" who drove to a Planned Parenthood clinic "that ran on 'informed consent' lines." Joyce writes, "After a brief chat, a nurse showed Helena how to inject testosterone and gave her a prescription for more. When Helena left for college two days later, she did so [identifying] as a boy." But soon, her situation deteriorated, and she told Joyce, "I was supposed to be this cute Tumblr transboy living his truth. Instead, I had transformed from a little girl with short hair into this testosterone-addled thing." Helena soon realized she had made a mistake, but she was met with resistance. Joyce explains, "When she finally admitted that she regretted transition, her therapist said she was making no sense; that the only cure for dysphoria was transition." Luckily, Helena persisted. Joyce writes, "Re-identifying as a woman was a great relief, and she is grateful she never progressed to surgery. But she worries about how her time on testosterone will affect her future health. And the psychological issues are far greater. 'I feel like a cult survivor, a thousand percent. That cult robbed me of my adolescence.'"[49]

References to cults were made again and again by those familiar with transgender activism. Dr. Jeffrey told me, "When you expose young and stressed children to ideas like this, and then you flood them with positive reinforcement when they claim to be transgender and there's a lot of fanfare . . . detransitioners who share their stories online are often explicit about this 'lovebombing' drove them into this identity. There's huge parallels to the cult world. It's a very similar experience that many of them describe."[50]

Arielle Scarcella, a popular lesbian YouTube star with over 700,000 subscribers, compared the transgender craze to a cult as well. Scarcella says her opposition to the transgender movement began "when the far Left became increasingly entitled in regards to women's bodies and women's spaces." On why people are gravitating toward this new identity, she told me, prefacing with the fact that she herself isn't religious, "People are searching for a deeper meaning to life. Usually people find that with religion. But people aren't as religious these days. And the people that are the least religious, if you look, are the people who are claiming these thousand genders. You'll never see non-binary people claim to be religious . . . Their new religion is this leftist/progressive ideology. Instead of the Word of God, I call it The Word of Woke."[51]

This "religion" isn't just a danger to families like the Littlejohns or to young women like Kay. Its doctrines are warping the perceptions of an entire generation, among other things, reviving stereotypical understandings of gender that we threw out decades ago as antiquated and sometimes oppressive. In *Trans*, Joyce writes about transgender activists and materials: "The stereotypes they promote teach children ideas about what is proper for boys and girls that feminists had thought consigned to the dustbin of history. This is just one of the ways in which gender-ideology harms all children, not merely those who end up identifying out of their sex. As queer theory conquered campuses, and the simplistic 'wrong body' version conquered popular culture, writing about transkids proliferated: storybooks for children, novels for teenagers and workbooks for readers of every age. Memeified versions circulate on social media. All express the same contradiction. Gender identity is an innate, ineffable sense, unrelated to body types, behavior and presentation. But that inner truth is manifested by stereotypes."[52] It's ironic that a movement all about ending oppression would simultaneously promote limiting stereotypes.

This is only one way that many old-school feminists like Joyce and author J.K. Rowling, who are nicknamed by their detractors trans-exclusionary radical feminists, or TERFs, see today's gender ideology as harmful to women. These feminists are speaking for a generation of girls who are victimized by the ideology in any number of ways, like losing private, women-only spaces—not just school bathrooms, changing rooms, and prisons, but even breastfeeding support meetings facilitated by La Leche League filled with new mothers learning how to breastfeed.[53]

Parents are facing an existential threat to their children's safety and well-being, both physical and mental, but it doesn't just include the real and frightening possibility that these children could themselves be sucked into the cult and secretly transition to another gender. It also puts their daughters into physically unsafe situations, like what happened in Loudoun County, Virginia, in 2021.

In June of 2021, Loudoun County Public Schools (LCPS) sought to pass a controversial transgender policy. The plan would provide bathroom and locker room access based on a student's gender identity, as well as allow transgender student athletes to participate on teams based on their gender identities; teachers and staff would be required to use students' preferred pronouns. In late 2021, Luke Rosiak broke the story for the *Daily Wire* in a groundbreaking piece of investigative journalism.

In the midst of that controversy, LCPS concealed that a ninth-grade girl was allegedly raped by a "gender fluid" student in a Loudoun school bathroom just three weeks prior. During the June school board meeting, the superintendent repeatedly said that the school system had no record of any bathroom assaults of any kind, nor any incidents involving transgender students, calling the idea a "red herring" and saying "the predator transgender student or person simply does not exist."[54] One man, Scott Smith, was arrested at that meeting opposing the bathroom policy and became the mascot for the media's vilification of contentious school board meetings, with footage of his arrest played endlessly on

TV. He has been portrayed as an unruly bigot by the mainstream media and the National School Boards Association. But Smith wasn't there as just any concerned parent: he was the father of the rape victim. Smith was at that meeting because of what happened to his daughter, and he was angry because the school system was pretending it never happened.

The boy was charged with four felony counts of forcible sodomy for what he did to Smith's daughter on May 28. He pled no contest to charges of sexual battery in November 2021. Instead of counseling the victim (remember #BelieveAllWomen?), LCPS merely transferred the student to a different school, and on October 6, the boy was arrested again in the alleged abduction and sexual assault of another girl in a different Loudoun County classroom.[55] If this boy had not been "gender-fluid," one can only imagine how different the response would have been.

The harms caused by the acceptance and promotion of radical gender ideology are innumerable and shared by troubled children, their parents, their peers, and society at large. Transgender ideology has provided an "out" (that actually solves nothing) for a generation of girls struggling with self-esteem, self-acceptance, and self-love while simultaneously placing them in dangerous situations. Children are being told that their psychological traumas are caused by gender confusion and that there's an easy solution to their crisis: transition. Though transition is easily accessible, little in the way of informed consent takes place for young people and their parents, who are often unaware of the scope of the side effects of the treatment that they or their children are given.

The conspiracy to promote this idea is widespread and has saturated the institutions we should be able to trust most implicitly with our children's health and safety: the medical profession and schools are more concerned with being affirming than with looking out for the true well-being of their young and impressionable patients and students. Parents trust doctors, therapists, and teachers with their children, but that trust is very often misplaced. And it's the parents who are left to pick up the pieces when transition, the magic cure their children have been sold, doesn't drive off their children's demons.

If you had a time machine and could go back to the average American fifteen years ago and tell them that there was a popular and powerful ideology with a stranglehold on all corners of childhood that was promoting "medical treatments" that maimed and sterilized troubled youth, especially gay and lesbian teens, it would have been assumed that it was the radical religious right at the controls, not the far Left. But the reality is teen mental health is already in the toilet, thanks in no small part to progressive messaging about doomsday, race and gender wars, and the omnipresent nature of brain-melting technology. And it is the woke elites in charge of our institutions who are throwing a match on the fire, sending already-troubled kids down an irreversible path of physical modifications and further confusion and turmoil.

Writing as a research fellow for the Heritage Foundation, Ryan Anderson, the author of the book *When Harry Became Sally: Responding to the Transgender Moment*, explains, "The most thorough follow-up of sex-reassigned people—extending over 30 years and conducted in Sweden, where the culture is strongly supportive of the transgendered—documents their lifelong mental unrest. Ten to 15 years after surgical reassignment, the suicide rate of those who had undergone sex-reassignment surgery rose to 20 times that of comparable peers."[56]

What can parents do to protect their children from the gender ideology cult? What might January Littlejohn tell her past self if she were given a time machine? As a parent, the first and most important step that you can take is one that you are currently taking: learn about all the ways in which the system is pitted against parents and kids. The loyalty to The Narrative regarding gender dysphoria is what takes precedence over the health and safety of our children. By spreading the truth about the impact of this ideology on our society and on individual children, public opinion will further shift in favor of medical sanity: a June poll by NPR/Ipsos found, for example, that 63 percent of Americans already opposed the participation of biological males in female sports.[57] Such poll results make it easier to convince legislators to do the right thing. In Florida, for example, a bill critics misleadingly called the "Don't Say Gay" bill requires any discussion of gender identity to be age appropriate: "Classroom instruction by school personnel or third parties on sexual orientation or gender identity may not occur in kindergarten through grade 3 or in a manner that is not age appropriate or developmentally appropriate for students in accordance with state standards."[58] The law also protects parental notification rights and includes a mechanism to challenge the school district over violations of the new rules. When the *Wall Street Journal* polled the specific text of the bill, it found that 61 percent of the public supported it.[59]

Meanwhile, after the 2021 Virginia governor's race turned on parental input in student curricula, other states took notice: North Carolina and Nebraska took steps toward increasing parents' choice in where to send their children to school, and the Michigan Democratic Party apologized for criticizing parents who wanted a say in their children's education.[60]

The pandemic made school board meetings the hottest place in town to meet other moms with similar concerns. With the restrictions winding down and masks coming off, this is not the time for parents to get complacent. It's time to ask questions about how gender ideology has seeped into the classroom, the school library, and perhaps most importantly, into the policies governing how the school operates. Every parent must question those in power at their kid's school: when it comes to sports, locker rooms, sleepover field trips, and more, does the school group students by their biological sex or by their gender identity? If it's the latter, it's time to organize to change the policy in the district. What do the school's policies say about parental notification and consent if a child wishes to go by another name and pronouns? School district officials are finding that they cannot avoid answering these questions anymore, and the pressure and public outrage from parents is working. Laws are changing, curriculum transparency and parental consent are expanding, and the increase in school choice means parents aren't simply stuck with whatever their district gives them.

7

SEXUALIZED CHILDHOOD

There is a great deal of overlap between the impact of gender ideology and how it causes the over-sexualization of children. Ultimately, the woke progressive view is that children are inherently sexual beings, and that they can and should assert that sexuality through their gender identification and through sexual acts.

The sexualization of childhood is a phenomenon that predates woke ideology and isn't exclusive to the present moment. Woke ideology, however, enables abusers to harm children by giving the abusers opportunities to use politics as a way to provide moral cover.

How did we get here? The assault on the notion that children are and should remain sexually innocent and should be protected from sexual content and relationships long predates our current political moment. In France, for example, a shift was recognized following the May 1968 demonstrations, according to psychiatrist and President of the Traumatic Memory and Victimology Association Muriel Salmona, as reported by *The Atlantic*. In part of this cultural revolution "children were viewed as having the right to be considered sexual beings" and, as Salmona puts it, "pedophilia was considered a sexual orientation . . . It was all part of a vision of freedom."[1] In France, the legal age of consent was only decided upon in 2021, set at fifteen years of age.

France isn't alone in its waffling on the matter of stigmatizing "child love" in the name of progressivism. A disturbing long-form article in the *New Yorker* told the stories of young men victimized by a state-sponsored pedophile cabal carried out in Germany called the "Kentler experiment" in the 1980s and 90s, named after psychologist Helmut Kentler whose idea it was to hand over homeless teenagers to foster parents who happened to be known pedophiles. The author, Rachel Aviv, explained, "In a 2020 report commissioned by the Berlin Senate, scholars at the University of Hildesheim concluded that 'the Senate also ran foster homes or shared flats for young Berliners with pedophile men in other parts of West Germany'" and that the "authors wrote that 'these foster homes were run by sometimes powerful men who lived alone and who were given this power by academia, research institutions and other pedagogical environments that accepted, supported or even lived out pedophile stances.'"[2] According to Kentler, these would make loving homes because he believed sexual contact between adults and children was harmless.

The origins of Kentler's work were Marxist in nature. In the same *New Yorker* article, Aviv explains, "He was inspired by the Marxist psychoanalyst Wilhelm Reich, who had argued that the free flow of sexual energy was essential to building a new kind of society. Kentler's dissertation urged parents to teach their children that they should never be ashamed of their desires."[3] The Marxist roots of this argument should be no surprise: left-wing revolutionary ideologies target the "institution" of the family as a way to turn people who would otherwise be products of their environment into blank slates.

Similar ideas existed elsewhere as well. In the *Weekend Australian* in 2016, Jennifer Oriel writes, "During the 1970s, pedophile groups capitalising on the sexual liberation movement sought to redefine their exploitation of youth as an expression of children's sexual rights, self-determination and autonomy. Groups such as the North American Man/Boy Love Association claimed children were sexual beings and sought to repeal age of consent laws to liberate their sexuality. They were welcomed by fringe elements of the neo-Marxist minorities movement that advocated sexual libertarian ideology under Queer and 'sex positive' politics."[4]

While the "sexual liberation" of children that occurred in the 1960s and 70s generally could be characterized as fringe, with few ordinary children experiencing the theft of their innocence in the name of radical political progress (outside of crazy communes, that is), in this new woke era, a new tactic is employed. Whereas overt political organizing to redefine the age of consent proved unsuccessful, new efforts in the name of childhood sexual liberation are far more discreet and sinister in nature.

Consider a 2002 book called *Harmful to Minors: The Perils of Protecting Children from Sex* by Judith Levine, the winner of the *Los Angeles Times* Book Prize. Levine's objective was to introduce the idea that "children and teenagers can have sexual pleasure and be safe too," as she writes, positing that children are inherently sexual beings and that adults should respect and encourage openness when it comes to sexuality with children.[5] Here's one particularly thought-provoking excerpt: "Just like the word *abuse*, the word *consent* is subject to multiple meetings. Negotiation is part of children sex play. It may involve bribes and trickery, conflict, trade-offs, and power imbalances, like all other interactions between children. Older and bigger does not necessarily add up to more powerful, though. And a wide spectrum of behavior involving power differences between children seems to be normative (or if I've soured you on normative, then apparently harmless). Psychologists Sharon Lamb and Mary Coakley surveyed 300 psychologically healthy Bryn Mawr students about their childhood sexual experiences. The young women wrote about thrilling games of porn star, prostitute, rape, and slave girl, all at ages in the single digits, indicating that the pairing of sex and aggression or sex and power differences, too, might be normal."[6] Levine's assertion is that anything goes.

One Amazon reviewer praised this book and gushed, "The most important thing we can do is let them do [whatever] feels good with [whomever] they choose, no matter the gender, the partner's age, the types of sexual activity as long as its CONSENSUAL."[7] The reviewer went on with this eye-popping boast, "My daughters were 7 and 8 when I discovered, as awkward as it sounds, they had both been using my electric toothbrush to masturbate. [Without] mentioning it [I] had them both come sit down with me at my computer that following Saturday. I opened my partition with all my adult links and opened 3 quality adult toys website[s]. I told them [I] felt it was time they had some big girl toys and I let them pick whatever they wanted with no shame."[8]

This kind of sexual liberation for children is now being encouraged in schools across the country, spearheaded largely by teachers. The discourse on children's sexual rights and the belief they are sexual beings are invoked to justify school programs that sexualize youth at ever younger ages.

Over the spring of 2022, we saw the natural byproduct of this ideology. Writing for *City Journal*, Christopher Rufo explained, "The principles of queer theory have escaped from the college campus and made their way into a summer camp for children in rural Kentucky. Last year, a nonprofit coalition called Sexy Sex Ed organized a series of 'Sexy Summer Camp' events targeted toward minors that included lessons on 'sex liberation,' 'gender exploration,' 'BDSM,' 'being a sex worker,' 'self-managed abortions,' and 'sexual activity while using licit and illicit drugs.'"[9] Rufo went on, "In a saner world, these statements and materials would all be red flags. Yet Sexy Summer Camp has received lavish praise in the media. *Yes!* magazine told readers that the program 'helps rural young people feel more comfortable discussing their bodies, sex, and reproductive health to empower them to advocate for themselves.'" According to Rufo, "CNN reported that Sexy Sex Ed is 'what women in Appalachian Kentucky really want,' framing the summer camp as a way to 'bring honest conversations to young people to fill the void left behind by homes and schools.'"[10]

Rufo concludes: "Programs like Sexy Summer Camp are unfortunately becoming more common in the United States. Another organization in Indiana was recently exposed for hosting a camp for children as young as eight that featured an instructor who encourages children to explore 'gender identity,' 'kink,' and 'condom demonstration[s].' Activists have tried to launder this type of material into schools and nonprofit programs through the guise of 'comprehensive sex education,' another euphemism that might lull the public into complacency.

Parents should proceed with caution: summer camps, which once taught archery, fishing, and hiking, might now be teaching kink, polyamory, and BDSM."[11]

These behaviors look strikingly like "grooming." RAINN (Rape, Abuse & Incest National Network), the nation's largest anti-sexual violence organization, defines grooming as "manipulative behaviors that the abuser uses to gain access to a potential victim, coerce them to agree to the abuse, and reduce the risk of being caught."[12] The act of grooming follows a pattern, beginning with victim selection: "Abusers often observe possible victims and select them based on ease of access to them or their perceived vulnerability." Identifying children who are struggling socially or mentally would fit this pattern. Another aspect of grooming is attempting "to gain trust of a potential victim through gifts, attention, sharing 'secrets' and other means to make them feel that they have a caring relationship and to train them to keep the relationship secret."[13] This secret-keeping is actually mandated in many schools where teachers are instructed to encourage students to keep their gender transition secret from their parents. Commenting on the phenomenon, a transsexual man, Buck Angel, commented on Twitter, "Number one rule! Never teach children to keep secrets from parents!! This is groomer tactics you f*cking morons."[14]

Yet this is now standard practice. In Canada, for example, an Ottawa-Carleton school board allows students to change their names without their parents' knowledge. Not just without their consent, but without their knowledge! Reporting on the phenomenon of schools and "queerness," Roberto Wakerell-Cruz explained in the *Post Millennial*, "According to an email sent to OCDSB [Ottawa-Carleton District School Board] colleagues, students will have the option of being referred to by their chosen name and pronouns, and will be able to change their names on all non-legal documents used by the school. The email states that parents or guardians 'do not have to be involved in their children's new identities. Parents will be able to see any changes to a student's chosen name or gender marker.'"[15]

Writing for her Substack newsletter in late 2021, journalist Abigail Shrier wrote about how activist teachers recruit kids for their gender and sexual orientation activities. Lori Caldeira, teacher and LGBTQ-club leader, says on an audio clip Shrier received from a conference attendee from California, "Because we are not official—we have no club rosters, we keep no records . . . In fact, sometimes we don't really want to keep records because if parents get upset that their kids are coming? We're like, 'Yeah, I don't know. Maybe they came?' You know, we would never want a kid to get in trouble for attending if their parents are upset."[16] Shrier writes, "The advice to those who run middle school LGBTQ clubs is: keep no records, so you can plead ignorance of the membership with the members' parents."[17]

The result of those efforts in California were brought to light in December of 2021, when a California mother, Jessica Konen, went viral for screaming at her daughter's school board in the Spreckels Union School District. At the deceptively named LGBTQ "Equity Club" meetings, Konen alleged that teachers at the school had coached and affirmed her daughter's transgender identity without talking to her first. Brad Jones for the *Epoch Times* reported, "Near the end of sixth grade, Konen's daughter told her she might be bisexual, and by the middle of the seventh grade, Konen was called to the school for a meeting with her daughter, a teacher, and the school principal."[18] Konen says she was "blindsided" and was crying at the meeting, "trying to absorb everything." How did the teacher respond? Jones writes, "The teacher accused Konen of not being 'emotionally supportive' of her daughter, who was to be called by a new name and male pronouns and would be using the unisex restroom at school." *The Epoch Times* reported that Konen said the teacher "completely coached" her child into her new gender identification, but this coaching could be viewed another way: she was groomed.[19]

The scariest part of this school-based transition is the interference of the state and of government officials in these very private and charged situations. *The Bridgehead* reported on what happened next to the family: "Within a few days of the meeting, the King City Police Department showed up at her door and told her that there had been a complaint made to Child Protective Services (CPS). The police questioned her two children and asked them if they wanted to be removed from the home."[20] Thankfully, "CPS dropped the case and did not demand she call her daughter by masculine pronouns as her teacher had insisted." However, the message had been received: "Throughout the school year, Konen was afraid to ask questions about her daughter or her school activities, fearing that CPS could take her children away."[21]

Not only did the school deliberately conceal their gender coaching, they also concealed other vital information for a parent to know: "After several meetings with the teachers, Konen discovered the school knew her daughter had searched online for information about suicide, but never told her about it."[22] When teachers take over, parents are left to pick up the pieces.

I discussed the topic of transgender-identifying children in the previous chapter, but it's important to note how much these "gender" issues can cross-pollinate into how the woke have taken aim at sexualizing an entire generation of children. Ultimately, encouraging kids with gender dysphoria to transition is a way of sexualizing them. The most influential and powerful radicalizers on issues related to gender and sexuality for kids are in far too many cases their own teachers.

The young woman who runs the viral Twitter account "Libs of TikTok" spends hours scouring the site in order to expose the most lunatic fringes of the social media platform built around the sharing of short videos. She described to me how often teachers pop up in her research on the most outrageous, most woke accounts and videos circulating the web. Most of the videos are made by millennial teachers, in their mid- to late-20s and 30s, who create content for other teachers on the app. She explained that sexuality is "their essence and their being. It's all they talk about. It's every single video. Everything they say, it circles back to their sexuality and their gender. And these are people we're putting in front of our kids to teach them." How pervasive is it? "I think it's everywhere and it has been for a couple years and nobody was paying attention. Because of social media, they have a platform now to shout it out for the world to see. . . . It's everywhere. I've spoken to teachers from every single state." She continued, "These people shouldn't be allowed near kids. They are indoctrinating them, even if they're not doing it on purpose. If your entire identity is about your sexuality, it's impossible to separate it. They're coming to school dressed in rainbow clothing and slogans from head-to-toe and [claiming] they aren't indoctrinating kids."[23]

TikTok isn't just a niche social media platform; TikTok's users now spend more time each month watching content than YouTube users.[24] Young people are spending more time on TikTok than any other social media platform.[25] As such, what is posted on TikTok has an outsized influence; whereas a tiny fraction of teachers and users are actually using the app, which skews extremely liberal, they have a way of influencing a potentially massive audience.

TikTok was the center of a 2021 *Wall Street Journal* investigation which uncovered how the app targets users with content revolving around sex, drugs, eating disorders, and more, calling it an "addiction machine."[26] Investigators created thirty-one accounts registered to young teens and turned them loose "to browse TikTok's For You feed, the highly personalized, never-ending feed curated by the algorithm." The article explained, "An analysis of the videos served to these accounts found that through its powerful algorithms, TikTok can quickly drive minors—among the biggest users of the app—into endless spools of content about sex and drugs. TikTok served one account registered as a 13-year-old at least 569 videos about drug use, references to cocaine and meth addiction, and promotional videos for online sales of drug products and paraphernalia. Hundreds of similar videos appeared in the feeds of the *Journal's* other minor accounts."[27]

TikTok isn't the only place where young people are exposed to sexually explicit content. On Instagram, it's common for models to tease barely allowable explicit content, while providing links off the app to subscription sites like OnlyFans for users to view the "full picture."

What happens to their brains when preteens and early teens are exposed to pornography? Brian Willoughby, professor of Family Life at Brigham Young University (BYU), sounded the alarm. More and more young people, he says, are seeing sexual content before puberty—not because they're seeking it out, but because it's been delivered to the smartphones their parents are buying them. In the current generation of young people, their first orgasms are tied not to real-life experiences, but to pornography. We know from brain research how influential first experiences are for mapping the brain, which could explain how year after year, we're seeing fewer and fewer young people interested in sex, dating, and committed relationships.

Thanks to the COVID era, we know how capable social media apps and platforms are of policing the content users post, as anyone who has posted anything about COVID can tell you. Within minutes of posting text, audio, or video related to the virus, a banner appears on the bottom of the story to direct users to an approved information hub. If this can be done for a virus, it could also be done with pornography. The fact that it isn't speaks volumes about companies' commitment to curbing explicit content. These companies could choose to remove pornography, especially when children appear. These companies could choose to remove access to sites like OnlyFans and Pornhub from their platforms; they choose not to.

BYU's Willoughby told me, "A lot is just driven by capitalism and making money. These pornographic sites are some of the most heavily trafficked sites on the internet. They make money via ads and revenue sharing."[28] Pornography is ubiquitous and literally chasing our children around the internet, stealing not only their innocence, but also their ability to maintain healthy sexual practices and boundaries in the future.

However, pornography doesn't just live on the internet inside private bedrooms, and its effects don't either. Over the course of 2020 and 2021, the ready availability of explicit content in school and public libraries became a hot-button topic. In Texas in November 2021, Governor Greg Abbott "sent a letter to Texas Education Agency (TEA)

Commissioner Mike Morath directing the agency to investigate any criminal activity in public schools involving the availability of pornographic material that serves no educational purpose. The governor also directed the agency to report any instance of pornography being provided to minors under the age of eighteen for prosecution to the fullest extent of the law."[29]

One of the 850 problematic books on the radar in Texas, for example, is a graphic novel memoir marketed to a young adult audience called *Gender Queer: a Memoir* by Maia Kobabe, which aims to describe "what it means to be nonbinary and asexual."[30] This is how the book is described by one reviewer—and no, there are no typos found within the following paragraphs: "In 2014, Maia Kobabe, who uses e/em/eir pronouns, thought that a comic of reading statistics would be the last autobiographical comic e would ever write. At the time, it was the only thing e felt comfortable with strangers knowing about em. Then e created Gender Queer. Maia's intensely cathartic autobiography charts eir journey of self-identity, which includes the mortification and confusion of adolescent crushes, grappling with how to come out to family and society, bonding with friends over erotic gay fanfiction, and facing the trauma and fundamental violation of pap smears."[31]

Erika Sanzi, outreach director for Parents Defending Education, explained that *Gender Queer* "is so sexually graphic that [she] could not describe it in detail in a recent radio interview because of FCC guidelines." She reports, "When a parent in North Kingstown recently raised concerns [about *Gender Queer*] to the superintendent, he defended the book in an email, likening it to Michelangelo's art, The David, and contrasting it with Playboy magazine. He argued the author intended 'to be concerned for the sexual health of those who are transgender and clearly not to be pornographic.'"[32]

Unfortunately, this is not unusual. Sanzi writes, "In recent weeks, I've been contemplating the departure from age-appropriate books to the gender-obsessed, hyper-sexualized and even pornographic books pouring into schools and children's sections of public libraries in the name of 'diversity, equity and inclusion.' . . . I am not clutching my pearls. These are not the days of protests over books such as author Judy Blume's coming of age novel, *Are You There God? It's Me Margaret.* The books of concern today contain graphic sexual images and descriptions of sex between children, teens and even adults and minors. Some are graphic novels that look like comic strips. The content is pornographic and represents a disturbing agenda by activists that targets youth, hiding behind seemingly virtuous and innocuous words such as 'diversity' and 'inclusion.' . . . Images of sex acts, regardless of who is in them, are wildly inappropriate for a school library or classroom. There is no justification for having different rules around pornography and sexually explicit content based on the gender identity and sexual orientation of a book's characters."[33]

Sanzi prompts an important question: "Is all of this hypersexual content a form of societal grooming?" Progressives insist that "grooming" can only apply to purposeful preparation for sexual abuse, and, therefore, the hypersexual education of a minor doesn't count. But that argument fails on its own merits. After all, if progressives believe children are just small adults, and should be treated as such for the purposes of sexual awareness, these ideologues will effectively erase the bedrock safeguard of the "age of consent." The only sure outcome of that would be the enabling of sexual predation. This is obvious to everyone who is unencumbered by ideological blinders. For example, in the fall of 2021, Old Dominion University professor Allyn Walker (a biological female born as Allyson but who identifies as a transgender male) ignited a firestorm resulting in his resignation. In a twenty-nine-minute interview with the Prostasia Foundation (more on that later), Walker said "Minor Attracted People" or "MAPs" should be used to describe people who are attracted to children but don't act on that attraction. "It's less stigmatizing than other terms like 'pedophile.' A lot of people, when they hear the term pedophile, they automatically assume that it means sex offender. And that isn't true. And it leads to a lot of misconceptions."[34] His defense and attempted legitimization of pedophilia caused a national scandal, precisely because most people naturally understand the danger in removing protections for minors in this area.

The attention garnered by Walker's interview, meanwhile, put the term Minor Attracted Persons (MAPs) on the radar of millions of Americans, and with it the realization that there is a concerted effort among a certain segment of academics and woke elites to normalize these feelings. The academic discussion of MAPs is a trial balloon, as anyone familiar with the normalization of radical gender ideology can attest. The idea that gender is a social construct originated in academia and eventually became mainstream enough that its influence became the subject of an entire chapter of this book. Radical gender ideology became a threat because it was no longer relegated to obscure academic circles, and if parents aren't careful, MAPs could follow the same path.

In September of 2021, journalists and self-described social liberals Katie Herzog and Jesse Singal addressed a particularly noteworthy proponent of this ideology on their podcast "Blocked and Reported." In their September 2 episode, they turn their attention to Noah Berlatsky, a widely published progressive writer with bylines in *The Atlantic*, NBC *Think*, and the *Washington Post* who also happens to be the Director of Communications of Prostasia, a "child protection organization that combines our zero tolerance of child sexual abuse with our commitment to human and civil rights and sex positivity."[35] If you know what the group actually does, that's like saying that *Playboy* is a women's appreciation magazine, or that Pornhub is a women's appreciation website. The reality? Herzog says Prostasia does "advocacy for what they call Minor Attracted Persons, commonly known as pedophiles."[36] She later quotes an article about the group on a site called 4W, which she describes as a feminist publication. "The organization's efforts," writes the author of the article, Anna Slatz, "have dedicated themselves to crusades against child pornography bans, letter-writing campaigns to state representatives demanding child-likeness sex dolls be kept legal, and funding research into 'fantasy sexual outlets' for pedophiles."[37]

In their campaign to keep child sex dolls legal, Prostasia suggests calling legislative offices and explaining that banning child-likeness sex dolls is unconstitutional, "won't help children," and "that rather than reducing child sexual abuse, a ban could actually increase it by removing a victimless outlet for some people who might otherwise target a real child."[38]

Prostasia claims they to want to "cure" pedophiles by giving them outlets for their urges and desires via sex dolls and child pornography, but a great deal of their activism actually involves desensitizing the public to adults who are attracted to minors. Instead of channeling sexual urges away from content (dolls and pornography) involving minors, they want to preserve their legal right to access such materials. Their argument hinges on the distinction made between people who are attracted to children but don't act on it and people who molest children for any number of reasons. This mindset sees pedophilia "like a sexual orientation" and, therefore, as something that should not be stigmatized. Paying lip service to the still socially required idea that child abuse is wrong, they say that their efforts will allow MAPs to seek help in the form of counseling and support groups, as well as resist the temptation to act on their sexual attraction to minors.[39] Despite its attempts to present as a progressive activist organization, all of Prostasia's goals and campaigns lead to the exact same outcome: the total normalization and acceptance of 'minor attraction,' better known as pedophilia.

It should be noted that Herzog goes on to acknowledge that there is no data or literature that answers this question of whether these tactics, publishing child pornography literature and legalizing child sex dolls, are "harm-reducing," i.e., if they make pedophiles more or less likely to offend.[40] While Singal and Herzog happily and frequently describe Berlatsky as the worst person on the internet, they question if he's actually a pedophile. I'm not so sure. But the fact that someone as problematic as Berlatsky, who remains a card-carrying progressive, is quite telling in regard to their willingness to accept the transformation of the taboo of pedophilia into the more benign-sounding term "minor-attracted person," normalizing sexual attraction to children.

This is only part of a larger agenda to "dismantle" the "innocence of children" by sexualizing them every way possible, to quote James Lindsay. In the summer of 2020, Lindsay wrote a Twitter thread that explained the woke assault on childhood: "The most obvious way Wokeness goes after the innocence of children is in the Queer variant of trans activism, especially by having trans strippers perform for children in schools [Drag Queen Story Hour], for example. Why would they do this? The belief is that the innocence we encourage in children is part of the systems of power (specifically generated through performativity) that enforce heteronormativity and cisnormativity and thus lead to dysphoria or oppression of gay and potentially trans kids. The logic isn't terribly complicated: there might be gay or trans kids in the class, say, who would be more comfortable in their sexual identity (if that makes sense for a kid -- it doesn't) and gender identity if they saw disruptions to the usual 'binaries' being celebrated."[41]

Further in his thread, Lindsay compares the sexual innocence of childhood to racial innocence (where children don't see race) that woke ideologues find "suspect" and "problematic" and believe must be "intervened upon." He explains, "CRT insists that racial innocence is, because of the operation of whiteness, only available for white (passing) people, though others will covet it and act white or take up white adjacency. That is, CRT argues that racial innocence (in young children) is a privilege afforded only to white (passing) people, and therefore, rather than aiming to expand it (which it deems impossible), it seeks to obliterate it to put everyone on equitable footing."[42] By this logic, innocence is a sign of privilege and, therefore, something to be ashamed about— and something to be destroyed as soon as possible. As Lindsay summarizes, "Children can't be innocent; they must be activists."[43]

In a podcast published in November of 2021, Lindsay explains that there is a long-running ideological project to groom children out of childhood innocence so that they can become politically moldable. And if there happens to be abuse and sexual grooming and sexual and psy-chological abuse of children along the way, so be it.[44]

Sexual education classes have adopted the "queer" model as well; they're not just about preventing pregnancy and sexually transmitted diseases anymore. Now, sexual education includes theories about gender and sexuality, in the form of lessons on "The Genderbread Person" and the "Gender Unicorn" as is happening in classrooms around the country. On its LGBTQ+ 101 website, Geneseo University explains the former: "One way to simplify the many components of gender identity, gender expression, sexuality, and biological sex is by using the Genderbread Person model, created and illustrated [by] Sam Killerman, author of itspronouncedmetrosexual.com and LGBT advocate."[45] These theories are the ways in which children and gullible adults are indoctrinated with gender theory, with about as much science behind it as the now-defunct FDA food pyramid. (Wouldn't it be nice if carbs were really supposed to form the base of our diet?)

Schools and libraries are at the center of on-the-ground efforts to de-stroy childhood innocence and create gender activists. There was once a time where the idea of having drag queens performing in any way, even reading books for children, would have been a bright red line in the sand for almost any American parent concerned about their child's innocence. Now "drag queen story hours" are ubiquitous in libraries and other child-centric settings around the country. A set of parents in Austin, Texas, wrote this letter to their school superintendents in May of 2021, "Two weeks ago . . . our kindergartener came home and told us he learned about drag queens in school. 'Drag queens are boys that dress up like girls for some reason . . . they wear makeup, sing, dance, and have fun,' he said. He also sang a lyric from the book: 'The hips on the drag queen go swish, swish, swish' to the tune of the innocent song 'The wheels on the bus . . . ' We were horrified . . . And we were even more horrified to discover that he was exposed at the place we least suspected: his ele-mentary school—during 'library time,' despite our understanding that human sexuality curriculum would be disclosed to us ahead of time."[46]

This kind of programming, taking place at libraries around the country, provides an opportunity for abusers to create sexualized events with children present. In March of 2021, Brett Blomme, a Milwaukee judge and former president of an LGBTQ organization that sponsored Drag Queen Story Hour (DQSH) events, was arrested on child pornography charges.[47] In 2019, the Houston Public Library was forced to apologize "after a man charged for sexually assaulting a child was allowed to entertain children at Drag Queen storytime."[48] Writing for *The Bridgehead* in October of 2019, Jonathon Van Maren discussed "a disturbing photo taken at a Minnesota public library featuring a drag queen sitting in a chair with his legs spread open, revealing his crotch to the children sitting in front of him."[49] Van Maren writes, "The photo was taken mid-movement, with the presenter clearly in the middle of a performance, and looks accidental." He went on to explain, "It is unclear if nudity is involved, but the image perfectly demonstrates the concern of conservatives and parents everywhere. Adult entertainment is not suitable for children."[50]

This is "queer theory" and the dismantling of childhood innocence in practice. In the span of roughly ten years, the progressive Left has hit the gas on the sexualization of children while dressing it up (literally, in the case of drag) as morally righteous progress. When we treat children merely as small adults, they are able to do a host of things: become activists, make grown-up decisions about their gender, and yes, even consent to sexual contact. It's all part of the same effort. The sooner parents realize that, the better.

8

CHILD SOLDIERS

On Valentine's Day 2018, nineteen-year-old Nikolas Cruz opened fire on students and staff at Stoneman Douglas High School in Parkland, Florida, killing seventeen people. It was the deadliest school shooting in American history. What followed would create a road map for activists on how to use children for their political causes, from gun control and climate change to, as discussed in previous chapters, queer theory and remote schooling during COVID. The woke discovered that if they could get children to parrot their ideas and advocate publicly, they would be far more successful.

Although leftist activists would blame it all on gun laws, the tragedy in Parkland actually began when law enforcement failed to do their job. Three days after the shooting, Emma González, a senior at the school, gave an eleven-minute speech at an anti-gun rally in Fort Lauderdale that would instantly go viral. "The people in the government who were voted into power are lying to us. And us kids seem to be the only ones who notice and our parents to call BS. Companies trying to make caricatures of the teenagers these days, saying that all we are is self-involved and trend-obsessed and they hush us into submission when our message doesn't reach the ears of the nation, we are prepared to call BS. Politicians . . . [say] that us kids don't know what we're talking about, that we're too young to understand how the government works. We call BS."[1]

The reality was, there wasn't much gun control measures could have done to stop the shooting, and nothing about that was BS. Cruz had been known to the school, to his county sheriff's office, and to the FBI as a threat. Between 2008 and 2017, Broward County Sheriff Israel had been tipped at least forty-five times about Cruz and his brother. A few months before the shooting, Cruz had posted a comment on a YouTube video warning, "I'm going to be a professional school shooter."[2] They did nothing. Worse still, "Three deputies from the Broward County Sheriff's Office remained outside the freshman building of Marjory Stoneman Douglas High" during the shooting.[3]

González's speech went viral and represented a real shift in our culture. It was like a lightbulb went off for leftist activists as they realized they could use children to make their arguments for them.

A week after the shooting, with emotions still understandably very raw, CNN hosted a "Town Hall." After experiencing extreme trauma at the hands of one of their classmates, the students of Stoneman Douglas High School were then subjected to the secondary trauma of being thrust on the main stage of the media's efforts to capitalize on their narrative to push a gun control message.

According to CNN, Sheriff Israel "fired up the crowd in the arena, saying, 'My generation, we did not get it done. You will get it done.'"[4] That was the first of many opportunities Israel took to shift blame from his own hapless department to others on the stage and, in the process, shift the responsibility from adults to children.

Survivors of the shooting confronted National Rifle Association (NRA) spokeswoman Dana Loesch, as well as Sens. Marco Rubio and Bill Nelson and Rep. Ted Deutch. It was a disaster. Survivors of the shooting, and relatives of those killed, got to take their aggression and anger out on people unrelated to what happened. The crowd chanted "Our blood is on your hands" at the start of the event.[5] Student Michelle Lapidot asked of the NRA, "Was the blood of my classmates and teachers worth your blood money?"[6]

At one point Israel harkened back to the González speech, responding to Loesch, "We're calling BS on that!"[7]

Loesch told me, "I believe Parkland was the first time, on a national level, that leftist activists realized they could dodge the basic responsibility in any debate, providing reasoned and well-articulated disagreement, if they could simply defer to a child as a substitute. That way, disagreement with their position equals hating children and the media supported them in this effort entirely."[8]

Cameron Kasky, one of the student activists, stood up on the stage and said, "Senator Rubio, it's hard to look at you and not look down the barrel of an AR-15 and not look at Nikolas Cruz, but the point is you're here, and there are some people who are not. And I need to ask two things of you."[9] At that point Kasky asked his friend Chris Grady to stand up. Kasky said Grady was joining the military and he needed Sen. Rubio to tell him that he was going to live to make it to serve our country. Rubio did that and also assured Kasky that he and his friends would bring about the change they wanted to see. Kasky seemed satisfied with this answer and told the audience it wasn't about red or blue or Democrat or Republican, but about who would agree with them.

Kasky then added, "This is about people who are for making a difference to save us and people who are against it and prefer money."[10] The accusation was as if the Senator was collecting piles of money in exchange for dead children. It was so deeply childish that even Jake Tapper, the CNN personality hosting the event, seemed uncomfortable. But the optics of a damaged teenager pinning a school shooting on a Republican senator was great for the Left, so it continued.

"So Senator Rubio," Kasky demanded, "can you tell me right now that you will not accept a single donation from the National Rifle Association?"[11] The crowd went wild. It had hit all the notes. He had compared Rubio to the actual school shooter, pretended that the issue of gun control wasn't partisan but simply right and wrong, and finally pushed a policy solution that would not do anything, since support for the Second Amendment does not begin or end with the NRA and their donations.

Journalists on the Left, predictably, loved this exchange. None of the anti-gun activists had actually been in the same room with Cruz to "look down the barrel of an AR-15," but it didn't matter. Writing in the

New Yorker, Evan Osnos praised Kasky as accomplishing something that liberal journalists could not: "As a moment in American politics, the pummeling of Rubio felt like an expression of collective rage at the falseness of so much that happens in Washington: the pivot, the dodge, the pallid follow-up question. Authenticity has rarely been more sought after in our public life—and, at once, so elusive. Accountability—the knowledge that the men and women we elect will act, foremost, in our interest and not that of their donors—has become a civic myth. Until a week ago, the students and parents of Marjory Stoneman Douglas High School never intended to be part of politics in this way, so they reject its pieties and rhythms. In several minutes on a weeknight, they laid bare Rubio's central political flaw—inauthenticity—more vividly than I ever could in a magazine profile."[12]

The Florida Politics website described Rubio's explanations on why banning certain guns is not possible, or not likely to be helpful, as falling "flat, sounding as if he was nickel-and-diming the issues on technicalities."[13] They further vilified him, saying, "And he was doing so in front of young people who had stared down a blazing AR-15 just days ago, and in front of grieving parents and siblings."[14]

I asked Loesch if, given the chance, she would do that town hall again. She said, "It wasn't my choice to do the town hall, but I would do it again because someone had to be the adult in the room. It was a free-for-all, and CNN reveled in the ratings. I was fully aware that I wasn't on stage to win some debate on the Second Amendment. I was simply there to hold the line and serve as a hurdle in the Left's race to vilify everyone who supports it."[15]

The realities of the situation could not be discussed at all. Unable to rage at Nikolas Cruz, they treated Loesch, Rubio, and the rest as murderers, and the Left loved every second of it. The politicians were caught in an impossible situation, and leftist activists noticed this and took notes. It sowed the idea that there really isn't a way to argue with children, and so using kids as political weapons is the perfect solution to shutting down any debate.

The child activists became heroes. Liberals were thrilled. The children were unassailable mascots to the cause. How could we not listen to the children?

Emma González, David Hogg, and Cameron Kasky would form the "Never Again MSD" movement and put on the "March for Our Lives" in Washington, DC, a month after the shooting. They would be interviewed on their anti-gun views by news outlets and treated as the great American hope. Former President Barack Obama called them, and three other members of their group, "the most influential Americans in 2018," in a piece written for *Time* magazine.[16] The former president concludes, "Our history is defined by the youthful push to make America more just, more compassionate, more equal under the law. This generation—of Parkland, of Dreamers, of Black Lives Matter—embraces that duty. If they make their elders uncomfortable, that's how it should be. Our kids now show us what we've told them America is all about, even if we haven't always believed it ourselves: that our future isn't written for us, but by us."[17]

But missing from all that adulation was Stoneman Douglas High School shooting survivor Kyle Kashuv. Kashuv was an outspoken supporter of the Second Amendment and frustrated that the anti-gun solutions presented would do little to stop shootings. Writing on the *Daily Wire* website three months after the shooting, Kashuv lamented, "The most unfortunate part of the never-ending push for gun control is that it distracts from pursuing real solutions. There are things we can do to reduce and prevent these atrocities from happening."[18] Kashuv's ideas included sane solutions like taking "school security seriously" and educating students and teachers "on the warning signs of a person in crisis."[19] These weren't flashy enough for the media, however, so he was ignored.

Kashuv was not featured on magazine covers celebrating his bravery. He did not appear in films like *After Parkland* or *Us Kids*. He was not portrayed as the future of our country. It turned out that it wasn't so much that we should listen to children, rather that we should listen to the children parroting what the leftist adults in their lives wanted them to say, and only those children.

Kashuv told me he felt like he had to speak up after the shooting. He saw all the media coverage telling a story that didn't seem true: "I had been peripherally interested in politics in high school, but the extent of that was watching an occasional YouTube video. I was never interested in entering the arena of politics, and my political beliefs were never a big part of my identity. After the shooting, I saw my peers pushing un-pragmatic policies in addition to imposing dangerous infringements on the rights of good law-abiding citizens. There was a short window of opportunity to pass solutions—and they would have to be sensible and bipartisan. I looked around and saw no one was willing to stand up— and so I did."

Kashuv credits his family's support with being able to be an "ad-vocate," a term he prefers instead of "activist." Kashuv told me, "The interesting thing about my high school—and you wouldn't get this im-pression from the media coverage—is that 30-40 percent of my class-mates were conservative. After speaking out, I would have around 5 students a day coming up to me in the hallway, in between walking to classes, and [expressing] their appreciation for what I was doing. It was always hushed and hurried, however. There was a frenzy from the media that painted you as evil if you spoke out in defense of the Second Amendment, and said 'hey, there's a better way to go about this than calling half of Americans scum who want more children dead.'"[20]

On March 14, 2018, schools around the country participated in the national walkout organized by EMPOWER, "the youth branch of the Women's March." The walkout took place at 10 a.m. and lasted sev-enteen minutes, one minute for each life lost at Stoneman Douglas High School. Kids as young as five marched.[21] Ten days after the walkout, the Stoneman Douglas student activists held their own event. "Here's a time to talk about gun control: March 24. My message for the people in office is: You're either with us or against us. We are losing our lives while the adults are playing around," junior Cameron Kasky said at the time.[22]

The walkouts were powerful. And they had the added benefit of instructing kids how to be activists for the Left.

The lesson was learned. Kids could be used to push one-sided, leftist talking points and no one could push back. It certainly would not stop with just gun control.

One of the next big targets, thanks to the sensational activism of one Swedish girl, was climate change.

Greta Thunberg is a Swedish environmentalist who, in August of 2018, began striking for climate change. At the time, Greta was fifteen years old. When Greta was eight years old, "She was shown a film of an armada of plastic assailing our oceans. She couldn't get it out of her head. She started to read about it, and became more and more terrified."[23] She would quickly become a worldwide celebrity.

In December 2018, Greta delivered a TED talk on the subject of her environmental activism. Sporting two long braids and looking even younger than her age, Greta told the story of when she first learned about climate change and how deeply it affected her: "So when I was 11, I became ill. I fell into depression. I stopped talking and I stopped eating. In two months, I lost about 10 kilos of weight. Later on, I was diagnosed with Asperger syndrome, OCD and selective mutism. That basically means I only speak when I think it's necessary. Now is one of those moments. For those of us who are on the spectrum, almost everything is black or white. We aren't very good at lying and we usually don't enjoy participating in the social game that the rest of you seem so fond of."[24]

She urged world leaders to be similarly uncompromising on the climate change issue: "I think in many ways that we autistic are the normal ones and the rest of the people are pretty strange, especially when it comes to the sustainability crisis where everyone keeps saying that climate change is an existential threat and the most important issue of all and yet they just carry on like before. I don't understand that because if the emissions have to stop, then we must stop the emissions. To me that is black or white. There are no gray areas when it comes to survival. Either we go on as a civilization or we don't. We have to change."[25]

Of course, there is quite a lot of gray in the climate change debate regarding what can be done to help the environment and what are feel-good solutions without any effect. But a teenager from a wealthy family in Stockholm—her father is an actor and her mother was an opera singer until Greta convinced her to stop traveling to help the climate—cannot be expected to see it.[26]

In an interview, Greta unsurprisingly said that it was an adult environmental activist who gave her the idea for her school strike: "Bo [Thorén from Fossil Free Dalsland] had a few ideas of things we could do. Everything from marches to a loose idea of some kind of a school strike (that school children would do something on the schoolyards or in the classrooms). That idea was inspired by the Parkland students, who had refused to go to school after the school shootings."[27]

Regarding her mom's career being halted in the name of helping the climate, Greta responded as any child might. In *The Guardian*, an interviewer notes that Greta's family had "made huge sacrifices" and rearranged their lives for her cause. Greta responded, "Yep. They changed their lifestyles. My mum stopped flying, and by doing that she stopped her international career, and I really appreciate it."[28] The interviewer then asked if she felt "guilty about stymieing her mother's career," and Greta, seeming "surprised by the question" said, "It was her choice. I didn't make her do anything. I just provided her with the information to base her decision on."[29] In the early 2000s—the early days of woke—it was common to hear the refrain "check your privilege." But no one ever said that to Greta, and Greta never checked her own privilege by acknowledging that her family could afford for one parent to drop out of the workforce because the child in the family wanted it.

By the time Greta spoke at the 2018 United Nations Climate Change Conference in December, she was already famous. But it was her performance at the same summit nearly a year later, in September 2019, that turned her into a full-fledged star. Holding back tears, she demanded "How dare you?" from an applauding audience.[30]

She was frequently in the media and was the perfect foil for then-President Donald Trump.

When Greta was photographed scowling at Trump at the 2019 UN event, the media went wild for it. "Greta Thunberg stares down Trump as two cross paths at UN" read one *Guardian* headline.[31] She was a hero. A child hero.

Science classes in America became a study of Greta. There was a period of time when my older son was in the first grade where the curriculum seemingly revolved around Greta Thunberg. Whenever I asked, "What did you learn in school today?" I always got the same answer: Greta.

But it went far beyond simple hero worship. Greta had become to America as Pavlik, whom you learned about in the first chapter, was to the Soviet Union: a symbol, a story, a calling.

Teachers across the world seized the opportunity to hold Greta up as an example and encouraged their students to walk in her footsteps. Greta, inspired by the students of Parkland, had stopped going to school because she felt so deeply the urgency of protesting climate change. Naturally, that's what schools across the country pushed onto children. On September 20, 2019, kids across not just America but the world walked out of their classes, led by their teachers of course, to protest climate change in homage to Greta. Globally, the total number of protesters was around four million.[32]

The kids had been carefully taught that the Earth was on death's door, we would all perish with it, and that evil people who only cared about money were causing the climate to shift. A child had led them, and it showed.[33]

What went ignored about the actual Greta is how deeply scarred she was because of her obsession with climate change. Greta had detailed her deep depression before starting her movement. It's no surprise that her followers exhibit the same struggles with mental health. But, like everything else, this fact was used to further support the woke cause rather than as a sign to examine whether political activism is good for children's well-being.

In September of 2021, researchers from the University of Bath released the results of the largest study about anxiety in children due to climate change. They found that 63 percent of the 10,000 kids surveyed in ten different countries said that they feel anxiety over the climate, that 68 percent feel sad, and that another 68 percent feel afraid.[34] As summarized in the journal *Nature*, "When asked about how governments are responding to climate change, 65% of respondents agreed with the statement that governments are failing young people, 64% agreed that they are lying about the impact of actions taken and 60% agreed they were dismissing people's distress."[35] In other words, the governments' failure to prevent and reverse climate change was causing the children's mental health struggles.

The Guardian reported in October of 2021 that "the climate crisis is taking a growing toll on the mental health of children and young people" and called this "eco-anxiety."[36] Though not a diagnosable condition, at least not yet, "eco-anxiety" was the cause of "complex psychological effects" and had a "disproportionate" impact on children.[37]

Who could argue with traumatized children, sad that the world was ending? No one. That was the point.

Many believe it's a good thing that kids are deeply worried about climate change: it's worrisome that the climate is changing, and kids should be concerned. Never mind the impact on the health and happiness of this generation of children taught that the world would end before their thirtieth birthday. It's a small price to pay to promote a political agenda.

But why? What will a child worrying in their bed at night do to help the climate?

In the 1980s, kids were deeply afraid of "acid rain." But even the *New York Times* had to admit by 1990, "Worst Fears on Acid Rain Unrealized."[38] In 2006, environmentalist Al Gore, whose house uses more than thirty times the energy of the average American home,[39] said, "Politicians and corporations have been ignoring the issue for decades, to the point that unless drastic measures to reduce greenhouse gasses are taken within the next 10 years, the world will reach a point of no return."[40] The best argument to quell children's fears regarding the environment is to show them how lavishly, and unconcerned, most environmental activists live.

But it's irrelevant whether climate change will end in catastrophe as predicted or whether it will fizzle out like "acid rain" in terms of forcing children to become agents of social change. After weeks of learning about Greta, my then-first grader internalized that the world would be imminently flooded. He came up with a plan that involved helicopters on autopilot to Antarctica and a Plan B that involved humans living in caves underground. As I wrote at the time to woke activists, "You wanted my 1st grader on it, he's on it."[41] Adults are meant to protect kids and make it so they don't worry about things out of their control. Using kids to play activist and echo adult talking points is wrong, and we shouldn't let our kids be used in that way.

This activism also takes the place of actual knowledge—in this case, scientific knowledge. Emotional responses become far more prevalent than intellectual ones. As discussed in previous chapters, when woke talking points become the primary focus of education, other things take a back seat.

In a 1999 study for the Competitive Enterprise Institute, Michael Sanera, PhD, wrote, "Making children aware of environmental problems can encourage them to think critically and creatively. Too often, however, environmental education skips the basics, pushing students into complex and controversial topics such as endangered species and global warming without establishing a scientific basis of knowledge. Education can play second fiddle to emotionalism and political activism."[42] Furthermore, this emphasis can lead to disturbing ideas completely unrelated to science, such as one parent notes in a letter to the *New York Times* that Sanera mentions: "I have noticed a disturbing trend. With each passing school year, my children are more convinced that humans and technology are bad for the planet. . . . While teachers are helping to ensure a 'greener' future, I do not think they understand that children may infer a condemnation of humanity."[43] Not only are kids not learning actual science, but they're also being indoctrinated with unfounded beliefs that can lead to mental health problems, all in the cause of training child activists to promote woke causes.

Here's another example. In 2021, the National Education Association (NEA) New Business Item 39 that admitted critical race theory is used in K-12 schools (see chapter three of this book) also added another goal to be pushed in schools: "Join with Black Lives Matter at School and the Zinn Education Project to call for a rally this year on October 14—George Floyd's birthday—as a national day of action to teach lessons about structural racism and oppression."[44] Howard Zinn was a far-Left activist who wrote *A People's History of the United States*, a book tucked under every wannabe socialist's arm at university. As Mary Grabar, author of *Debunking Howard Zinn: Exposing the Fake History that Turned a Generation against America*, wrote in a 2020 essay, "Zinn advanced Communist Party USA Chairman William Z. Foster's interpretation of American history as an Edenic land subjugated by greedy capitalists. . . . Both Zinn and Foster trace every bloody event—Indian massacres, slavery, wars, riots, factory fires—to capitalism."[45] Now the Zinn Education Project has "free lessons and resources for teaching people's history in K-12 classrooms."[46] The casualness with which the NEA adds protesting as a required subject for children's education while partnering with extreme leftist organizations should be concerning to parents.

That trend has continued and grown. Children's books like *Our 1st Protest* or *What's That Noise?: A Children's Book About Protesting for Equal Rights and Justice* are now standard. Elementary school students get invited to workshops where they "learn to use a bullhorn and participate in a practice march/rally."[47] Children protesting is becoming ever more commonplace, and it's the adults who are pulling the strings.

When the pandemic hit, the trend spread to this new cause. On January 11, 2021, students at several schools attempted a walkout to protest the lack of a remote option during the Omicron COVID-19 spike in New York City. In their first notice about the walkout, the student group Teens Take Charge announced, "Our partners at Students Break the Silence, PRESS NY, MORE-UFT Caucus, Student Success Network, & The YA-YA Network are organizing A STUDENT WALK-OUT!"[48] The only problem was that MORE-UFT is part of the United Federation of Teachers Union. Its far left-wing, not surprisingly. The group then sent out an update: "*** CORRECTION: The Student Walk Out is organized by a concerned group of New York City public school students, not any existing organization."[49]

Sure it is.

The problem with schools turning our kids into little activists is you can't just deprogram kids at home. The chilling example of Nazi Germany is again helpful. Anti-Semitic beliefs didn't randomly become fashionable in Germany. It wasn't that people suddenly hated Jews. Rather, there was a concerted effort to make that the "right" opinion of the land. And in much the same way as now, children are the clearest conduit. A 2015 study on "Nazi indoctrination and anti-Semitic beliefs in Germany" found that "between 1933 and 1945, young Germans were exposed to anti-Semitic ideology in schools, in the (extracurricular) Hitler Youth, and through radio, print, and film. As a result, Germans who grew up under the Nazi regime are much more anti-Semitic than those born before or after that period: the share of committed anti-Semites, who answer a host of questions about attitudes toward Jews in an extreme fashion, is 2–3 times higher than in the population as a whole."[50] What children learn outside the home matters quite a lot.

When any mention of Nazism occurs, there's an immediate move to discount the example. Nothing is as bad as Nazism, that's true. But the Left uses this comparison too, arguing that indifference in the face of evil is what caused the horrors of World War II. "Silence is violence" goes the woke mantra—that means children can't stay quiet either.

In his book *Woke Racism*, John McWhorter argues that woke ideology is "actually a religion in all but name and that this explains why something so destructive and incoherent is so attractive to so many good people."[51] It sounds cultish because it is. Proselytizing is a big part of this new "religion" and is why the conversion of small children is moving full speed ahead. And just like with cults, it will take a lot to remove kids from the grip of this ideology.

Seven months after confronting Senator Rubio on the town hall stage, Cameron Kasky apologized and admitted he regretted what he had said and did. On the *Benson and Harf* Fox News radio show, Kasky said, "But, looking back on that . . . I'm not going to kick myself for it because I'm 17. Despite the fact that I thought I did at the time, I don't know everything. But, I look back on that and I say, you know what, there were people who had just been buried and when you're looking at somebody that you find might in some way have been complicit in this murderer obtaining the weapon, it's hard not to say something like that. But I went into that wanting less conversation and more to embarrass Rubio and that was my biggest flaw."[52] Kasky started a podcast called "Cameron Knows Nothing" and told Benson and Harf, "My whole message is I was [p]ropped up as an expert. The whole message was these kids are the real experts. Look, I have some very intelligent friends. Some friends who can intellectually run circles around me, but I'm not the expert in pretty much anything."[53] Kasky was a kid on that stage, but he was being given adult responsibility and authority. Not surprisingly, that didn't end well. His contrition is very admirable, but the lesson is clear: kids aren't supposed to be activists. They shouldn't be used to make arguments on behalf of adult leftists. Let the kids be kids.

It's up to us, their parents, to act.

I'll be the first to admit it's very hard to put a spotlight on your kid and pull your child from school-organized protests. My son, in first grade at the time of the climate strike, participated in it with his class, making a sign that read "Earth dies, we die." I thought about having him sit out, but he had just switched schools after the school year had already begun, and I didn't want to make him a target. I was mad at myself for a long time after that. I knew my child was being used as a pawn in a larger political game, and I hated that I allowed it. I vowed to never let that happen again, no matter the circumstances.

It often takes one solid voice to stand up and say no to this kind of thing. No, my child won't be used for your political statements. No, I do not consent to any sort of political activity during school hours. No, my child won't participate in sign-making or chanting. These things should not be mandatory in a politically free country.

When it's hard to pull your child from something other kids are doing, think about the people who have had no choice in the matter. Don't let your kid be an ideological foot soldier if you can stop it. So many people don't have that chance. But we still do—at least for now.

PART IV

WHERE DO WE GO FROM HERE?

"We cannot protect our children from life.
Therefore, it is essential to prepare them for it."

— RUDOLF DREIKURS

"Since it is so likely that [children] will meet cruel enemies,
let them at least have heard of brave knights
and heroic courage."

— C.S. LEWIS

9

IN PRAISE OF RESILIENCY

What is perhaps the most worrisome overarching trend in this current political moment is the fetishization of victimhood. Even the appearance of too much resilience is discouraged. From social media trends and influences to celebrities to mental-health professionals, the message is clear: everything wrong in the world is the fault of racism or some other strain of bigotry. As a result, children are being taught to externalize responsibility for anything negative that happens to them. And their internal struggles are elevated to the level of mental illness, absolving them of the need for self-reflection. Some go even further and embrace their newly clinicalized identity as the golden ticket into a protected class. Not only are they faultless but any objection to their actions is beyond the pale. There is nothing they can, or should, do to improve their situation.

Josh, a clinical psychiatrist, predicted that this mindset will increasingly produce "kids who are brittle, kids who think that everything needs to be catered to them. That that's the natural state of being. Anything that's adverse or a challenge will be misperceived and misconceived and will be turned into an -ism, as we've seen increasingly. I think you're going to see kids who are more depressed, who don't know how to relate to one another, and don't know how to express disagreements effectively. Increasingly, you'll see kids whose only answer to conflict isn't to deal with it but to go to an authority figure."[1]

A good friend made an astute observation about the goal of woke propaganda for children: "I think all the different stuff is basically under the heading of promoting fragility in kids. They do not want kids under any circumstances to be strong, happy, independent, able to think for themselves and look after themselves. You will never have a revolution, or at least a manipulable citizenry that seeks paternalistic government, with people like that. And even less grandiosely, happy, resilient people will never be dependent on woke leftists, and for many woke leftists, it's quite virtuous to be fragile, self-pitying, and constantly offended. To put it crudely: woke leftists are basically [messed] up people, and [messed] up people don't want everyone else to be healthy and happy—they want everyone to be [messed] up like them. . . . And so of course they are promoting this stuff to kids, because misery loves company. And because the Left, on a very basic level, wants people to be victims, because that is politically helpful to the Left."[2]

Not only are young people made to believe that unseen forces are at work, but they're also taught that they are ill-equipped to confront these forces on their own. Both the problems and the solutions must come from somewhere else. Consider this prototypical TikTok introductory post from a woke librarian: "Hey y'all, outfit of the day. My vaccine is Moderna. My birth control is Mirena. My antidepressant is Zoloft and my anti-anxiety is trazodone and I accessorize occasionally with ibuprofen for migraines."[3] Her mental illness is part of her identity. According to Comscore, in 2020 nearly a third of TikTok users were between the ages of ten and nineteen.[4] (Certain features are restricted for users under thirteen.) Young people are thus told that even in adulthood, dependence is the healthy norm.

Writing for *Fortune* in September of 2021, Sophie Mellor commented on the danger of making mental illness seem trendy: "As mental health awareness improves, there comes a troubling trend of young people diagnosing themselves with a mental illness, which can be a mood, personality, or anxiety disorder, but can also range to disabilities like autism or Tourette's. And while some may relish finally being able to relate to feelings that they're having, others might be creating new problems in their own minds. This is mental illness and disability appropriation: the perfect marriage between the rise in mental health awareness in the midst of an 18-month-long pandemic and the unabating teenage desire to be different and unique."[5] It becomes a cool status symbol to self-identify with any number of mental illnesses.

Plus, being able to name a mental illness as part of your identity is an easy way to land yourself in the club of the oppressed, and thus escape the category of the privileged oppressor.

Charlie Jacobs, the mother in the San Francisco Bay area discussed briefly in the introduction, told me that her daughter, who fell down a rabbit hole of rapid-onset gender dysphoria, saw her self-diagnosed mental illness as a way to "rectify" her whiteness and affluence. Jacobs told me, "They have to pick something that marginalizes them. They have long discussions online trying to one-up each other on mental illness; one says she has ADD, but that's below OCD. If you have a therapist, you go up a notch, and if you have a psychiatrist and a therapist, that's another. They want to be put into a victimhood box. You hold more sway the more mental illness you have." Jacobs then commented that this becomes "a self-fulfilling prophecy" in which children "start to believe what they're putting on the internet" and start to feel mentally ill, which everyone used to agree is not a good thing. Jacobs said of her daughter, "She freaked out that she was [in fact, as she had claimed online] a schizophrenic."[6]

Appearing on a podcast with Benjamin Boyce, who concluded that we might define wokeness as a "trauma-inflation regime," Seerut Chawla, a London-based anti-woke therapist, explained how wokeness has infected her clients. She said, "When you look at [refugee experiences and] compare that to what we're seeing in the West, which is some of the most ungrateful, angry, fragile group[s] of people, and they've not had anything . . . of the same sort of [traumatic] experience . . . I think something happens to human beings when you have too much comfort; I think you start to malfunction . . . The conditioning of young people into postmodernist thinking . . . I think that causes mental health problems."[7] She defined postmodernism as "deconstructing things" and explained that many of her clients who attended university in the West (Europe or North America) were educated in applied postmodernism, which we call wokeness. She explained, "When you upend someone's sense of reality, you do something really profound to their mind because you're taking away from somebody that 'down is down' and 'your feet are there' and 'you're grounded' and 'this is what the world is.' 'This is the truth, and you can hang your hat on it.' That's taking away from a cast . . . swathe of people, and . . . nothing has meaning," says Chawla. "That's a feature of clinical depression, where the world literally becomes meaningless and pointless, and you have affective disorders—they're rising; the numbers are rising. And I don't think this is an insignificant factor."[8] In other words, the woke ideology is a systematic infliction and inflation of trauma on young people in order to destabilize our society.

Writing in the March issue of *Commentary* magazine, Robert Pondiscio explained that this dynamic is taking place in classrooms as well. It isn't confined to influences young people find on their own volition and in their free time; it's force-fed to them by authority figures at institutions where attendance is mandatory and which are designed to shape their character. The result, according to Pondiscio, is that the misery children see in the culture is reinforced by educators. "When education becomes activism, it dwells exclusively in the bad and the broken; at least tacitly it encourages children to see their community and country as nothing more than a collection of problems to be solved, with none of the virtues and blessings of citizenship," he writes.[9] Believing that the world is a hostile, horrible place doesn't do wonders for young psyches. Believing it *only* contains hostility and horrors is a recipe for disaster. Pondiscio continues, "Fair-minded people can see that gratitude for what works and outrage at what's not working are equally important in a well-functioning civil society. But when only the latter is emphasized, it creates in the minds of students the impression that their country is reflexively antagonistic to their interests: what we have, what we have been given, and what some may wish to preserve is wrong, unjust, and must be dismantled, root and branch."[10] This is indeed what progressives wish to do: dismantle society in order to rebuild it, but this mission carries a significant mental health toll on an individual basis.

The woke approach is to work to prevent children from finding their way through everyday challenges and upsetting situations by making them all a part of a larger, opaque crisis, the solutions to which must be handed down from above. Basically, they're being set up for failure. As Josh asked me, "Emotional intelligence is an essential part of success. . . . We won't let them feel negative emotions; so how can they develop emotional intelligence?"[11] This makes them dependent, incompetent adults as well because they never develop the resilience they would otherwise have at their disposal.

To understand why I place so much stock in the importance of resilience, I'd like to tell you about a chapter in my own life.

When I was three years old, my parents divorced after years of trying to align their lives with the obligations of parenthood. My father deeply loved all manner of illegal narcotics and had no desire to end his relationship with them. My mother, from the moment she discovered she was pregnant with me, knew I deserved more than that. They bonded over their drug use early on, but inevitably it would be the major driving force behind their separation and divorce.

Until I was seven, my father and his drug use would make appearances in my everyday life. Despite a crystal-clear recollection of my time spent with my mother, which was 98 percent of the time, my occasional weekends at my father's remain opaque. As an adult, I'm still not entirely sure what happened on those weekends, but I trust that my brain is doing me a solid by blurring those memories.

When I was seven years old, my father's increasingly sporadic visits came to a close, thanks to the tens of thousands of dollars my impoverished single mother paid in legal fees. I would not see him again until a year after my mother's death.

I was sixteen years old and in the middle of a junior year study abroad program in Belgium when I found out she was seriously ill from complications from lupus, an autoimmune disorder. After I learned how sick she was, I flew home the next day and went straight to the hospital. When I walked in, I looked at my mother and knew she was sick in a way she'd never come back from. I said aloud, "Oh, (expletive). This is going to mess me up for the rest of my life."

I was told that if her kidneys didn't start producing urine in the next few hours, they would be permanently inoperative. I sat next to her bed until 3 a.m. and watched the bag, and I prayed. I had never done that before. I yelled, I pleaded, I cried, and I watched the bag. At 3 a.m., the window had passed. Not a drop of urine fell from my mother's body.

I went back to my friend Kaitlin's house and slept in her guest room. At 6 a.m. I woke up and crawled into Kaitlin's bed and cried on the foot of her bed in a ball. Her mother heard me and came in, and soon the entire house was awake. I was inconsolable. My mother's friend Tina had called the doctors at my request, and they told her that they placed my mother's chances at 10-50 percent, depending upon if she woke up after they took her off the medication they had used to induce her into a coma the night before. They told Tina that even if she survived, my mother would be on dialysis for the rest of her life, which would not be very long. She would not have a chance to receive a transplant for her liver or kidneys, given that she was now in multi-organ failure.

My mother had placed Tina, a nurse, as her healthcare proxy, but it was made clear to myself and Tina at the time of this decision that it was ultimately my wishes that would be honored. I was too young to be the proxy legally, so Tina agreed to act as my advisor and above all promised to respect my wishes.

Tina and I had a face-to-face meeting with my mother's doctors, and we agreed to keep her in a medically induced coma until my grand-parents arrived so that she wouldn't have to suffer on her last day. We went through her potential care plan if we decided to sustain her on life support and she survived. The doctors started the meeting looking at Tina, but by the end they knew I was the one in charge.

I knew walking into the meeting that day that it would be my mother's last day on Earth, and walking out, I felt more certain that it was the right decision. Kaitlin's mother and Tina suggested that I wait with them in the lobby, and not sit in the room with my mother, but I knew that these were my last hours with my mother and that I would never forgive myself if I spent them in a hospital lobby with other people. I sat with my mother alone in her room for the next five hours.

I wrote in my diary a few years later, "As much changing as I did in Belgium, as much changing as I have ever done, those five hours completely shaped who I am today. I walked into her hospital room at noon one person and out at 5 p.m. someone completely different. Of those five hours I'm not sure what I want to divulge about what I said and what happened. They are the most precious hours of my life, and they always will be. They were the best hours of my life, and the absolute worst. For everything that happened between my mother and me, for the fact that she was leaving me a virtual orphan at sixteen years old, I made peace with it, and I made peace with her. I ultimately needed her to know that she raised me well enough for me to survive without her. Her not being around, the trauma that I had experienced between her and my father, all of it, I realized in that room with her, it was all my warm-up for that moment. Everything I had gone through up until that moment had prepared me to make the decision to let her go, to let her escape away from the pain she had been in her entire life. The physical pain, as well as the mental pain. I realized in those five hours that I ultimately loved her more than I loved myself. That I loved her enough to let her go. I loved her enough to put myself at the whim of the world in exchange for her freedom. And I wanted nothing more than to give it to her."

When my grandparents arrived, they somehow had the impression that my mother was extremely ill but not on her last day. When they walked into her hospital room, they were shocked at my mother's appearance. She looked nothing like anyone had remembered her. All of her teeth had fallen out while I was in Belgium, and the medication they had given her to hydrate her had swelled her body to literally over double its normal size (three times the size my grandparents remembered her as, since they hadn't seen her in years). She was unconscious, another surprise. They just stared at her. When we walked out, they realized the gravity of the situation. I told them that I was taking her off of life support at 8 p.m.

Soon after, while we were sitting in my mother's room, a group of a half-dozen doctors, interns, and medical students came in. They asked that we leave the room so that they could examine a piece of machinery that had been placed into my mother a year earlier to regulate her spinal cord fluid. My grandparents stood to leave, but I remained seated and asked why they needed to examine her. The doctors were taken aback by me, at sixteen years old, taking control of my mother's medical care. I asked them, abruptly, if they had bothered to look at her chart, and if they had seen that we were taking her off of life support in an hour. They mumbled that yes, they had seen that on her chart. I told them, "While I understand that this is a teaching hospital, you need to realize that this is someone's daughter and someone's mother. This is our last few minutes with her alive, and you can examine her after we've unplugged her, because this is our time with her." They quietly apologized and scurried out of the room. My grandparents were incredibly impressed with me, and I like to think that my mother was too. I like to think that after our five hours together, my having done this convinced her that I would be all right without her, that I was strong enough to survive.

She continued to lie there, silent, immobile, still comatose. They had stopped the sedative medication hours before, but she still hadn't woken up. She never would.

When the time came to take out the ventilator tube, we were asked to leave the room for a moment while they did so. We walked back in, and my mother lay there peacefully. They didn't have a heart monitor in the room, and we had no way of knowing if she was alive or dead. Her breath had already been so shallow before that it was hard to tell. Soon, however, she started to take gasping, violent breaths that shook her entire body. She thrashed, and we had to hold her down so that she wouldn't fall off the bed. She was struggling for every breath, suffocating before our eyes. It was the most excruciating few minutes of my life. Maybe it was a few minutes, maybe a half hour, I don't know, but it felt like an eternity. My grandmother started screaming, hysterically screaming. I tried to stay calm; I didn't want my mother's last moments on Earth to include a look of anguish on my face. My grandmother screamed at my mother to "go into the light." She started grabbing at her, screaming it in her ear, over and over. I ripped her hands off of my mother, grabbed her arms, and with a death stare and a tight squeeze said, "Shut up or get out." My grandmother looked at my grandfather in horror that I had spoken to her like that. My grandfather looked at me and knew I was serious, and told her to do as I said or that she would have to leave. I like to think my mother loved hearing me scream at her mother in her last moments. They shrunk away silently, and I was the only person at her bedside.

I grabbed my mother's head, the only part of her body still recognizable, and tried to keep it steady as the rest of her body thrashed. I whispered in her ear that I was OK, that she could go, to stop fighting, that I loved her, and then I sang to her. I sang, "You Are My Sunshine"—I'm not sure why, or where it came from in my brain, but it was the first thing that popped into my mind. I sang it over and over until she stopped thrashing, until the doctor walked in to tell us that her heart monitor had flatlined. But I already knew. Seconds before he walked in, she had opened her eyes, the first time since I had stepped off the plane. She looked at me, straight at me, and I saw in her eyes that she was scared, that she was sorry, and that she loved me. A tear rolled down her cheek. A moment later, she closed them, and she was gone.

I share all of that with you because challenges await everyone at some point, even if my mother's death was an extreme example, and building resilience is crucial to meeting these challenges.

How did my mother raise a child who could go through such an experience and not only remain intact but also go on to thrive? This is a question I've been asked countless times, and the answer is in direct conflict with what woke ideology promotes to its adherents.

The assertiveness and clear hierarchy of power my mother modeled in our home was a blueprint for me, and it's one I model in my own home now. My mother, in her role as the head of our household of just the two of us, took seriously her duty to train me to be a fully functioning adult, because unfortunately, due to her illness, she recognized I would be thrust into that role far earlier than my peers. While still in middle and high school, I was getting a crash course in what is now facetiously referred to as "adulting": paying bills, making meals, doing laundry, plus dealing with the bureaucracy of health insurance claims and navigating the healthcare system in general. I was put in charge of all of these tasks in our family in part to help my disabled mother with household management but also so that I could gain experience while still wearing the "training wheels" of having my mother present to troubleshoot or answer questions.

That assertiveness and training prepared me for life after her death just shy of my seventeenth birthday.

Just as important as this training, however, was that Mother believed in a concept that has become frowned upon by parenting "experts": discipline. Remember the "look" that our parents once gave us, the one that froze us dead in our tracks? How often have you seen that same look in modern parenting settings? We are told as parents that any discipline should be "gentle" and that the relationship between parent and child is more cooperative than authoritative. This model of parenting leaves children without clear boundaries and breeds less capable, less happy, less functional adults because the "training wheels" never come off.

John Rosemond, a family psychologist and syndicated columnist on parenting topics, told me his perspective on the shift: "In the late '60s and early '70s, we (being the American parents) bought into the very utopian-sounding idea that the parent-child relationship was only of psychological benefit to the child if the relationship was democratic, if the child was in any discussion in the family on a level-playing field with his parents. We shifted from the understanding that the raising of a child was about the proper training of the child and the teaching of a proper moral worldview to the idea that it was all about having a wonderful relationship with your child. [This] was clearly a denial of the very concept of legitimate authority." Instead of parents whose primary goal is to raise children to be competent, confident adults, as Rosemond says, we now "have two generations of children raised by parents who are trying to be liked. These are kids who have received a lot of unconditional love but virtually no authentic authority in their lives."[12] Without that authority, they learn neither clear boundaries nor how to model that authority in their own adulthoods.

One striking result of this approach is a drop in self-esteem. That may sound counterintuitive, but such self-esteem comes from capability and competence, not constantly being told how great you are without ever having the chance to prove it to yourself. Many parents notice this problem but are at a loss as to how to help. A 1999 profile of Rosemond in the *New York Times* delivers a succinct explanation of his view of the link between discipline and self-esteem: "If held accountable for their behavior and allowed to experience hardship and frustration, children will develop self-esteem on their own."[13] Too many parents, particularly mothers, "are guilty of rushing in the minute the child begins feeling unhappy or distressed." This short-circuits the process by which children develop a sense of their own ability to handle challenges. As Rosemond says in the profile, "If there are two words that underlie self-esteem . . . they are 'I can.'" He continues, "I was in a school recently. I walked into the boys' bathroom. Above the mirror, there was this sign that said, 'You are now looking at the most special person in the whole world.' This isn't self-esteem. This is narcissism."[14] Woke ideology teaches parents to build up their children's self-concept by constantly praising them and protecting them from difficulty. But that only makes them more

vulnerable to difficulty later on. Learning the skills to handle challenges, often through the hidden blessing of failure, is how humans
develop resilience.

The growth in popularity of "gentle parenting" and an aversion to
discipline and authority in millions of American homes is a clear
problem for anyone familiar with the goings-on across college campuses. Again, the inmates are running the asylum. And they demand
to be kept safe from unpleasant ideas and feelings to the degree that
professors have to tiptoe around any possible "triggers" that might
offend their students, rather than teaching the subjects in which they
are recognized experts. It's as if they still need their parents to cut the
crust off their sandwiches and offer to make "noodles and sprinkle
cheese" if there's nothing in the dining hall to their liking. A popu-
lation-wide shift in parenting away from discipline and clear consequences and toward making sure children only experience positive
emotions has created a proliferation of young adults incapable of
taking on not just the hard aspects of adulthood but any aspect of
"adulting." This is a societal catastrophe. Just look at the increasing
number of "children" in their twenties and even thirties who are still
living at home, extending their adolescence indefinitely.

They lack, in a word, resilience—an essential aspect of which is
moving forward from past traumas and taking ownership over your life,
something I was fortunate to learn when I was in college.

Almost three years following my mother's death, my father committed suicide. We never did resolve the issues between us. Considering all that had happened, I somehow wasn't a basket case. But I
wasn't OK, either.

In the weeks following my father's death, I didn't act much differently
than I had before, but given all I had gone through, everyone in my life
insisted I go to therapy, and so, I made an appointment at University
Health Services. When I arrived, they had an input form asking why I
was there for mental health services. There were three lines to list why
I was there.

I wrote on the intake form:

— My mom died when I was sixteen.

— My dad committed suicide last week.

— Do I really need a third reason?

The woman who did my intake salivated when she saw my form. She was a doctoral student in psychology and, I think, sick of listening to kids talk about stress from finals or their significant others. I think she thought, "*Finally*, someone with *actual* problems." It took me over an hour to tell her my life story up to that point in our intake meeting, and I'm pretty sure she called dibs on my case.

I spent the rest of that year of college, my sophomore year, making orphan jokes. The hat my friend knitted me became my "orphan hat." The jacket whose buttons popped off that I couldn't afford to replace became my "orphan jacket." That was how I defined myself. That is, until my therapist confronted me during one session, saying, "I know that's how you see yourself. But is that all you want to be? An orphan?" She told me that I couldn't change what had happened to me, but I could control my response to it. I could decide that I would be something more than just an orphan.

I'm incredibly grateful for this woman's tough love, that she challenged me to be more than a victim. Sadly, fewer and fewer therapists are willing to push their patients in this way today. Instead, too often they perpetuate the problem. As we noted in our earlier chapter on how wokeness has invaded every aspect of mental health, from training programs to professional organizations, the fox is already in the henhouse. Embracing victimhood is seen as a goal in itself, rather than, as my therapist (correctly) saw it, a stumbling block to self-sufficiency.

On the Boyce podcast, the anti-woke therapist Chawla emphasized this trend of reinforcing victimhood: "I don't know whether it's because therapy is less scientific than psychology, and whether therapy is closer to social work . . . But all of the woke ideas of identity-first instead of humanity, and over-validating and coddling . . . It has insidiously burrowed its way into therapy, but it's at the cost of the client."[15] Boyce asked Chawla, "What are the outcomes you see for clients who are given the woke model of therapy?" Chawla responded, "They don't cope very well because one of the rhetorics that I hate is that they are now problematizing resilience. They're saying you shouldn't *have* to be resilient because the world is oppressive . . . The oppression should be removed and then you can be as you are. What kind of stupid bollucks is this to tell people?"[16]

If the objective of the woke is to emotionally cripple an entire generation of children by teaching them that they are fragile and that the world is dangerous, COVID was the perfect opportunity for absolute destruction.

Commenting on Twitter about the woke response to the pandemic and its assault on pediatric mental health, Erika Sanzi, outreach director for Parents Defending Education, noted, "Kids [are] being told they are viral vectors, that they shouldn't be high-fiving or hugging their friends, that they can't let that mask slip or else. Hysterical adults with no sense of costs/benefit have projected their neurosis onto children."[17] This paranoia about staying safe was termed "safetyism," which, in a column for *Mishpacha* magazine in January of 2022, Jonathan Rosenblum explained "ramps up anxiety and hysteria, one consequence of which is to cause people to view one another with suspicion, if not as direct mortal threats."[18] He continues, "Safetyism did not begin with COVID-19. For decades, American children have been less and less likely to ride a bike or walk to school, or play sports after school unsupervised by adults. As a consequence, they grow ever more fragile, and less resilient and independent."[19]

In the age of COVID, it was often the progressive Left opportunistically repeating the mantra, "Kids are resilient," as a blanket defense for their preferred policies, which were deeply harmful to children. They told parents over and over that it was OK that schools were closed, and that kids were masked, because kids were able to withstand any and all abuse our society shoved upon them. This cohort of adults historically has exhibited the least amount of resiliency themselves but felt no qualms demanding resilience of toddlers and young children, whose entire childhoods were upended and demolished by a virus that held for them statistically zero chance of serious illness or death. The woke—many of whom have a diagnosed mental illness themselves and are in therapy hashing out their emotional trauma from their own childhoods—didn't pause to consider the significant damage extended isolation and virtual schooling might cause for an entire generation of young people. Whereas we once heard "check your privilege" repeatedly, there was a deafening silence about the fact that schools were more likely to be closed in inner cities than in wealthy suburban districts. While children whose parents could afford private schooling were more likely to return to in-person learning, poorer public-school children were shut out for well over a year.

All of this is to say that the woke ideology places children in an impossible situation. They are prevented from developing the emotional skills they need to flourish as adults at the same time that they are expected to handle anything woke activists throw at them.

So, what next? Where does a parent go from here? How can we raise resilient and emotionally mature children in an environment where everyone is entitled to participation trophies but is also burdened with the emotional baggage of a world destroyed by climate change? Or, more recently, how can we protect children from the notion that they could kill grandma by simply breathing near her and so must be tasked with the responsibility of wearing an N95 mask outside at the playground to protect her but also expected to gather in crowds to protest for woke causes?

This is the million-dollar question and perhaps the reason you've read this entire book. The answer isn't simple, but the most succinct way to explain it is this: our duty to our children is to raise them into capable adults. It's our responsibility to teach them about living in the world without stripping them of their innocence. And by innocence, we don't mean naivete or ignorance or weakness. We mean the ability to look at the world around them without the woke filter of cynicism that distorts everything they see into ideological signposts of a wicked world. The woke see children as child soldiers in their cultural revolutions, isolating them from their parents and radicalizing them. In such a climate, parents need to assert their right to raise their own children rather than leaving that to forces like teachers, media, and peers who seek to sexualize and politicize their existence. It requires limiting, supervising, and monitoring the exposure children have to authority figures and messages that seek to usurp their parents' proper role. The task is exhausting, and things will inevitably slip through the cracks. Those are learning opportunities, chances to explain to children that some things are not meant for them. Guarding their innocence will also help protect them against an assault on their mental and emotional health.

Before reading this book, the overwhelming nature of the many ways childhood innocence is being targeted by political activists may have been unimaginable to you. Who would suspect a child's therapist, teacher, pediatrician, or librarian of being part of widespread effort at indoctrination and manipulation? Now, the scope of the threat is clear. It can be overwhelming when you come to the realization that the elites of every major cultural institution are stacking the deck against traditional American families. How can we possibly fight a machine as well funded, well organized, and shameless as the woke progressive Left?

The task is immense, but you've already taken the first step. We mirror what every episode of *G.I. Joe* would end with: "Now you know. And knowing is half the battle."

The solution starts with us. American moms and dads are the answer to this crisis, and our power cannot be doubted after how we changed the electoral tide at the conclusion of the pandemic.

We know the lion's den that awaits our kids in classrooms, in libraries, and even in therapists' offices, so we need to exert power over the most sacred space, the place where kids are most influenced and most connected: our homes. We control the movie night choices, the read-aloud selections, the internet-enabled devices, and the individuals with whom our kids form personal relationships. Parents need to wield that control unashamedly, deliberately, and mercilessly.

And outside the home, we parents owe it to our children to make our voices heard. Staying quiet is a luxury our kids cannot afford; it might make day-to-day relationships easier without conflict or friction, but it will lead to a lifetime of regret if your kids are indoctrinated into basket cases by overzealous ideologues. COVID taught parents how powerful our individual and collective voices are, and we cannot forget that lesson. The stakes are too high and our kids too sacred.

The hardest aspect of this is becoming comfortable with the idea of making *other people* uncomfortable. It's OK to set clear lines in the sand and establish boundaries. When your son's teacher begins a first-grade class by telling the children his pronouns, you'll be perceived as a bigot for saying, "In our family we believe that one's gender is immutable. Please do not introduce the idea to him that it's subject to change according to one's whims." You'll have to become comfortable with the idea of being perceived as a troublemaker and even a bigot; be in contact with your kid's teacher, principal, and the school board. Keep tabs on what they're doing and give them feedback. Connect with other parents concerned about these issues as well. You are far from alone.

Don't be afraid of establishing boundaries, even quietly. When a form at your pediatrician's office asks if you have guns in the house or what your child's pronouns are, you can and should leave them blank. If you're asked directly, you can decline to answer as well, and if you're feeling cheeky, suggest they add questions more directly applicable to more statistical safety risks such as, "Do you own a pool?" or "Is your young child riding in a rear-facing car seat?"

Boundaries are important with children too. They need to understand the family's values, and that means they might not get an iPhone before high school and open access to every book, movie, or television show, even if they've been marketed to children. There must be a culture of work and respect, of discipline and responsibility.

Plenty of things are out of our control, like the woke training that our kids' teachers, doctors, and therapists receive. While it's crucial to know what goes on outside the home, we can only control what takes place in our own homes, doing our best to raise resilient children able to withstand a woke assault on their values and sanity. It's our hope that in this book we've given you the motivation and the tools to do so.

HOW TO PULL YOUR KIDS OUT

What if you've seen all there is to see here, and you've decided to take your ball and go home? What if you believe that existing fully in this culture—sending kids to school, consuming modern media, having your kids socialize with public school friends, and playing on TikTok with them—is just no longer an option?

In what was arguably her most famous novel, *Atlas Shrugged*, Ayn Rand created a new civilization in what she called "Galt's Gulch." There is, unfortunately, no such place (unless there is, in which case, please contact me). American families have to decide how best to "go Galt" while still living in modern America.

Where are your kids most likely to encounter a toxic brand of wokeness that endangers their innocence and safety? In public school and libraries, doctors' offices, in media content like books, movies, and television shows, and on the internet. Karol will give you the blueprint for trying to navigate those worlds while still keeping your children safe if that's the path you've envisioned for your family. But I don't think that's a viable long-term solution. Instead, I am convinced the only way to protect our children is to disconnect them almost completely from those conduits.

In just the time it took us to write this book, the material we had to work with exploded. Between the time of this writing and when the book will go to print, more stories and revelations will inevitably break, only serving to accelerate the progressive assault on childhood innocence and traditional families. The reason is clear: they want to totally remake American society, but in order to do that, they need to ideo-logically capture the next generation. They're not having kids, so they must capture ours. It's our job as parents to stop them, and drastic mea-sures are necessary.

Let's start with public schools: you have to pull your children out of them, and we have to recapture what takes place inside of them. We cannot cede control of these schools to the woke, but we also can't allow our own children to become collateral damage if we can help it while we wage that battle.

"Let me tell you about homeschool." That's the quip I always tweet, along with stories about institutional rot in public schools. Well, you've bought the book, so I owe it to you to actually tell you about homeschooling.

Due to COVID, the popularity of homeschooling exploded. The Census Bureau found that, by October 2020, the nationwide proportion of homeschoolers had risen to more than 11 percent, from 5 percent at the start of the pandemic. For black families, the growth was sharper.[1] Around 3 percent of black students were homeschooled before the pan-demic; by October, the number had risen to 16 percent.[2] Public schools sent a message to families over COVID: schools are non-essential. Parents received that message loud and clear.

Now, I want to acknowledge that, for every family with the ability and will to homeschool, there are countless more without the option. There are families that cannot, for any number of reasons, homeschool. For them, we need to ideologically recapture schools via school boards (as Karol will discuss), and we need to support viable private schools by offering families school choice to be able to take their money with them and allow the funding to follow the student. But if you can manage it, I highly recommend homeschooling your children.

Where does a parent even start? First, you have to find out the laws in your state and ensure you're able to legally meet the standards set by your local legislatures. You can check all of the requirements on the Home-school Legal Defense Association (HSLDA) website and consider joining in order to fund their efforts to protect homeschool freedom and give yourself an insurance policy with HSLDA's lawyers, who will be on call if your family runs afoul of authorities in the course of your homeschooling.

The question then becomes: How do I do school at home? My first answer is: You don't. You don't have to recreate school at home, with lectures, desks, worksheets, and tests. You can totally reimagine what education is and how to home-educate your children. I have a few resources for further reading:

- John Taylor Gatto was a schoolteacher-turned-education activist and writer. After teaching for nearly thirty years, he wrote several treatises against modern education not just in public schools but traditional schools more generally. *Dumbing Us Down* was released in 1991, and *Weapons of Mass Instruction* (which isn't at all about politics despite the name) was released in 2008. Both books will leave you completely reimagining what education can and should look like.

- *For the Children's Sake* by Susan Schaeffer Macaulay: When you listen to old-school homeschoolers discuss how they first discovered homeschooling, this is the book almost all cite as the bedrock for their educational philosophy. Macaulay popularized the teaching of a nineteenth-century English educator named Charlotte Mason for the modern homeschooler, and it is her philosophy that we follow in our own homeschool.

- Read living books: The backbone of Charlotte Mason's teaching is an emphasis on reading "living books." Good-quality books that inspire, that open a window into a person's life, a time period, or important ideas. Mason wrote that within living books there is "the fit and beautiful expression of inspiring ideas and pictures of life."[3] A living book doesn't just contain facts—it is narrative and is full of literary merit. It's a book that stays with you. It makes you think. It opens a window to the world and how we want to walk in it. *Charlotte's Web*, *The Chronicles of Narnia*, these are living books. *Captain Underpants* and textbooks, not so much.

The power of reading out loud cannot be understated. I have three book recommendations on that topic. Perhaps that sounds excessive, but they all have their own flair, and when you're done, you'll be fully on board the cult of books; and honestly, there are worse cults.

- *The Read-Aloud Handbook* by Jim Trelease is the original of the genre, and it contains not just the "why" of reading aloud, but also what exactly you should be reading aloud.

- An even more science-based version is found within Meghan Cox Gurdon's book *The Enchanted Hour*, which is a modern view on the importance of reading aloud in the age of nonstop screens and distraction. Gurdon is the children's book critic of the *Wall Street Journal* and a journalist worth following for her coverage of the children's literature and education space.

- Sarah Mackenzie created the *Read-Aloud Revival*, a website, community, podcast, and book focusing on how and what to read aloud in a busy family. Mackenzie isn't just recommending what to read based on ages, interests, and even months of the year; she's also working on creating a wholesome children's book publisher of her own.

- More inspiring content includes *The Brave Learner* by Julie Bogart, a popular personality in the homeschooling world, and *The Call of the Wild + Free* by Ainsley Arment, about bringing natural wonder into your homeschool.

- I found a lot to take away from a classic in the homeschool genre, *The Well-Trained Mind* by Susan Wise Bauer and Jessie Wise, but I'm overall not personally a fan of their execution. *The Well-Trained Mind* has a lot of helpful resources, including the popular *Story of the World* narrative textbook series, but if you take a look at Susan's Twitter feed of late, you'll bemoan her own turn toward wokeness. In their book *Consider This: Charlotte Mason and the Classical Tradition*, Karen Glass and David B. break down a lot of the modern "classical" education philosophy, including *The Well-Trained Mind*. Glass is the author of two other incredibly worthy books on home-schooling as well, *In Vital Harmony* and *Know & Tell*.

But homeschooling isn't just about books and sitting in your home; it's about being out in the world. One of the most annoying questions I get, which I am always on the receiving end of while I'm out in the world, is, "What about socialization?" Ironically, I usually get these questions as my children are socializing. I have started to just point at them and make a circle motion with my finger; it's like asking me, "What about breathing?" They're doing it *right now*.

Homeschooling isn't possible without a tribe, and if I can find it in deep-blue Montgomery County, Maryland, you can find it wherever you are too. It isn't easy, but nothing that's worth having comes easy.

The key to forming a friend group of homeschoolers is putting yourself out there—investigate homeschool classes, groups, field trips, and conferences. You only need to meet that one good friend, and they'll introduce you to one or two more. The key is consistency: try to have a standing hangout (ours is on Wednesday afternoons). You'll have more luck among religious folks, even if you're not religious yourself. I have three homeschool friend groups I see with varying frequency: a contingent of other observant Jews in my immediate area, a group of a few core families of all different faiths (from atheist to LDS to Catholic), and a large group of fellow Charlotte Mason homeschoolers from all over Maryland. In addition to playdates, we join and form classes to-gether for our kids (and we hang out while they're doing it): tae kwon do, art, pottery, rock climbing, and more.

But outside of the question of how to homeschool, the "why" is even more important. The reason you choose to homeschool cannot just be because you don't want to send your kids to public school and because the private options are untenable for any number of reasons: cost, dis-tance, educational philosophy, etc. In *Consider This: Charlotte Mason and the Classical Tradition*, Glass and Hicks encourage parents to reimagine what education is, what it once was for "classical educators," and what it could and should be again. They write, "Intellectual prowess was not the primary concern of the classical educators. Their reason for education had an altogether different goal. When we understand what motivated their educational efforts, we will see that there is a sharp difference between the historical, classical approach to education and our modern one. It is not a difference merely of methods, but a difference of purpose."[4]

Think about why you send your children to school. To learn, obviously. But to learn what, and why? And to what end? These are fundamental questions that parents have been conditioned by their own upbringing and through taking part in compulsory schooling not to reflect upon, and that lack of reflection has led us to sleepwalk into sending our children to become educated, without a clear idea of what they are going to be educated in.

Glass and Hicks go on, "What the educators of history have to tell us is that education is about developing a vision of goodness and virtue, and then—most importantly—bringing that knowledge to bear on actual conduct . . . Only within the past several generations has education become entirely divorced from moral development, and we see the results around us every day."[5]

Teachers and administrators recently have begun to take on the mantle of moral education, but it's not any sort of morality most American parents are comfortable passing on to their children. Even moderate parents don't want their kids' moral instruction happening at the hands of woke twenty-five-year-olds, but that's what's happening when they choose to send them to school. They aren't just learning math or English (if, as evidenced by test scores, they're even learning at all); they're spending the vast majority of their waking hours taking in the life lessons of their woke teachers and peers. There is no metric that makes the loss of a child's moral compass worth it.

Pulling your children out of public schools will go a long way to protect them from woke moral indoctrination, but you can't stop there. The media is also extremely powerful.

The question of how to handle media depends a great deal upon the social lives of your children. I can tell you from experience that home-schooling has a lot of tangential benefits, and one of the biggest is that question of "socialization" that I mentioned previously. Not only are my homeschooled kids "socialized" (whatever that means), but they are also not spending most of their waking hours with kids from families that don't share our values. They aren't picking up on the media habits of friends who are allowed to stay up all night watching anything they want and playing video games. When your kids don't hear about this kind of content from friends all day, it's a great deal easier to place some boundaries around what they're watching and doing.

In our home, the television is always off during the week and on the Jewish Sabbath (Saturday). If Sunday happens to be a busy workday for me and my husband and/or the weather makes the outdoors impossible, we'll allow the kids to stream a television show or movie that we've vetted or are already familiar with from our own childhoods.

You may have noticed (like our editor did) that in the chapter on media, there wasn't much mention of live television or going to the movies; and that's due to our own families' viewing habits. We don't watch almost any modern children's content on live television; and we're not alone. According to a site called Pirates & Princesses, the ratings for Nickelodeon are stagnating. They reported, "Since July of 2017, Nickelodeon's viewership has dropped from 1.3 million average viewers per week to a June of 2021 average of only 372,000. In only four years, Nickelodeon has dropped more than two-thirds of its audience."[6]

Their viewers are doing what we are: streaming. When you stream old episodes of *Boy Meets World* or *Full House*, you know what you're getting. When families decide to watch Disney classics instead of content that producers have promised will be awash in ideological content, you know what you're getting will be in line with your values.

Families are voting with their feet and their wallets when it comes to media content. Will it have an effect? When we went to print, it was too early to say when it came to Disney. But a survey conducted by Trafalgar

Group of 1,000 respondents in April of 2022 spells trouble for the brand.[7] According to the results, 68.2 percent of overall participants said they were less likely to do further business with the media giant. That includes over 48 percent of participants identifying as a Democrat (39.3 percent of the total group), over 85 percent of those identifying as a Republican (35.6 percent), and over 72 percent of those who did not identify as non-partisan or some other party (25.1 percent). What's more, 69.1 percent of overall participants said they were likely to support family-friendly alternatives to Disney. That includes 58.6 percent of Democrats, 77.6 of Republicans, and 72.1 percent of those unaffiliated with a political party.[8] That bodes well for sending a message to woke corporations, but it also signals good news for alternative upstarts, like our publisher the *Daily Wire*, which are committed to producing more age-appropriate media content for children.

Smartphones are even more important to avoid. In 2019, Naomi Schaefer Riley wrote the book *Be the Parent, Please: Stop Banning Seesaws and Start Banning Snapchat: Strategies for Solving the Real Parenting Problems*. Riley discussed the critical importance of getting kids off screens—most importantly, cellphone screens—and how to do it. That need has only become more pronounced since her book was published.[9] In a *New York Times* piece published in the spring of 2022, "'It's Life or Death': The Mental Health Crisis Among U.S. Teens," the negative effect of screen time, especially on cellphones, was a common theme in the deterioration of the mental well-being of teenagers. Parents usually meant well, as in the following example: "At 10, M got a smartphone. Linda and her husband, Tony, both of whom had busy work schedules, worried that the device might lead to heavy screen time, but they felt it was necessary to stay in touch."[10]

Smartphones are not necessary to stay in touch. There are flip phones available with every major carrier. Alternatively, kids can have a walkie-talkie one-touch phone that operates on a cellphone network with built-in GPS (there are a few options like this; we use one called Relay). Your preteen does not need a phone. I repeat: *Your preteen does not need a phone.* Your young teenager doesn't need one either. You might have the only kid in school who doesn't have one—or so they tell you. Remember when we used to groan when our parents told us, "If everyone else jumped off the Brooklyn Bridge, would you too?" You know what they say: we all turn into our parents one day. So, turn into your parents and try that Brooklyn Bridge line out on your kids; keep them off of smartphones and off of social media as long as humanly possible.

I spoke to a captivating young woman, Mary, a recent college graduate from a small liberal arts school who arrived on campus as a woke and troubled pink-haired bisexual atheist and left as a self-described "TradCath," or traditional Catholic. Mary explained where her parents went wrong: "I was given unmitigated access to the internet as a twelve-, thirteen-year-old. That's insane, but that's normal. I got into Tumblr wokeness; I became convinced that my gender issues were driving my unhappiness, not my family life. I turned my dissatisfaction with my life [into dissatisfaction with the] basic facets of reality. Neglect is what drove so much of the drive [toward dysfunction and wokeness]." How will she raise her children differently? She told me, "I'm not going to let my kids have access to screens until they're teenagers. I'm going to homeschool them. Raise them with present, positive values. Our parents' generation were able to coast with a social safety net, of having these values be enforced; even if you didn't grow up in a devout household, you could still be shunned if there was adultery. You have to be intentional about the values you give to your children [now]; society won't fill in the gaps. Morality is gone from public life. The family is where they're getting their sense of right and wrong; our parents thought they could outsource goodness and childrearing to people who don't have their kids' best interest in mind."

Shielding kids is a full-time job, and mistakes will slip through the cracks. Parents need to do the best they can to screen friends, television, books, and messaging on issues like gender, guns, and climate change. But we also need to have open, honest, and difficult conversations with kids to prepare them for the inevitable time that someone asks them their pronouns or tells them that we're all going to drown in the melted polar ice caps. We'll all have our own talking points on how to address those issues when they come up, and it's up to individual parents to decide what theirs are. But making an intentional decision to protect children will pay dividends in their improved mental health over the entirety of their lives. We must shield them from the doom and gloom; we must protect them at all costs from messaging that the world is ending, that they are "the oppressors" or "the oppressed," and that they'll find true happiness living in someone else's body.

For one tearful mother I spoke with, Kavita, it was too late to save her relationship with her own daughter, a recent college graduate with whom she has barely communicated in the last several years because of politics. Kavita, an immigrant of Indian descent, isn't woke enough for her daughter, who objects to Kavita and her white husband's lack of commitment to abortion rights, Black Lives Matter, and more. She told me, "I started becoming aware of politics when it was too late; we didn't raise our kids to be religious; we [just] raised them to be good kids. I used to tell them, 'Do the right thing because it's the right thing to do.' I regret we were never religious, reading about how important faith is to children." But her biggest regret is not taking advantage of opportunities to have real, honest conversations with her daughter, no matter how difficult. She said, "I lost so many teachable moments with her during her high school years," and wished she could tell parents, "You guys have to talk to your kids about these things at such an early age, and I didn't. I regret that, and I'll live with that for the rest of my life. I think that I could have changed her."[11] It is essential to talk about things clearly and openly with your kids when woke concepts inevitably come up.

Don't shy away from these discussions out of fear they'll turn into arguments. And don't assume it's just a phase or a form of teenage rebellion, because the consequences of wokeness are long-term and sometimes (as in the case of gender reassignment surgery) permanent. An ideology that is specifically designed and propagated to engineer conflict does not need much time to do a lot of damage. Keep the lines of communication wide open and talk through with them what they're thinking, what they're learning, and where they're learning it. And use the stories in this book as a guide to fill in the blanks: teens in thrall to woke authority figures aren't hearing the cautionary tales and the sad endings. They aren't being told about what happens on the other side of this, what becomes of the once-promising individuals used as foot soldiers and then discarded into adulthood, unprepared and broken and alone. They aren't presented with the massive weight of medical and scientific knowledge that debunks the propaganda they're fed. This isn't simply a clash of values; these children are being lied to, and you—their parents—know the truth. And at the very least, you'll know what they're being told and by whom, because now you know the full menu of options at your disposal. You are neither powerless nor alone.

Conclusion

HOW TO FIGHT FROM WITHIN

As you've learned throughout this book, wokeness isn't just attacking your kids at school. It's coming from every direction. There's only so much you can do to opt out of society to protect them.

Our three children are twelve, nine, and six. They have gone to public school since kindergarten. They each have an iPad, bought by their grandparents, which they are allowed to use in moderation. They watch current movies and shows and read modern books. They are not on any social media. For our family, limited yet intentional exposure to wokeness is a way of combating it.

In fifth grade, in New York City, our daughter suddenly had friend after friend come out as trans, all girls, generally declaring themselves "nonbinary." We talked about showing respect toward people who may be struggling, and we talked about what it actually meant that so many girls suddenly didn't feel right in their bodies. We couldn't, and didn't, pretend this social contagion wasn't happening around her. We kept the lines of communication open with her and engaged on the topic on any level she felt comfortable.

Our older son and I recently had a good laugh over him carrying his "Earth dies, we die" sign (mentioned in chapter eight) at the climate march in first grade. Currently in third grade, he understands the absurdity of having a bunch of kids protest for any reason, much less that the climate is changing. He's our most outspoken child, ready to challenge the world. I don't want my children to be political at such a young age, but he's a history buff (don't get him started on Napoleon's misunderstood place in history), and that leads him to having a wide range of opinions, on many topics, that he enjoys sharing with others. That wasn't easy in Brooklyn when he was pointing out to his friends that masking to stop an airborne virus made no sense, but we knew it was more important that he hear the truth from us.

Our younger son is six years old and too young to understand a lot of the concepts that come with explaining and battling woke culture. We start small. He knows he must have his own opinion. He does not need to copy what his friends believe. He knows we expect him to be a leader and not a follower. We lay the basics so when it comes time to challenge ideas he hears, he'll know that is what's expected of him.

There are many ways to fight for your children. Bethany describes "The Benedict Option," a retreat from society into tight-knit communities, based on the Rod Dreher book, *The Benedict Option: A Strategy for Christians in a Post-Christian Nation*. The option, named after the sixth-century monk St. Benedict of Nursia, argues that Christians "embrace exile from mainstream culture and construct a resilient counterculture."[1] Obviously it's not just for Christians. It may include homeschooling, tuning out mainstream television shows, and shunning modern books and movies.

This is the most extreme option and the one hardest for most people to achieve. I understand why people do it, and I advocate making the best decisions for your own family, but I don't want to surrender the society we've collectively built to the forces of leftism. The fewer non-woke people there are participating in public schools or in wider culture, the more power the fringe will amass. I don't want to capitulate to these conformist extremists.

Another option is selective flight. You can take your children away from woke spaces while still participating in overall culture. That might mean having to skip story hour at a library where the librarian is in indoctrination mode. It might mean switching schools for your kids. It might mean moving to another state.

That's what it meant for our family. Our reasons for the move from Brooklyn to south Florida were pandemic related: our youngest child had never been maskless at school, and we saw it having a real negative effect on his education. We also could not forgive that schools had closed and rich New Yorkers simply got their kids an education via private school or private tutors, while not fighting to open schools for the kids who didn't have that access. We could not unsee what we saw during COVID, and so my husband and I, both lifelong New Yorkers who had planned to raise our children the same, knew we had to get our kids out.

It was the response to the pandemic that galvanized our resolve, yes, but there have been so many other pluses about the move in terms of fighting wokeness. Governor Ron DeSantis has been at the forefront of making policies to challenge wokeness aimed at children. He has three small kids himself, and he has the urgency to give his kids a good, normal, healthy life. This isn't a fight down the road for him. It matters to him right now just like it matters to us.

In April of 2022, the Florida Department of Education rejected fifty-four math textbooks because they contained inappropriate material. One lesson on polynomials was titled "What? Me? Racist?"[2] It's a giant positive for my new state that they realize racial indoctrination can be happening in their math books. But it's also a testament to the fact that it really could happen anywhere.

That's the problem with flight as a general solution. As we've shown through the book, wokeism is spreading. The idea that it is limited to coastal regions or cities is simply false. We can only run for so long. Our family is lucky to have Governor DeSantis at the helm right now, but what happens when he's no longer governor? The fight is on, and it isn't up to just any one politician to mount it. It will require all of us.

We have to engage more in our local politics. Before 2020, I did not think the governor of my state had that big an effect on my life. New York Governor Andrew Cuomo had been my governor for over a decade at that point, and I never felt his presence one way or another. That changed dramatically during the COVID pandemic. It was scary to see just how much power the governor could have over my everyday life. I could never go back to not paying attention.

It was further terrifying to see how much unelected officials, like those at New York City's Department of Education, could affect the lives of my children. I had been coasting. Now I know we have to fight.

Will Johnson, a parent-turned-activist with FAIR (Foundation Against Intolerance and Racism) in Douglas County, Colorado, told me the battle is front and center in schools. "K-12 education is where the soul of our country is being decided. Too often today, the K-12 system is wedging itself between parent and child and training our children in a worldview antithetical to parents' values and America's founding principles." Johnson's suggestions for parents who want to get involved are the following: "1. Be present in the school and volunteer where possible. As they say, half the battle is just showing up. 2. Use Freedom of Information Act Requests to uncover withheld information. 3. Link up with other like-minded parents. There is strength in numbers and many more people agree with you than it seems! 4. Join groups like Parents Defending Education, FAIR, and Moms for Liberty. They and others have great resources and communities to empower you to act! 5. Reinforce your values at home. Don't assume the school system is doing it for you."[3]

With either path, whether your family participates in culture like mine does or isolates from it like Bethany's, you can't just tune out. Wokeness demands conformity from all, not just the woke. Bethany spent much of the pandemic fighting her county's absurd mask mandate. You might not be interested in wokeness, but wokeness is interested in you.

Fighting involves finding other like-minded people and standing your ground. All over the country, parents have reached their breaking points and are standing up for their children. It is a long battle, but in some places, they are winning or have won. It is not impossible. There will be tough times in that fight. You will be called names. You will be targeted. But the reward is standing up for your child and forging a better path for children everywhere.

None of these options are easy, but there's no other way around the avalanche of indoctrination being aimed at your child. The Left knows the strategies to shut down debate, to force conformity, and to make sure no one steps out of line. It's not enough to drift along and imagine someone else will take on the fight for you. You're the parent. Your kids are yours and no one else's. You know what is best for them. You know what you believe and what's important. The leftists are coming for the kids, and you're the last line of defense. Fight.

ACKNOWLEDGEMENTS

This book would not have clawed its way to print without our literary agent who shaped the project from start to finish, shepherding it from an idea to a powerful proposal. It would not have found a home were it not for his belief in our project and our vision. Keith Urbahn, and the entire team at Javelin, the best in the business—thank you.

Thank you to Alyssa Cordova at the *Daily Wire* for showing as much excitement about our premise as we had, for having faith in our ideas and our ability to put them into words. We are honored to be one of the first class of *Daily Wire* books. Your bravery to publish a book every major publisher wanted to buy but was too scared to touch is what sets *DW* apart from the pack, and that fearlessness will make it a power-house moving forward.

To our editor Natasha Simons, you shaped this manuscript with such incredible skill; encouraging us when we were going in the right direction, and gently guiding us when we went down the wrong path. You understood exactly what we were trying to do, and understood better than we did what we needed to do to make it great. This book wouldn't exist in anything resembling its current form without your brilliance, your insight, your kindness, and your encouragement.

Thank you to Rebecca Curry for keeping us on track and getting this book to the finish line. Thank you to Mara Eller for the line edits that brought the whole project together. We're so appreciative of both of you.

Neera Deshpande, when you first DMed Bethany on Twitter a year ago, your message was so sharp, so astute, so wise beyond your years, she instantly had to get you on the phone. We were in the market for an assistant; and G-d knew it had to be you. You helped us with the mad dash to the finish line with research, edits, ideas, and connections with other insightful members of your generation to help us perfectly sculpt our draft into an actual book.

BETHANY:

It's overwhelming considering all of the people who I want to thank; not just for making this project into what it is, but also for all of the people who helped get me to this place where I'm lucky enough to be writing an acknowledgements section of a book I've written.

My career in politics started at the Heritage Foundation, and I'd like to thank everyone there for giving me a chance fresh off the plane from Cambodia. Thank you to Nat Ward and Amanda Reinecker Callanan for helping me gain footing and confidence in this industry, and for remaining friends long after we all left Heritage.

The man I consider my professional Jewish uncle, John Podhoretz, you brought me to work for you at *Commentary* magazine alongside my husband when we were young and rudderless. You launched our careers, and we consider ourselves forever honored to be part of the *Commentary* family. Jonathan Tobin, you believed in my writing and my voice and have been a dear friend and cheerleader every step of the way. Abe Greenwald, I keep forgetting we don't talk multiple times a week because I'm lucky enough to hear your insights on the *Commentary* podcast, but please, do America a favor and write a book. Stephanie Roberts, I'm still very sorry about being the cause of the Great Fruit Fly infestation of 2013 in the office. Thank you for everything you do to make the *Commentary* ship run smoothly.

When I was a brand-new mother trying to imagine what would come next professionally after I left *Commentary* to freelance while staying home to raise my family, Mollie Hemingway took my crying call, made in a postpartum daze of emotions, and mentored me at a critical moment in my life and in my career. I will never forget it, and deeply appreciate being part of *The Federalist* in its infancy.

To Scott Immergut at *Ricochet*: Thank you for always meeting me where I was and being the most kind, considerate, and forgiving boss imaginable. There were more calls for my head than I can possibly remember, and it was always comforting to know you would not yield to any mob. Max Ledoux, you were the best part about Ladybrains (besides our listeners!), and were such a joy to work with, and you are what we miss most about our girlfriends podcast. Jon Gabriel, thank you for being such a rock of a colleague and never wavering in your beliefs and opinions.

Christine Rosen, you were the first editor who paid me actual money for my ideas at Acculturated, and you got some of my best because you helped cultivate me as a new writer. Thank you for your wisdom and kindness as a writer and as an editor. Naomi Schaefer Riley, it was an honor to work with you at Acculturated, as well. The work that you're doing now is so important and should be read by everyone in Congress and the White House every time you hit publish.

My dear Batya Unger-Sargon, you made me into a neo-Nazi for the pages of The Forward, and never stopped apologizing for running a headline that I myself suggested! You are the most talented and versatile opinion editor in the country, and it has been a true joy watching you get red-pilled over the last few years.

To my Deseret colleagues, who publish all of my Big Family propaganda with delight. Hal Boyd and Jennifer Graham, if only every editor of every major publication in America were like the two of you, our country would be in a far better place.

To my Heroes of Liberty colleagues: I believe G-d made our paths cross at the moment they did so that we could work on this endeavor to save the bookshelves and minds of America's children together. Rotem, Gadi, and Tal: Thank you for your brilliance, your shared vision, and the talents you each bring to execute that vision flawlessly, every single month, as we bring heroes to life for kids who desperately need to be inspired by their stories.

In an industry like ours, you'd be surprised to learn how many genuinely wonderful women there are who delight in encouraging and mentoring young women like me. Dana Perino, Janice Dean, and Megyn Kelly: Thank you for being a true light and source of inspiration.

There are so many women we walk alongside in this fight, too many to thank properly, and yet, I'll boldly attempt to do so. Bari and Suzy Weiss, your courage and love of the Jewish people is a force to be reckoned with. Abigail Shrier, it's no mystery why people around the country are erecting billboards to advertise your book, and I'm proud to own a galley copy of such a groundbreaking project, and be a friend to such an inspiring woman. Lahav Harkov, the worst part about not living in Israel is not being able to delight in your company and baking skills in person, but I deeply appreciate your friendship from across the ocean. Katie (and Tim) Carney, Noa (and Phil) Klein: Thank you for helping keep us sane in MoCo, for being allies in this industry and in our crazy county. Erielle Davidson, you came to my house within hours of my having given birth; there are not many people I trust to call in that vulnerable a state. I knew I could count on you, and I'm so grateful for your friendship. Cat Forbes: You have an incredible ability to text right at the moment I need it the most, and you always know exactly what to say. Allie Stuckey, your friendship has been a real blessing as we have babies together and try to preserve the world they're being born into. Megan Phelps-Roper, when I first read your book years ago, I sent you what is now an embarrassing fan email trying to befriend you (please, don't try to go back and find it), and I'm so glad my plan finally worked out. Salena Zito, you are my surrogate momma-slash-mentor-slash-hero, and I'm forever grateful for your patience and faith in me as a writer, a mother, and a friend, even when I don't deserve it.

I don't recommend starting a book project twelve weeks postpartum with your fifth child and submitting your edits while eight weeks pregnant with your sixth. I especially don't recommend it without having childcare. The only way I survived is thanks the grace of my local crew: Suri and Eric, Aravah and Yair, Oneg and Yoni, Brit and Elad, Andrea and Kevin, Michelle and Yoni, Nachama and Menachem, Tal and Liora, Naomi and Nate, Susannah and Nic, Olga and Emily.

There is nobody I'd rather write a book with than you, Karol. For the last decade, every time I've read something you've written, I have bemoaned that you got to it first and wrote it better than I ever could have. You are brilliant and fearless and the best girlfriend and coauthor I could have ever dreamed of. I look forward to talking you into the next book project after we recover from this one.

To my sharks, aka the Ladybrains: Elisha Krauss, we first met when you saved my job when you were at Hannity and I was at Heritage. I immediately knew you were the kind of friend a girl keeps around, and I'm so glad you stuck with me after over a decade of friendship. Lyndsey Fifield, I think we first met when I offered my couch to you, never having met you in person, when you first moved to DC. You are loyal and sharp, and I'm so grateful for your friendship. Kelly Maher, in the middle of writing this acknowledgements section, you called to cheer me on because you knew I needed it. Your strength is a pillar in my life, and I know I can always count on you, and I'm so grateful for it. Emily Zanotti, my on-call lawyer, expert witness I'll call in all things true crime, Catholicism, cosplay, clown attacks, and inner strength. You are the most versatile and fascinating person I know, and I'm lucky to count you as my friend. Mary Katharine Ham, you have been my best friend since we first realized we were pregnant with our first babies at the same time. You get all of the calls from me that start with "I just have to say something really dark right now," and talking to you every single day, multiple times a day, keeps me sane and grounded when I'm otherwise surrounded by people significantly shorter than me.

To Sal, who always was meant to walk me down the aisle. Along with you, I got a bonus stepmother and stepbrother, Linda and Neil, who are my family in every way.

To Lori and Jacob, without whom I'm genuinely unsure how I would have survived my late teens. Scott, Erica, Hal, and Karen: thank you for being the only family I could rely upon in the best and worst of times.

Jonathan, Autumn, and Sara: It's not often you discover cousins in adulthood, and I'm in awe of how lucky I am to have found you.

To the Krupnick and Mandel families: I married Seth, and by default was blessed to be inducted into the greatest *mischpacha* in all of New Jersey.

To my mother, Vera Jean Murphy: I've lived over half of my life without you, and yet, I still hear your voice every day. Every time I have a baby, right at the end when I think I'm dying, I'm oddly comforted by the idea that at least I'll see you again. You are my sunshine, always.

To my children: You are the greatest joy I have ever known. You come along for every ride, and every crazy idea I have to go alone with all of you to Colonial Williamsburg or to a work meeting; you are my road warriors. Witnessing you grow into men and women, and hopefully guiding your path, is the most sacred honor I will ever have in this life. You make me laugh every day, and make me thank G-d every night for the privilege of being your mother.

Seth: You are the best person I've ever known, and literally your only fault is that you are too nice. That's it, that's my only complaint. I always knew I wanted to write a book, but I never knew what it would be about. I have always known, though, what I'd write in my acknowledgements about you: You saved me. You are my best friend and my soulmate, and I love that we still sneak kisses in the kitchen as our kids and dog violently try to vie for our attention. I am honored to be your wife and the mother of your children, thank you for trusting me with it all. My first two decades of life were rough sailing, and you were the rainbow at the end of a very dark storm.

KAROL:

I would be nothing without my incredible family. I thank G-d for you all.

The biggest thank you to my husband, Shai. The greatest man I've ever met and my inspiration. I do what I do to make you proud. Thirteen years (right?) in and I'm still completely obsessed with you. I could not have written this book, or anything else, without you. I blew up the plan for our lives, more than once, and you were down for all of it every step of the way. Me, you, everything.

To my children. You three are the absolute best. So clever, beautiful, funny, and good. I'm so deeply proud of you. I will always fight for you. Everything is for you. Sadie, thank you for your late-night visits with jokes and memes and also for finding errors (whoops) in this book. I hope to someday be as wise and brave as you. Jack, I will always be available to listen to all of your long-winded, alternate takes on history. You are quirky and hilarious, and I hope you always stay that way. Jude, your little face poking into the office with a "hi mama" made the work easier on so many long afternoons. I was always happy to discuss that yes, I do think you're going to the NFL but, no, I don't think you need to decide quarterback or wide receiver right now.

Ronnie, my amazing brother and best friend. You thought I was worth listening to before anyone else did. That meant so much. Having you in my corner always made me stronger. Yes, you're right, I should be on YouTube. Thank you, Becca, for your warmth and kindness and for my incredible nieces, Miri and Ruby. I can't wait to watch them grow.

Thank you to my mom, Nina, who has always been supportive of me and who will now have no choice but to acknowledge that writing is a real career. I love you, mama.

I lucked out into the greatest in-laws anyone could have. Gilly and Simon, you've been so wonderful to me. I've always felt such love and encouragement from you both. Thank you. Shearly and Ron, you treated me like family from day one. No one I'd rather watch bad movies and fast with on Yom Kip. The Florida Markowiczes and the Florida and Israel Kupermans, thank you for your unfailing support.

Sarra and Raya, I loved writing your story in this book. I always wish you had gotten to see how things turned out.

To my extraordinary friends. More, please. More DiFarasgivings and old-school Italian nights, weddings on islands, birthdays in Vegas, parties in Loveland, and everything else. If you've been to any or all of those, yes, I mean you. More texting, more jokes, more trips, more time together. We're so lucky to have each other. You're always who I reach for, my people. I love you all.

Thank you to my coauthor Bethany Mandel. You're so freaking talented and startlingly prolific, and it's not clear how you do it all. But I feel most connected to you because we are two women with less-than-ideal family origin stories who know the importance of protecting our children, and guarding our families. I hope that comes through in the work we have done together.

Thank you to all of my fantastic colleagues at the *Post*. I've had the best editors in the game: Mark Cunningham, Seth Mandel, Sohrab Ahmari, Kelly Jane Torrance, and the rest of the team. Being a columnist at the very finest paper in the country has been a dream job.

There are too many fellow writers and editors to thank, but Bethany did such a good job I can just say: same, me too, all of those. But seriously, I've been blessed to be surrounded by such smart, talented writers who have lent me their wisdom along the way. If you think I mean you, I do.

I've always felt so championed by my "Russian" community in Brooklyn and elsewhere. It makes me feel untouchable that my community is with me. I have such pride in us. Our families have survived so much, and now we are free. I love us. We are the upright Jews. Am Yisrael Chai.

Our family very publicly moved to Florida while I was writing this book. Living in Florida meant I didn't have to worry about my kids needlessly wearing masks in school and what that was doing to their development. I didn't have to worry about schools arbitrarily closing. I didn't have to worry, as much, that my kids were getting indoctrinated in the classroom. The freedom is glorious. I have been recognized by so many strangers with a friendly "Welcome to Florida!" I'm incredibly grateful to our new state for taking our family in and to Governor and Mrs. DeSantis for giving our family back a life of sanity. Also, thank you to my Florida crew for making life in the free state comfortable and fun. We've got a good thing to protect.

Thank you to everyone who has read me along the way. Your comments, notes, tweets, likes keep me going. I appreciate every single one.

I wasn't born in America and there isn't a day that goes by that I don't think about how differently my life could have gone. Living in the greatest country in the history of the world has been my immense privilege.

Thank you, G-d.

ENDNOTES

INTRODUCTION

[1] Ibram X. Kendi, *Antiracist Baby*, New York: Kokila, 2020.

[2] This and the preceding four quotations are all from an interview with Alison, April 25, 2022.

[3] This and the preceding four quotations are all from an interview with Charlie Jacobs, April 26, 2022.

[4] *Broward County Public Schools LGBTQ Critical Support Guide*, (Fort Lauderdale, FL: BCPS, 2020), https://defendinged.org/wp-content/uploads/2022/05/BCPS-LGBTQ-Critical-Support-Guide-III-Edition-2020.pdf.

[5] Brandon Drey, "California Science Camp Accused of Allowing Biological Male Counselors in Female Elementary Students' Cabins," *The Epoch Times*, February 22, 2022, https://www.theepochtimes.com/california-science-camp-accused-of-allowing-biological-male-counselors-in-female-elementary-students-cabins_4296008.html.

[6] Brandon Drey, "California Science Camp Accused of Allowing Biological Male Counselors in Female Elementary Students' Cabins."

[7] Parent of child in Los Alamitos, email message to author, February 22, 2022.

[8] Parent of child in Los Alamitos, email message to author, February 22, 2022.

[9] Hannah, email message to author, February 22, 2022.

[10] This and the preceding quotation are from an interview with Hannah, April 29, 2022.

[11] "Greta Thunberg Teaching Resources | Teachers Pay Teachers," Teachers Pay Teachers, accessed July 10, 2022, https://www.teacherspayteachers.com/Browse/Search:greta+thunberg/.

CHAPTER 1

[1] "Gulag," Britannica, accessed May 3, 2022, https://www.britannica.com/place/Gulag.

[2] Michael T. Kaufman, "Solzhenitsyn, Literary Giant Who Defied Soviets, Dies at 89," *The New York Times*, August 4, 2008, https://www.nytimes.com/2008/08/04/books/04solzhenitsyn.html.

[3] Aleksandr Isaevich Solzhenitsyn, *The Gulag Archipelago, 1918-1956: An Experiment in Literary Investigation*, ed. Thomas P. Whitney, vol. 2 (New York: Harper Perennial Modern Classics, 2007), 463.

[4] Solzhenitsyn, *The Gulag Archipelago, 1918-1956: An Experiment in Literary Investigation*, 465.

[5] "Woke Definition & Meaning – Merriam-Webster," Merriam-Webster, accessed July 17, 2022, https://www.merriam-webster.com/dictionary/woke.

[6] Lee Brown, "Merriam-Webster Lists 'Sexual Preference' as 'Offensive' after Amy Coney Barrett Spat," *New York Post*, October 15, 2020, https://nypost.com/2020/10/15/merriam-webster-lists-sexual-preference-as-offensive-after-scotus-spat/.

[7] "James Carville: 'Stupid Wokeness Is a National Problem for Democrats,'" CNN, accessed May 3, 2022, video, 2:49, https://www.cnn.com/videos/politics/2021/11/05/don-lemon-james-carville-democrats-stupid-wokeness-newday-vpx.cnn.

[8] Bill Maher (@billmaher), "Why are @TheDemocrats who Support so Many Issues that Benefit the Middle Class Still Considered 'Out of Touch' by 62% of America? #DemIntervention #Midterms2022 #WokeIsAJoke," Twitter, November 20, 2021. https://twitter.com/billmaher/status/1461938829946880002.

[9] Steve Rose, "How the Word 'Woke' Was Weaponised by the Right," *The Guardian*, January 21, 2020, https://www.theguardian.com/society/shortcuts/2020/jan/21/how-the-word-woke-was-weaponised-by-the-right.

[10] John McWhorter, "How 'Woke' Became an Insult," *The New York Times*, August 17, 2021, https://www.nytimes.com/2021/08/17/opinion/woke-politically-correct.html.

[11] Bill Maher (@billmaher), "Why are @TheDemocrats who Support so Many Issues that Benefit the Middle Class Still Considered 'Out of Touch' by 62% of America? #DemIntervention #Midterms2022 #WokeIsAJoke."

[12] Lydia Saad, "U.S. Political Ideology Steady; Conservatives, Moderates Tie," *Gallup*, January 17, 2022, https://news.gallup.com/poll/388988/political-ideology-steady-conservatives-moderates-tie.aspx.

[13] Bill Pan, "Amazon Donated Hundreds of Copies of 'Antiracist' Book to Virginia Public School, Report Says," *The Epoch Times*, June 23, 2021, https://www.theepochtimes.com/amazon-donated-hundreds-of-copies-of-antiracist-book-to-virginia-public-school-report-says_3871295.html.

14 "Instead of Donating Hot Spots for Remote Learning, Amazon Donated Money for Anti-Racism 'Stamped' Books and Spent $8,000 for 45-Minute Talk with Author," Parents Defending Education, June 21, 2021, https://defendinged.org/incidents/instead-of-hot-spots-amazon-donates-for-stamped -books-and-author-talk/.

15 Thomas B. Edsall, "The Law of Unintended Political Consequences Strikes Again," *The New York Times*, January 5, 2022, https://www.nytimes.com/2022/01/05/opinion/progressive-philanthropy-critics.html.

16 Luke Rosiak, "Behind the Network of Outside, Left-Wing Groups Pushing Racial Policies in Cities, Counties Across America," The Daily Caller, October 8, 2019, https://dailycaller.com/2019/10/08/liberal -network-racial-equity-policies/.

17 Rosiak, "Behind the Network."

18 Saul McLeod, "Solomon Asch − Conformity Experiment," SimplyPsychology, December 28, 2018, https://www.simplypsychology.org/asch-conformity.html.

19 Emma Flynn, Cameron Turner, and Luc-Alain Giraldeau, "Follow (or Don't Follow) the Crowd: Young Children's Conformity Is Influenced by Norm Domain and Age," *Journal of Experimental Child Psychology* 167 (March 2018): 222–33, https://doi.org/10.1016/j.jecp.2017.10.014.

20 Flynn, et al., "Follow (or Don't Follow) the Crowd."

21 Sai Sun and Rongjun Yu, "Social Conformity Persists at Least One Day in 6-Year-Old Children," *Scientific Reports* 6, no. 39588 (December 2016), https://doi.org/10.1038/srep39588.

22 Timur Kuran, preface to *Private Truths, Public Lies: The Social Consequences of Preference Falsification*, 1st Harvard University Press pbk. ed (Cambridge, Mass: Harvard University Press, 1997).

23 "Totalitarianism," Britannica, accessed July 8, 2022, https://www.britannica.com/topic/totalitarianism.

24 Eden K. McLean, *Mussolini's Children: Race and Elementary Education in Fascist Italy*, (Lincoln, NE: University of Nebraska Press, 2018), 148.

25 McLean, *Mussolini's Children: Race and Elementary Education in Fascist Italy*, 148.

26 Lisa A. Kirschenbaum, *Small Comrades: Revolutionizing Childhood in Soviet Russia, 1917-1932*, Studies in the History of Education (New York: RoutledgeFalmer, 2001), 5.

27 Kirschenbaum, *Small Comrades: Revolutionizing Childhood in Soviet Russia, 1917-1932*, 5.

28 Kirschenbaum, *Small Comrades: Revolutionizing Childhood in Soviet Russia, 1917-1932*, 6.

29 David R. Topor et al., "Parent Involvement and Student Academic Performance: A Multiple Mediational Analysis," *Journal of Prevention & Intervention in the Community* 38, no. 3 (2010): 183–97, https://doi. org/10.1080/10852352.2010.486297.

30 Callie Patteson, "McAuliffe Says 'Everybody Clapped' after He Said Parents Shouldn't Be Involved in Classroom," *New York Post*, November 1, 2021, https://nypost.com/2021/11/01/mcauliffe-claims-everybody -clapped-after-classroom-comment/.

31 Patteson, "McAuliffe Says 'Everybody Clapped' after He Said Parents Shouldn't Be Involved in Classroom."

32 Interview with friend of author, February 1, 2022.

33 Rone Tempest, "Communism Broke Grip of Tradition: Half a Century of Change Has Reduced Role of Family. But Overseas Relatives Are Imposing Old Values," *Los Angeles Times*, July 18, 1995, https://www .latimes.com/archives/la-xpm-1995-07-18-wr-25022-story.html.

34 Tania Branigan, "China's Cultural Revolution: Son's Guilt over the Mother He Sent to Her Death," *The Guardian*, March 27, 2013, https://www.theguardian.com/world/2013/mar/27/china-cultural-revolution -sons-guilt-zhang-hongping.

35 "A Soviet Legend Dies Hard," *Los Angeles Times*, November 12, 2002, https://www.latimes.com/ar- chives/la-xpm-2002-nov-12-fg-pavlik12-story.html.

36 Alexey Timofeychev, "A Boy Murdered in the Stalinist Era Still Divides Russia," *Russia Beyond*, November 28, 2018, https://www.rbth.com/history/329601-demon-or-hero-morozov.

37 Katya Soldak, "This Is How Propaganda Works: A Look Inside A Soviet Childhood," *Forbes*, December 20, 2017, https://www.forbes.com/sites/katyasoldak/2017/12/20/this-is-how-propaganda-works-a -look-inside-a-soviet-childhood/.

38 Soldak, "This Is How Propaganda Works."

39 Christian Caryl, "China: Year Zero," *Foreign Policy*, May 7, 2013, https://foreignpolicy.com/2013/05/07 /china-year-zero/.

40 Kathrin Hille, "China's 'Sent-down' Youth," *Financial Times*, September 20, 2013, https://www.ft.com /content/3d2ba75c-1fdf-11e3-8861-00144feab7de.

[41] Prak Chan Thul, "Cambodian Khmer Rouge's Chief Ideologist, 'Brother Number Two', Dead at 93," Reuters, August 4, 2019, https://www.reuters.com/article/us-cambodia-rouge-nuonchea-idUSKCN1UU0GU.

[42] "Khmer Rouge Ideology," Holocaust Memorial Day Trust, accessed May 3, 2022, https://www.hmd.org.uk/learn-about-the-holocaust-and-genocides/cambodia/khmer-rouge-ideology/.

[43] Jocelyn Gecker and Haven Daley, "San Francisco to Strip Washington, Lincoln from School Names," AP News, January 27, 2021, https://apnews.com/article/race-and-ethnicity-san-francisco-school-boards-education-dianne-feinstein-8ed10976d4041129917914f7dd73c14e.

[44] Alexandra Kelley, "At Least 33 Christopher Columbus Statues Removed since Spring Protests: Report," *The Hill*, September 25, 2020, https://thehill.com/changing-america/respect/equality/518193-at-least-33-christopher-columbus-statues-removed-since/.

[45] David Williams, "Protesters Tore down a George Washington Statue and Set a Fire on Its Head," CNN, updated June 19, 2020, https://www.cnn.com/2020/06/19/us/portland-george-washington-statue-toppled-trnd/index.html.

[46] Colleen Shalby, "7 Arrested in Vandalism of George Washington Statue near L.A. City Hall," *Los Angeles Times*, August 14, 2020, https://www.latimes.com/california/story/2020-08-14/7-arrested-in-vandalism-of-george-washington-statue-near-l-a-city-hall.

[47] Latisha Jensen, "Portland Man Describes Tearing Down Thomas Jefferson Statue: 'It's Not Vandalism,'" *Willamette Week*, June, 20, 2020, https://www.wweek.com/news/2020/06/20/portland-man-describes-tearing-down-thomas-jefferson-statue-its-not-vandalism/.

[48] Rachel Elbaum, "Portland Protesters Topple Statues of Abraham Lincoln, Theodore Roosevelt," NBC News, October 12, 2020, https://www.nbcnews.com/news/us-news/portland-protesters-tear-down-statues-abraham-lincoln-theodore-roosevelt-n1242913.

[49] Bill Chappell, "New York City Will Exile Thomas Jefferson's Statue from a Prominent Spot in City Hall," NPR, October 19, 2021, https://www.npr.org/2021/10/19/1047258467/thomas-jefferson-statue-removal-new-york-city-council-chamber.

[50] Zachary Small, "Theodore Roosevelt Statue Removal Begins at Museum of Natural History," *The New York Times*, January 19, 2022, https://www.nytimes.com/2022/01/19/arts/design/theodore-roosevelt-statue-natural-history-museum.html.

[51] Bill Chappell, "Statue Of Lincoln With Formerly Enslaved Man At His Feet Is Removed In Boston," NPR, December 29, 2020, https://www.npr.org/2020/12/29/951206414/statue-of-lincoln-with-freed-slave-at-his-feet-is-removed-in-boston.

[52] "Dr Seuss: Six Books Withdrawn Over 'Hurtful and Wrong' Imagery," BBC News, March 4, 2021, https://www.bbc.com/news/entertainment-arts-56250658.

[53] "Dr Seuss: Six Books Withdrawn Over 'Hurtful and Wrong' Imagery."

[54] Chris Morris, "EBay Removes Listings for 'Banned' Dr. Seuss Books," *Fortune*, March 5, 2021, https://fortune.com/2021/03/05/dr-seuss-banned-books-ebay-removes-listings/.

[55] Isaiah Mitchell, "Texas School Board Association Leaves National Group Over Letter Accusing Parents of 'Domestic Terrorism,'" *The Texan*, May 24, 2022, https://thetexan.news/texas-school-board-association-leaves-national-group-over-letter-accusing-parents-of-domestic-terrorism/.

[56] Michael Balsamo, "Garland Defends School Violence Memo against GOP Criticism," AP News, October 28, 2021, https://apnews.com/article/education-violence-school-boards-merrick-garland-school-violence-efbeb14afe3bb0d244848850251c7b72.

[57] Ashley Abramson, "Children's Mental Health Is in Crisis: As Pandemic Stressors Continue: Kids' Mental Health Need to be Addressed in Schools," *Monitor on Psychology* 53, no. 1, (January 2022): 69, www.apa.org/monitor/2022/01/special-childrens-mental-health.

[58] Zachary Rogers, "Elon Musk Says 'Wokeness' is 'Divisive, Exclusionary, and Hateful,'" ABC4 News, December 22, 2021, https://abcnews4.com/news/nation-world/elon-musk-says-wokeness-is-divisive-exclusionary-and-hateful.

[59] "About Us," China Media Project, accessed July 10, 2022, https://chinamediaproject.org/about/.

[60] Stella Chen, "The CMP Dictionary: Main Melody 主旋律," China Media Project, February 18, 2022, https://chinamediaproject.org/the_ccp_dictionary/main-melody/.

[61] Chen, "The CMP Dictionary: Main Melody 主旋律."

[62] Dan Levin, "A Racial Slur, a Viral Video, and a Reckoning," *The New York Times*, updated March 18, 2021, https://www.nytimes.com/2020/12/26/us/mimi-groves-jimmy-galligan-racial-slurs.html.

[63] Levin, "A Racial Slur, a Viral Video, and a Reckoning."

[64]Hannah Arendt, *The Origins of Totalitarianism* (Boston, Mass.: Houghton Mifflin Harcourt, 2011), 176.

[65]Rod Dreher, *Live Not by Lies: A Manual for Christian Dissidents* (New York City: Sentinel, 2020), 31.

[66]"Are Public School Students Required to Recite the Pledge of Allegiance?," Freedom Forum Institute, accessed February 1, 2022, https://www.freedomforuminstitute.org/about/faq/are-public-school -students-required-to-recite-the-pledge-of-allegiance/.

[67]Matthew Rozsa, "Why Have Millennials Stopped Celebrating Thanksgiving?," *Salon*, November 22, 2018, https://www.salon.com/2018/11/22/have-millennials-stopped-celebrating-thanksgiving/.

[68]Christian Allaire, "Why I'm Not Celebrating Thanksgiving This Year," *Vogue*, November 25, 2020, https://www.vogue.com/article/why-im-not-celebrating-thanksgiving.

[69]David Oliver, "Are You Ambivalent about Celebrating July 4? You're Not Alone," *USA Today*, published July 1, 2021, updated July 1, 2022, https://www.usatoday.com/restricted/?return=https%3A%2F% 2Fwww.usatoday.com%2Fin-depth%2Flife%2F2021%2F07%2F01%2Fjuly-4th-what-do-if-youre-not -feeling-patriotic-proud-american%2F5371042001%2F.

[70]Kate Sheehy, "AOC Warns Dems 'There's No Going Back to Brunch' Even If Biden Is Elected," *New York Post*, September 20, 2020, https://nypost.com/2020/09/20/aoc-warns-dems-theres-no-going-back-to -brunch-even-if-biden-wins/.

[71]Annie Karni, "A.O.C.'s Met Gala Dress Triggered Strong Reactions," *The New York Times*, published September 15, 2021, updated September 24, 2021, https://www.nytimes.com/2021/09/15/style/aoc -met-gala-dress.html.

[72]Salvador Rodriguez, "QAnon and Anti-Vaxxers Brainwashed Kids Stuck at Home—Now Teachers Have to Deprogram Them," CNBC, published September 4, 2021, updated September 7, 2021, https://www.cnbc .com/2021/09/04/qanon-and-anti-vaxxers-brainwashed-kids-stuck-at-home-during-pandemic.html.

[73]Corey DeAngelis (@DeAngelisCorey), "Joe Biden: 'They're All Our Children .. They're Not Somebody Else's Children. They're like Yours When They're in the Classroom,'" Twitter, April 27, 2022, https:// twitter.com/deangeliscorey/status/1519439933789937666.

[74]Emma Kerr, "Silicon Valley Parents Freak Out Over Sex Ed," *Daily Beast*, June 13, 2017, https://www .thedailybeast.com/silicon-valley-parents-freak-out-over-sex-ed.

[75]Jocelyn Gecker, "San Francisco Recalls 3 City School Board Members," PBS NewsHour, February 16, 2022, https://www.pbs.org/newshour/education/san-francisco-recalls-3-city-school-board-members.

CHAPTER 2

[1]Spectrum News Staff, "De Blasio: 'Very High Bar' to Shut Schools Down," Spectrum News NY1, March 13, 2020, https://www.ny1.com/nyc/all-boroughs/coronavirus/2020/03/13/mayor-bill-de-blasio -coronavirus-briefing—3-13-20.

[2]Sally Goldenberg, "De Blasio's Big Decision," *Politico*, March 16, 2020, https://www.politico.com /states/new-york/albany/story/2020/03/16/de-blasios-big-decision-1267377.

[3]"Governor Cuomo Announces New York City Cleared by Global Health Experts to Enter Phase Four of Reopening Monday, July 20th," July 17, 2020, https://www.governor.ny.gov/news/governor-cuomo -announces-new-york-city-cleared-global-health-experts-enter-phase-four-reopening.

[4]Valerie Strauss, "Cuomo Questions Why School Buildings Still Exist — and Says New York Will Work with Bill Gates to 'Reimagine Education,'" *Washington Post*, May 6, 2020, https://www.washingtonpost .com/education/2020/05/06/cuomo-questions-why-school-buildings-still-exist-says-new-york-will -work-with-bill-gates-reimagine-education/.

[5]Strauss, "Cuomo Questions Why School Buildings Still Exist."

[6]Anne McCloy, "Rep. Stefanik Calls Gov. Cuomo's Answer to Summer Camp Question 'Disgraceful,'" WRGB, April 30, 2020, https://cbs6albany.com/news/coronavirus/rep-stefanik-calls-gov-cuomos -answer-to-summer-camp-question-disgraceful.

[7]Dan Diamond, "Suddenly, Public Health Officials Say Social Justice Matters More Than Social Dis- tance," *Politico*, June 4, 2020, https://www.politico.com/news/magazine/2020/06/04/public -health-protests-301534.

[8]Mallory Simon, "Over 1,000 Health Professionals Sign a Letter Saying, Don't Shut Down Protests Using Coronavirus Concerns as an Excuse," CNN, June 5, 2020, https://www.cnn.com/2020/06/05/health /health-care-open-letter-protests-coronavirus-trnd/index.html.

[9]Simon, "Over 1,000 Health Professionals Sign a Letter."

[10]Annie Grayer, "The Preliminary Success of Reopening New York City Schools and What It May Mean

for Other Districts," CNN, October 22, 2020, https://www.cnn.com/2020/10/20/us/nyc-schools
-coronavirus-cases-success/index.html.

[11]"NYC Schools Reopening: What to Know About New COVID Policies Inside Schools," NBC New York,
August 27, 2021, https://www.nbcnewyork.com/news/local/nyc-schools-reopening-what-to-know
-about-new-covid-policies-inside-schools/3243782/.

[12]Kristina Sgueglia, "New York City Reports 0.17% Positivity Rate in Open Schools," CNN, October 20,
2020, https://www.cnn.com/world/live-news/coronavirus-pandemic-10-20-20-intl/h_1974e866938
b3070f5b037b1ea2f9cbc.

[13]Amanda Taub, "Pandemic Will 'Take Our Women 10 Years Back' in the Workplace," The New York Times,
updated July 29, 2021, https://www.nytimes.com/2020/09/26/world/covid-women-childcare-equality.html.

[14]Emily Rauhala et al., "How the Pandemic Set Back Women's Progress in the Global Workforce,"
Washington Post, August 28, 2021, https://www.washingtonpost.com/world/interactive/2021
/coronavirus-women-work/.

[15]Tami Forman, "Women's Workforce Participation has Plummeted. Here's How to Reverse the Trend,"
Fortune, February 4, 2022, https://fortune.com/2022/02/04/womens-workforce-participation-has
-plummetedheres-how-to-reverse-the-trend-pandemic-labor-shortage-diversity-economy-tami-forman/.

[16]"Reduced Screen Time for Young Highly Recommended for Well-Being," ScienceDaily, October 29, 2018,
https://www.sciencedaily.com/releases/2018/10/181029150931.htm.

[17]Greg Lukianoff and Jonathan Haidt, The Coddling of the American Mind: How Good Intentions and Bad
Ideas Are Setting Up a Generation for Failure (New York: Penguin Press, 2018), 163.

[18]Nicole Racine et al., "Global Prevalence of Depressive and Anxiety Symptoms in Children and Adolescents During COVID-19: A Meta-Analysis," JAMA Pediatrics 175, no. 11 (November 2021): 1142–50,
https://doi.org/10.1001/jamapediatrics.2021.2482.

[19]Stephanie Pappas, "What Do We Really Know about Kids and Screens?," Monitor on Psychology 51, no.
3, (April 2020): 42, https://www.apa.org/monitor/2020/04/cover-kids-screens.

[20]Nora Crumley, "More Screen Time During Pandemic Can Lead to Eye Strain," December 7, 2020, https://
publications.aap.org/aapnews/news/12053.

[21]Kurt Streeter, "'Everything Is Closed Down.' The Lack of Youth Sports Is a Crisis," The New York Times,
published October 12, 2020, updated October 14, 2020, https://www.nytimes.com/2020/10/12/sports
/covid-youth-sports-canceled.html.

[22]Streeter, "'Everything Is Closed Down.' The Lack of Youth Sports Is a Crisis."

[23]Jessica Dickler, "Virtual School Resulted in 'Significant' Academic Learning Loss, Study Finds," CNBC,
published March 30, 2021, updated Oct 12, 2021, https://www.cnbc.com/2021/03/30/learning-loss
-from-virtual-school-due-to-covid-is-significant-.html.

[24]Brian Dunleavy, "Study Links Kids' Screen Time during Pandemic with Rise in Mental, Behavioral
Issues," UPI, December 28, 2021, https://www.upi.com/Health_News/2021/12/28/canada-screen-time
-pandemic-study/6621640705849/.

[25]Dyani Lewis, "Mounting Evidence Suggests Coronavirus Is Airborne—but Health Advice has Not
Caught Up," Nature 583 (July 2020): 510–13, https://doi.org/10.1038/d41586-020-02058-1.

[26]Olafimihan Oshin, "Gottlieb: 'Nobody Knows' Origins of Six-Foot Social-Distancing Recommendation,"
The Hill, September 19, 2021, https://thehill.com/homenews/sunday-talk-shows/572926-gottlieb
-nobody-knows-where-six-foot-distancing-recommendation/.

[27]Oshin, "Gottlieb: 'Nobody Knows' Origins of Six-Foot Social-Distancing Recommendation."

[28]David Zweig, "Hybrid Schooling May Be the Most Dangerous Option of All," Wired, August 6, 2020,
https://www.wired.com/story/hybrid-schooling-is-the-most-dangerous-option-of-all/.

[29]Zweig, "Hybrid Schooling May Be the Most Dangerous Option of All."

[30]Amy Zimmer, "New York City's Long and Winding School Year Ends on a Full Day for Most Students,"
Chalkbeat, June 24, 2021, https://ny.chalkbeat.org/2021/6/24/22549165/nyc-last-day-school-day-full-half.

[31]Karol Markowicz, "Our Inept Leaders' Irrational Decision to Close NYC Schools," New York Post,
November 18, 2020, https://nypost.com/2020/11/18/our-inept-leaders-irrational-decision-to-close
-schools/.

[32]"NYC Middle Schools Reopen in Person for 1st Time in Months; Older Kids Stay Remote," NBC New
York, February 25, 2021, https://www.nbcnewyork.com/news/coronavirus/nyc-middle-schools
-reopen-in-person-for-1st-time-since-nov-mayor-hopeful-for-high-school-announcement-in
-weeks/2909251/.

[33]Peter Szekely, "New York Mayor Sees High School Classrooms Reopening in Current Academic Year," *Reuters*, February 24, 2021, https://www.reuters.com/world/us/new-york-mayor-sees-high-school -classrooms-reopening-current-academic-year-2021-02-24/.

[34]Jillian Jorgensen "Public High Schools to Reopen March 22," Spectrum News NY1, updated March 8, 2021, https://www.ny1.com/nyc/all-boroughs/news/2021/03/08/dates-set-for-in-person-nyc-public -high-schools-and-psal-sports-to-resume.

[35]Post Editorial Board, "Teacher-Union Boss Mulgrew Should Look in the Mirror When Bemoaning 180K Kids out of NYC Schools," *New York Post*, October 7, 2021, https://nypost.com/2021/10/07/mulgrew -should-look-in-the-mirror-when-bemoaning-180k-kids-out-of-nyc-schools/.

[36]Peter Szekely, "New York Mayor Sees High School Classrooms Reopening in Current Academic Year."

[37]Anya Kamenetz, "Lessons From Europe, Where Cases Are Rising But Schools Are Open," NPR, November 13, 2020, https://www.npr.org/2020/11/13/934153674/lessons-from-europe-where-cases-are-rising-but -schools-are-open.

[38]Interview with Corey DeAngelis, February 17, 2022.

[39]Karol Markowicz, "For Our Health and Economic Survival, We Need to Get Outside," *New York Post*, May 17, 2020, https://nypost.com/2020/05/17/for-our-health-and-economic-survival-we-need-to-get -outside/.

[40]Markowicz, "For Our Health and Economic Survival, We Need to Get Outside."

[41]Rosemond Crown, "Health Experts Warn Cloth Masks are Ineffective Against COVID-19," KWTX, January 7, 2022, https://www.kwtx.com/2022/01/08/health-experts-warn-cloth-masks-are-ineffective-against -covid-19/.

[42]Ronny Reyes, "Blue Surgical Face Masks are Only 10% Effective in Preventing COVID Infection, New Study Finds," *Daily Mail*, August 21, 2021, https://www.dailymail.co.uk/news/article-9914969/Popular -blue-surgical-face-masks-NOT-stop-people-infected-COVID-19.html.

[43]Mike Catalini, "Governors in Four States Plan an End to School Mask Mandates," *Los Angeles Times*, February 8, 2022, https://www.latimes.com/world-nation/story/2022-02-08/governors-four-states -plan-end-school-mask-mandates.

[44]Jim Acosta (@Acosta), "Fauci Tells CNN Updated Outdoor Mask Guidance Likely Very Soon: 'The Risk When You're Outdoors – Which We Have Been Saying All along – Is Extremely Low. And If You Are Vaccinated, It's Even Lower. So You're Going to Be Hearing about Those Kinds of Recommendations Soon,'" Twitter, April 25, 2021, https://mobile.twitter.com/acosta/status/1386424116492730377.

[45]Jesse O'Neill, "San Francisco Tightens COVID Vax Mandate for Customers and Workers," *New York Post*, August 13, 2021, https://nypost.com/2021/08/12/san-francisco-tightens-covid-vax-mandate-for -customers-workers/.

[46]Franklin Leonard (@franklinleonard), "London Breed said 'everyone was vaccinated and it was Tony! Toni! Toné!'s first live performance in decades. Yes, I danced without a mask. Come on, y'all. Raphael Saadiq! How can you NOT dance?,'" Twitter, September 20, 2021, https://twitter.com/franklinleonard /status/1440106366169849861.

[47]Leonard (@franklinleonard), "London Breed said 'everyone was...'"

[48]This and the preceding quotation are from an interview with Rachel, February 10, 2022.

[49]Mary Reece (@MaryPat105), "Dr. Deborah Cornavaca welcomes participants to NJ 5th Annual Women's Leadership Conference! @NJPSA @NJASANews @AASAHQ," Twitter, September 30, 2021, https:// twitter.com/marypat105/status/1443571851310116864.

[50]Interview with parent, December 26, 2021.

[51]Interview with Daniela Jampel, January 10, 2022.

[52]This and the preceding quotation are from Maud Maron, email message to author, January 10, 2022.

[53]Jennifer Sey, "Yesterday I Was Levi's Brand President. I Quit So I Could Be Free," *Common Sense* (blog), Substack Newsletter, February 14, 2022, https://bariweiss.substack.com/p/yesterday-i-was-levis -brand-president.

[54]Ryan Delaney, "Europe Is Locked Back Down, But Most Schools Stay Open," STLPR, November 18, 2020, https://news.stlpublicradio.org/education/2020-11-18/europe-is-locked-back-down-but-most -schools-stay-open.

[55]Perry Stein and Quentin Ariès, "As Schools Decide to Reopen or Go Virtual, Europe's Short-Term Closures Suggest Long-Term Costs," *Washington Post*, December 31, 2021, https://www.washingtonpost.com /world/2021/12/31/schools-reopening-europe/.

56Jim Salter and Leah Willingham, "Teacher deaths raise alarms as new school year begins," Ap News, published September 9, 2020, https://apnews.com/article/mississippi-education-michael-brown-randi -weingarten-virus-outbreak-3e97872bf3cd8697064014efcf2ec622.

57Donald Trump, "Remarks by President Trump on Safely Reopening America's Schools," (remark, East Room of The White House, July 7, 2020), https://trumpwhitehouse.archives.gov/briefings-statements /remarks-president-trump-safely-reopening-americas-schools/.

58"Return to School 2020: Learning Bridges Program," NYC Department of Education, n.d., https://infohub .nyced.org/docs/default-source/default-document-library/dece_learning_bridges_flyer_english_v2-(1).pdf.

59David Cruz, "Frustrated But Not Surprised: Weary Parents Grapple With Citywide Closure Of Public Schools," Gothamist, November 19, 2020, https://gothamist.com/news/frustrated-not-surprised -weary-parents-grapple-citywide-closure-public-schools.

60Sophia Chang, "Demand Grows For Learning Bridges Childcare Program As City's Public Schools Stay Closed," Gothamist, November 21, 2020, https://gothamist.com/news/demand-grows-learning -bridges-childcare-program-citys-public-schools-stay-closed.

61Jon Levine, "Powerful Teachers Union Influenced CDC on School Reopenings, Emails Show," *New York Post*, May 1, 2021, https://nypost.com/2021/05/01/teachers-union-collaborated-with-cdc-on-school -reopening-emails/.

62Levine, "Powerful Teachers Union Influenced CDC on School Reopenings, Emails Show."

63"Jake Tapper Presses CDC Director on Reopening Schools," CNN, accessed July 24, 2022, video, 6:19, https://www.cnn.com/videos/health/2021/02/14/cdc-director-rochelle-walensky-reopening-schools -tapper-sotu-vpx.cnn.

64Karol Markowicz, "Exhausted Teachers, Troublemaking Kids: The Result of Declaring Schools Non-essential," *New York Post*, November 21, 2021, https://nypost.com/2021/11/21/exhausted-teachers -troublemaking-kids-the-result-of-declaring-schools-nonessential/.

65Mark Moore, "Chicago Mayor Lightfoot Blasts Teachers Union for 'Illegal Walkout,'" *New York Post*, January 9, 2022, https://nypost.com/2022/01/09/chicago-mayor-lightfoot-blasts-teachers-union-for -walkout/.

66Julie Mack, "Flint and Detroit among Nation's Top 5 Poorest Cities, New Census Data Shows," MLive, September 26, 2019, https://www.mlive.com/news/2019/09/flint-and-detroit-among-nations-top-5 -poorest-cities-new-census-data-shows.html.

67Dylan Goetz, "Flint Schools Extends Virtual Learning Period Indefinitely," MLive, January 19, 2022, https://www.mlive.com/news/flint/2022/01/flint-schools-extends-virtual-learning-period -indefinitely.html.

68Alex Gutentag, "What They Did to the Kids," *Tablet*, November 21, 2021, https://www.tabletmag.com /sections/news/articles/school-closures-covid-alex-gutentag.

69Gutentag, "What They Did to the Kids."

70Wall Street Journal Editorial Board, "The Conformity Crackup of 2021," *Wall Street Journal*, December 30, 2021, https://www.wsj.com/articles/media-conformity-wuhan-covid-russia-crime-11640805471.

71Angie Schmitt, "Why I Soured on the Democrats," *The Atlantic*, January 7, 2022, https://www.theatlantic .com/ideas/archive/2022/01/democrats-botched-public-school-covid-policy/621183/.

72Angie Schmitt, "Why I Soured on the Democrats."

73Jackie Mader, "'The Reading Year': First Grade Is Critical for Reading Skills, but Kids Coming from Dis-rupted Kindergarten Experiences Are Way Behind," The Hechinger Report, November 14, 2021, http:// hechingerreport.org/the-reading-year-first-grade-is-critical-for-reading-skills-but-kids-coming-from -disrupted-kindergarten-experiences-are-way-behind/.

74Mader, "'The Reading Year.'"

75Philip Klein, "Teachers' Union-Led School Closures Are Disproportionately Harming Black and His-panic Children," *National Review*, April 12, 2021, https://www.nationalreview.com/corner/teachers -union-led-school-closures-are-disproportionately-harming-black-and-hispanic-children/.

76Emma Dorn et al., "COVID-19 and Student Learning in the United States: The Hurt Could Last a Lifetime," June 1, 2020, https://www.mckinsey.com/industries/education/our-insights/covid-19-and -student-learning-in-the-united-states-the-hurt-could-last-a-lifetime.

77Dorn et al., "COVID-19 and Student Learning in the United States."

78Philip Klein, "Teachers' Union-Led School Closures Are Disproportionately Harming Black and Hispanic Children."

[79] Anna Maria Della Costa, "COVID-19 Cases are Rising Fast. Can Schools Reopen Safely After the Holidays?" *The Charlotte Observer*, December 30, 2021, https://www.charlotteobserver.com/news/local/education/article256921762.html.

[80] "COVID-19 Cases Rise in Children Across US as Schools Begin to Open for in-Person Learning," FOX 5 DC, August 26, 2021, https://www.fox5dc.com/news/covid-19-cases-rise-in-children-across-us-as-schools-begin-to-open-for-in-person-learning.

[81] Scott Sutton, "Gov. Ron DeSantis Says 'Schools Will Remain Open for In-Person Instruction,'" WPTV, November 30, 2020, https://www.wptv.com/coronavirus/gov-ron-desantis-says-schools-will-remain-open-in-florida-for-in-person-instruction.

[82] Karol Markowicz, "The Future is Florida," *Washington Examiner*, January 29, 2021, https://www.washingtonexaminer.com/politics/the-future-is-florida.

[83] Markowicz, "The Future is Florida."

[84] Alyssa Hyman, "Three Broward Educators Die from COVID-19: Union," NBC 6 South Florida, published August 12, 2021, updated August 13, 2021, https://www.nbcmiami.com/news/local/schools-and-covid/three-broward-educators-die-of-covid-19-union/2528573/.

[85] Zoe Christen Jones, "Four Broward County Educators Die from COVID-19 within 24 Hours, as Florida's Battle over Masks in Schools Continues," CBS News, August 13, 2021, https://www.cbsnews.com/news/florida-covid-schools-broward-county-covid-19-deaths/.

[86] This and the preceding three quotations are all from an interview with Governor Ronald Dion DeSantis, March 1, 2022.

[87] Claire Farrow, "Welcome to Florida: Sunshine State among Top States People Moved to in 2021," WTSP, January 11, 2022, https://www.wtsp.com/article/news/regional/florida/who-is-moving-to-florida/67-e1aaee99-cd2d-48b8-965e-d7fb25ff721d.

[88] Francesco Fuso Nerini et al., "Personal Carbon Allowances Revisited," *Nature Sustainability* 4, (December 2021): 1025–31, https://doi.org/10.1038/s41893-021-00756-w.

CHAPTER 3

[1] "Full NSBA Letter to Biden Administration and Department of Justice Memo," Parents Defending Education, November 29, 2021, https://defendinged.org/press-releases/full-nsba-letter-to-biden-administration-and-department-of-justice-memo/.

[2] The Attorney General Merrick Garland to Director, Federal Bureau of Investigation, et al., memorandum, "Partnership Among Federal, State, Local, Tribal, and Territorial Law Enforcement to Address Threats Against School Administrators, Board Members, Teachers, and Staff," memorandum, October 4, 2021, https://www.justice.gov/ag/page/file/1438986/download.

[3] Rob Crilly, "Biden's Education Secretary Cardona ASKED National School Board Association to Send Letter Comparing Protesting Parents to Domestic Terrorists, New Emails Claim," Daily Mail Online, January 11, 2022, https://www.dailymail.co.uk/news/article-10391397/Biden-education-secretary-solicited-National-School-Boards-letter-comparing-parents-terrorists.html.

[4] Gabe Kaminsky, "A School Board Banned Ideology From Classrooms. The Schools Simply Ignored It," *Daily Wire*, January 17, 2022, https://www.dailywire.com/news/a-school-board-banned-ideology-from-classrooms-the-schools-simply-ignored-it.

[5] Kaminsky, "A School Board Banned Ideology From Classrooms."

[6] Kaminsky, "A School Board Banned Ideology From Classrooms."

[7] "Democratic vs. Republican Occupations," Verdant Labs, accessed May 4, 2022, http://verdantlabs.com/politics_of_professions/index.html.

[8] Sol Stern, "Pedagogy of the Oppressor: Another Reason Why U.S. Ed Schools are so Awful: the Ongoing Influence of Brazilian Marxist Paulo Freire," *City Journal*, Spring 2009, https://www.city-journal.org/html/pedagogy-oppressor-13168.html.

[9] Sol Stern, "Pedagogy of the Oppressor."

[10] Helen Pluckrose and James A. Lindsay, *Cynical Theories: How Activist Scholarship Made Everything about Race, Gender, and Identity—and Why This Harms Everybody*, First Edition (Durham, North Carolina: Pitchstone Publishing, 2020), 13-14.

[11] Daniel Buck and James Furey, "Units of Indoctrination: A Language Arts Curriculum Widely Used in U.S. Schools Ignores Academic Fundamentals in Favor of Radical Pedagogy," *City Journal*, November 24, 2021, https://www.city-journal.org/critical-race-theory-in-the-classroom.

[12]Jay Schalin, *The Politicization of University Schools of Education: The Long March through the Education Schools* (The James G. Martin Center for Academic Renewal, February 2019), 45.

[13]Schalin, *The Politicization of University Schools of Education*, 49.

[14]Schalin, *The Politicization of University Schools of Education*, 49.

[15]Schalin, *The Politicization of University Schools of Education*, 58.

[16]Overly-Woke Support Group, accessed July 8, 2022, https://vimeo.com/284986055.

[17]Theodore Kim, "Racism in Our Curriculums Isn't Limited to History. It's in Math, Too," *Washington Post*, December 8, 2021, https://www.washingtonpost.com/outlook/2021/12/08/racism-our-curriculums -isnt-limited-history-its-math-too/.

[18]Williamson M. Evers, "California Leftists Try to Cancel Math Class," *Wall Street Journal*, May 18, 2021, https://www.wsj.com/articles/california-leftists-try-to-cancel-math-class-11621355858.

[19]Karin Brodie, "Yes, Mathematics Can Be Decolonised. Here's How to Begin," The Conversation, October 13, 2016, http://theconversation.com/yes-mathematics-can-be-decolonised-heres-how-to-begin-65963.

[20]Catherine Gewertz, "Seattle Schools Lead Controversial Push to 'Rehumanize' Math," *Education Week*, October 14, 2019, https://www.edweek.org/teaching-learning/seattle-schools-lead-controversial-push -to-rehumanize-math/2019/10.

[21]Christopher Dubbs, "A Queer Turn in Mathematics Education Research: Centering the Experience of Marginalized Queer Students," (presentation, Annual Meeting of the North American Chapter of the International Group for the Psychology of Mathematics Education, Tucson, AZ, November 3-6, 2016), https://eric.ed.gov/?id=ED583735.

[22]Dubbs, "A Queer Turn in Mathematics Education Research."

[23]Aaron Sibarium, "Why Private Schools Have Gone Woke," *The Washington Free Beacon*, July 28, 2021, https://freebeacon.com/culture/why-private-schools-have-gone-woke/.

[24]Sibarium, "Why Private Schools Have Gone Woke."

[25]This and the preceding quotation are from an interview with Christopher Rufo, January 16, 2022.

[26]"Critical Race Theory 101," WNYC, July 21, 2021, https://www.wnyc.org/story/critical-race-theory-101/.

[27]Karol Markowicz, "The Rise of the Left-Wing Language Police," *Spectator World*, October 16, 2020, https://spectatorworld.com/topic/rise-left-wing-language-police-hirono-sexual-preference/.

[28]Michael Malice, "No, Amy Robach Is Not a White Supremacist," *New York Observer*, August 25, 2016, https://observer.com/2016/08/no-amy-robach-is-not-a-white-supremacist/.

[29]Malice, "No, Amy Robach Is Not a White Supremacist."

[30]Karol Markowicz, "Critical Race Theory Is Part of Woke Agenda —Parents Should Fight It," *New York Post*, June 27, 2021, https://nypost.com/2021/06/27/critical-race-theory-is-part-of-woke-agenda-parents -should-fight-all-of-it/.

[31]Ibram X. Kendi, "The Difference Between Being 'Not Racist' and Antiracist," recorded June 9, 2020, TED video, 51:05, https://www.ted.com/talks/ibram_x_kendi_the_difference_between_being_not_racist _and_antiracist.

[32]Asra Q. Nomani, "Receipts on Fairfax County Paying Ibram Kendi $20,000 for 1-Hour," *Asra Investigates* (blog), Substack Newsletter, September 24, 2020, https://asrainvestigates.substack.com/p/heres-the -receipt-on-fairfax-county.

[33]Ann Doss Helms, "Two Top NC Republicans Take Aim At CMS For Paying Anti-Racism Author Kendi To Speak," WFAE 90.7, June 29, 2021, https://www.wfae.org/education/2021-06-29/two-top-nc-republicans -take-aim-at-cms-for-paying-anti-racism-author-kendi-to-speak.

[34]The National Desk, "Maryland School District Spends $450K on Anti-Racist Audit," WJLA, June 3, 2021, https://wjla.com/news/nation-world/maryland-school-district-spends-450k-on-anti-racist-audit.

[35]Isabel Vincent, "Inside BLM Co-Founder Patrisse Khan-Cullors' Million-Dollar Real Estate Buying Binge," *New York Post*, April 10, 2021, https://nypost.com/2021/04/10/inside-blm-co-founder-patrisse -khan-cullors-real-estate-buying-binge/.

[36]Sean Campbell, "The BLM Mystery: Where Did the Money Go," *New York Magazine*, January 31, 2022, https://nymag.com/intelligencer/2022/01/black-lives-matter-finances.html.

[37]Zachary Rogers, "Black Lives Matter 'Delinquent' on Finances, Calif. AG Warns BLM Risks Tax-Exempt Status," ABC4 News, February 2, 2022, https://abcnews4.com/news/nation-world/black-lives-matter -delinquent-on-finances-calif-ag-warns-blm-risks-tax-exempt-status-california-department-justice -attorney-general-patrisse-cullors-influence-watch-rob-bunta-washington-examiner-doj.

[38]Carmen Black and Christy Olezeski, "We Should Be Teaching Critical Race Theory to Kids—but It Must

Be Done Right" *Newsweek*, February 9, 2022, https://www.newsweek.com/we-should-teaching-critical
-race-theory-kids-it-has-done-right-opinion-1677698.

[39]National Education Association, "New Business Item 39" July 5, 2021, https://web.archive.org
/web/20210705234008/https://ra.nea.org/business-item/2021-nbi-039/.

[40]National Education Association, "New Business Item 39."

[41]Leslie M. Harris, "I Helped Fact-Check the 1619 Project. The Times Ignored Me.," *Politico*, accessed
March 6, 2020, https://www.politico.com/news/magazine/2020/03/06/1619-project-new-york-times
-mistake-122248.

[42]"Denver Elementary School Announces Plans to Instruct Kindergartners and 1st Graders about Why It's
Important to Disrupt the Nuclear Family and Be Trans and Queer Affirming; They Host Racially Segregated Playground Nights Too," Parents Defending Education, January 19, 2022, https://defendinged.org
/incidents/denver-elementary-school-announces-plans-to-instruct-kindergartners-and-1st-graders
-about-why-its-important-to-disrupt-the-nuclear-family-and-be-trans-and-queer-affirming/.

[43]"Centennial A School for Expeditionary Learning," GreatSchools.org, accessed July 8, 2022, https://
www.greatschools.org/colorado/denver/417-Centennial-A-School-For-Expeditionary-Learning/.

[44]"Centennial A School for Expeditionary Learning."

[45]Michael H. Kater, *Hitler Youth* (Cambridge, Mass: Harvard University Press, 2006), 43.

[46]George Packer, "When the Culture War Comes for the Kids," *The Atlantic*, October 2019, https://www
.theatlantic.com/magazine/archive/2019/10/when-the-culture-war-comes-for-the-kids/596668/.

[47]George Packer, "When the Culture War Comes for the Kids."

[48]This and the three preceding quotations are all from an interview with Alvin Lui, February 16, 2022.

[49]Ann Marie Shambaugh, "Carmel Clay Schools Prepares to Address $2M Shortfall Caused by Declining
Enrollment," *Current*, September 22, 2021, https://www.youarecurrent.com/2021/09/22/carmel-clay
-schools-prepares-to-address-2m-shortfall-caused-by-declining-enrollment/#:~:text=Carmel%20
Clay%20Schools%20prepares%20to%20address%20%242M%20shortfall%20caused%20by%20
declining%20enrollment,-0&text=Carmel%20Clay%20Schools%20has%20found,small%20
number%20of%20teaching%20jobs.

[50]Interview with Alvin Lui, February 16, 2022.

[51]Interview with Inez Stepman, February 17, 2022.

[52]"Indoctrination Map," Parents Defending Education, accessed July 11, 2022, https://defendinged.org/map/.

[53]"Grant High School Gives Presentation Showing 'Pyramid of White Supremacy'; School District Promotes Gender Transitioning Material to Children," Parents Defending Education, January 13, 2022,
https://defendinged.org/incidents/grant-high-school-gives-presentation-showing-pyramid-of-white
-supremacy-school-district-promotes-gender-transitioning-material-to-children/.

[54]"Grant High School Gives Presentation Showing 'Pyramid of White Supremacy.'"

[55]"North Carolina Dept. of Instruction Pushed Racialized Preschool Teacher Training While Hiding Evidence,"
No Left Turn, June 8, 2022, https://www.noleftturn.us/north-carolina-pushed-racialized-training/.

[56]Emily Benedek, "California Is Cleansing Jews From History," January 27, 2021, *Tablet*, https://www
.tabletmag.com/sections/news/articles/california-ethnic-studies-curriculum.

[57]Benedek, "California Is Cleansing Jews From History."

[58]Luke Rosiak, *Race to the Bottom: Uncovering the Secret Forces Destroying American Public Education*
(New York: Broadside Books, 2022).

[59]Mark Miloscia, "Tracy Castro-Gill's Racist 'Leadership' Exemplifies the Moral Depravity of Public
School," Family Policy Institute of Washington, January 25, 2022, https://fpiw.org/blog/2022/01/25
/tracy-castro-gills-racist-leadership-exemplifies-the-moral-depravity-of-public-school/.

[60]This and the two preceding quotations are all from Luke Rosiak, *Race to the Bottom: Uncovering the
Secret Forces Destroying American Public Education* (New York: Broadside Books, 2022). Kindle.

[61]Tracy Castro-Gill, "The Failures of Ethnic Studies (And How to Fix Them)," Washington Ethnic Studies
Now, May 29, 2020, https://waethnicstudies.com/2020/05/29/the-failures-of-ethnic-studies-and-
how-to-fix-them-5/.

[62]Robby Soave, "Hispanic Students Were Forced To Learn Critical Race Theory. They Hated It," *Reason*,
January 31, 2022, https://reason.com/2022/01/31/critical-race-theory-taught-in-classroom-california/.

[63]Soave, "Hispanic Students Were Forced To Learn Critical Race Theory. They Hated It."

[64]Douglas Murray, *The Madness of Crowds: Gender, Race and Identity* (London: Bloomsbury Continuum,
2019), 3.

[65] Murray, *The Madness of Crowds*, 3.

[66] Dan O'Donnell, "Small-Town Wisconsin Schools Won't Tell Parents If Children Identify As Transgender," *The Federalist*, October 28, 2021, https://thefederalist.com/2021/10/28/small-town-wisconsin-schools -wont-tell-parents-if-their-children-identify-as-transgender/.

[67] Steven Stewart, "Leon School Officials Develop Gender Transition Plan Without Parent Approval," *Tallahassee Reports*, September 26, 2021, https://tallahasseereports.com/2021/09/26/leon-school-officials -develop-gender-transition-plan-without-parent-approval/.

[68] CS/CS/HB 1557: Parental Rights in Education, 2022-22 L.O.F. (2022), https://www.flsenate.gov/Session /Bill/2022/1557/?Tab=Citations.

[69] Christopher Rufo (@realchrisrufo), "SCOOP: The Evanston/Skokie School District Has Adopted a Radical Gender Curriculum That Encourages PK-3 Students to Celebrate the Transgender Flag, Break the 'Gender Binary' Established by White 'Colonizers,' and Experiment with Neo-Pronouns Such as 'Ze,' 'Zir,' and 'Tree,'" Twitter, April 21, 2022, https://twitter.com/realchrisrufo/status/1517198914784485377.

[70] Christopher Rufo (@realchrisrufo), "In Pre-Kindergarten, the Children Are Taught an 'Introduction' to the Rainbow and Transgender Flags. Teachers Then Provide the Basic Concepts of Gender Identity, Explaining That 'We Call People with More than One Gender or No Gender, Non-Binary or Queer,'" Twitter, April 21, 2022, https://twitter.com/realchrisrufo/status/1517199479480463361.

[71] Christopher Rufo (@realchrisrufo), "In First Grade, the Teacher Encourages Students to Experiment with Gender Pronouns Such as 'She, Tree, They, He, Her, Him, Them, Ze, Zir, [and] Hir.' The Students Read Gender Scripts and the Teacher Reminds Them: 'Whatever Pronouns You Pick Today, You Can Always Change,'" Twitter, April 21, 2022, https://twitter.com/realchrisrufo/status/1517201690365210624.

[72] Abigail Shrier, "The Chronicle Cries for Activist Teachers," *The Truth Fairy* (blog), Substack Newsletter, December 31, 2021, https://abigailshrier.substack.com/p/the-chronicle-cries-for-activist.

[73] Shrier, "The Chronicle Cries for Activist Teachers."

[74] Christopher Rufo (@realchrisrufo), "Winning the Language War: Use the Term 'Political Predators' for Describing Teachers who Indoctrinate their Students and Treat the Public School System as a Recruiting Ground for their Private Ideologies," Twitter, August 31, 2021, https://twitter.com/realchrisrufo/status /1432787777133760515?lang=en.

[75] Shrier, "The Chronicle Cries for Activist Teachers."

[76] Peggy Noonan, "Democrats Need to Face Down the Woke," *Wall Street Journal*, November 11, 2021, https://www.wsj.com/articles/democrats-face-the-woke-elections-socialists-critical-race-theory -schools-aoc-virginia-11636669165.

[77] Tyler Kingkade, "They Fought Critical Race Theory. Now They're Focusing on 'Curriculum Transparency,'" NBC News, January 20, 2022, https://www.nbcnews.com/news/us-news/critical-race-theory-curriculum -transparency-rcna12809.

[78] Kingkade, "They Fought Critical Race Theory. Now They're Focusing on 'Curriculum Transparency.'"

[79] Interview with Christopher Rufo, January 16, 2022.

[80] "Governor Ron DeSantis' State of the State Address," State of Florida, January 11, 2022, https://flgov .com/2022/01/11/governor-ron-desantis-state-of-the-state-address-3/.

[81] ACLU (@ACLU), "Curriculum transparency bills are just thinly veiled attempts at chilling teachers and students from learning and talking about race and gender in schools," Twitter, January 21, 2022, https:// twitter.com/aclu/status/1484573261967114247?lang=en.

[82] Karol Markowicz (@karol), "It's Amazing How Almost None of What the ACLU Works on Anymore Has Anything to Do with Civil Liberties and Is Just Leftist Wishlist Nonsense.(From a Fundraising Email I Just Got)," Twitter, March 31, 2021, https://twitter.com/karol/status/1377312452040404994.

[83] James Kirchick, "The Disintegration of the ACLU," *Tablet*, March 30, 2021, https://www.tabletmag.com /sections/news/articles/the-disintegration-of-the-aclu-james-kirchick.

[84] Kirchick, "The Disintegration of the ACLU."

[85] "Students Win with Recent School Board Decisions in Lyon and Clark Counties," American Civil Liberties Union, December 13, 2013, https://www.aclu.org/press-releases/students-win-recent-school -board-decisions-lyon-and-clark-counties.

[86] "ACLU-KY Reviews 'Bible Literacy' Courses in Kentucky Public Schools," American Civil Liberties Union, January 8, 2018, https://www.aclu.org/press-releases/aclu-ky-reviews-bible-literacy-courses -kentucky-public-schools.

[87] Interview with Jeff Myers, February 6, 2022.

[88]This and the preceding quotation are from an interview with Quisha King, February 6, 2022.

[89]The Editorial Board, "'Don't Say Gay' Is Popular? You Don't Say," *Wall Street Journal*, April 1, 2022, https://www.wsj.com/articles/dont-say-gay-is-popular-you-dont-say-ron-desantis-florida-law-elementary-school-11648849131.

[90]Inez Stepman, email message to author, February 17, 2022.

[91]Quisha King, email message to author, February 17, 2022.

CHAPTER 4

[1]Gabriela Schulte, "Poll: One-Third of Voters Identify as 'Woke,'" *The Hill*, July 16, 2021, https://thehill.com/hilltv/what-americas-thinking/563415-poll-one-third-of-voters-identify-as-woke/.

[2]Schulte, "Poll: One-Third of Voters Identify as 'Woke.'"

[3]Dana Goldstein, "Opponents Call It the 'Don't Say Gay' Bill. Here's What It Says," *The New York Times*, March 18, 2022, https://www.nytimes.com/2022/03/18/us/dont-say-gay-bill-florida.html.

[4]Goldstein, "Opponents Call It the 'Don't Say Gay' Bill. Here's What It Says."

[5]"Statement from the Walt Disney Company on Signing of Florida Legislation," The Walt Disney Company, March 28, 2022, https://thewaltdisneycompany.com/statement-from-the-walt-disney-company-on-signing-of-florida-legislation/.

[6]"Statement from the Walt Disney Company on Signing of Florida Legislation."

[7]Caroline Downey, "Disney Executive Producer Admits to 'Gay Agenda,' 'Adding Queerness' Wherever She Could," *National Review*, March 29, 2022, https://www.nationalreview.com/news/disney-executive-producer-admits-to-gay-agenda-adding-queerness-wherever-she-could/.

[8]Downey, "Disney Executive Producer Admits to 'Gay Agenda,' 'Adding Queerness' Wherever She Could."

[9]Timothy Nerozzi, "Disney Corporate President Says Next Generation 'Queerer,' Company Must 'Get With It,'" FOX Business, April 8, 2022, https://www.foxbusiness.com/media/disney-corporate-president-next-generation-queerer; https://reimaginetomorrow.disney.com/our-intentions.

[10]Ethan L. Clay, "Disney's Institutional Capture," *Quillette*, March 29, 2022, https://quillette.com/2022/03/29/disneys-institutional-capture/.

[11]Anika Burgess, "The Artful Propaganda of Soviet Children's Literature," *Atlas Obscura*, June 15, 2017, https://www.atlasobscura.com/articles/soviet-childrens-books-propaganda.

[12]This and the preceding quotation are from an interview with librarian, January 25, 2022.

[13]"Drabinski, Watson Seek 2023-24 ALA Presidency," American Library Association, October 5, 2021, https://www.ala.org/news/press-releases/2021/10/drabinski-watson-seek-2023-24-ala-presidency.

[14]"New President-Elect of American Library Association Is Also a Lesbian Mom," Mombian (blog), Dana B. Rudolph, LLC, April 14, 2022, https://mombian.com/2022/04/14/new-president-elect-of-american-library-association-is-also-a-lesbian-mom/.

[15]Joy Pullman, "21,400 Attend Library Conference Featuring Workshops on Drag Queens and Queering Elementary Schools," *The Federalist*, July 10, 2019, https://thefederalist.com/2019/07/10/21460-librarians-attend-major-conference-featuring-workshops-drag-queens-queering-elementary-schools/.

[16]Pullman, "21,400 Attend Library Conference Featuring Workshops on Drag Queens and Queering Elementary Schools."

[17]Meghan Cox Gurdon, "Children's Books: A Look at This Year's Newbery and Caldecott Winners," *Wall Street Journal*, January 28, 2022, https://www.wsj.com/articles/childrens-books-review-newbery-caldecott-winners-last-cuentista-watercress-firekeepers-daughter-unspeakable-tulsa-race-massacre-11643384726.

[18]"Top 10 Most Challenged Books Lists," American Library Association, March 26, 2013, https://www.ala.org/advocacy/bbooks/frequentlychallengedbooks/top10.

[19]Alex Gino, *George* (New York: Scholastic Press, 2015), 47.

[20]Alex Gino, *George* (New York: Scholastic Press, 2015), 47.

[21]Alison Flood, "Alex Gino's Children's Novel George Retitled Melissa 'to Respect Trans Heroine,'" *The Guardian*, November 2, 2021, https://www.theguardian.com/books/2021/nov/02/alex-gino-childrens-novel-george-retitled-melissa-to-respect-trans-heroine.

[22]"Top 10 Most Challenged Books Lists," American Library Association, March 26, 2013, https://www.ala.org/advocacy/bbooks/frequentlychallengedbooks/top10.

[23]"Norwegian Librarians Refuse to Arrange Harry Potter Events Because of J.K. Rowling's Transphobia," Trans Express, accessed May 4, 2022, https://trans-express.lgbt/post/640496884893483008/norwegian-librarians-refuse-to-arrange-harry.

[24]AJ Willingham, "Laura Ingalls Wilder's Name Stripped from Book Award Because of Racist Themes," KSLTV, published June 25, 2018, updated June 7, 2022, https://ksltv.com/397226/laura-ingalls-wilders-name-stripped-book-award-racist-themes/.

[25]NPR, "Classic Books Are Full Of Problems. Why Can't We Put Them Down?," Colorado Public Radio, February 26, 2019, https://www.cpr.org/2019/02/26/classic-books-are-full-of-problems-why-cant-we-put-them-down/.

[26]Mark Pratt, "6 Dr. Suess Books Won't Be Published for Racist Images," AP News, March 2, 2021, https://apnews.com/article/dr-seuss-books-racist-images-d8ed18335c03319d72f443594c174513.

[27]Pratt, "6 Dr. Suess Books Won't Be Published for Racist Images."

[28]Vanessa Riley, "A Jane Austen Museum Addressing Regency-Era Slavery? How Sensible," *Washington Post*, May 12, 2021, https://www.washingtonpost.com/opinions/2021/05/12/jane-austen-museum-regency-slavery/.

[29]John Daniel Davidson, "In An Affront To Its Namesake, The Tolkien Society Goes Woke," *The Federalist*, June 18, 2021, https://thefederalist.com/2021/06/18/in-an-affront-to-its-namesake-the-tolkien-society-goes-woke/.

[30]Davidson, "In An Affront To Its Namesake, The Tolkien Society Goes Woke."

[31]Lauren J. Young, "Educators Weigh In on Summer Reading Lists in SLJ/NCTE Survey," *School Library Journal*, April 14, 2022, https://www.slj.com/story/educators-weigh-in-on-summer-reading-lists-in-slj-ncte-survey.

[32]Young, "Educators Weigh In on Summer Reading Lists in SLJ/NCTE Survey."

[33]Daniel Buck (@MrDanielBuck), "They'll Tell You This is about Diversifying Curriculum. It's Not. It's about Getting Rid of any Commitment to Excellence, Aesthetic Beauty, or Canons," Twitter, April 18, 2022, https://twitter.com/MrDanielBuck/status/1516065506490564611.

[34]Daniel Buck (@MrDanielBuck), "The Irony. The List of Books They Want to Remove Would Make a Brilliant High School Curriculum," Twitter, April 18, 2022, https://twitter.com/MrDanielBuck/status/1516066129436938240.

[35]This and the preceding quotation are from an interview with librarian, January 16, 2022.

[36]This and the preceding quotation are from an interview with Susan, January 19, 2022.

[37]Juniper Fitzgerald, *How Mamas Love Their Babies* (New York: Feminist Press at the City University of New York, 2018).

[38]"Stonewall Book Awards - Children's and Young Adult Award," American Library Association, accessed July 11, 2022, https://www.ala.org/awardsgrants/stonewall-childrens-and-young-adult-award.

[39]Jennifer Vanasco, "New Diverse Children's Books That Actually Reflect The Lives Of NYC Kids," Gothamist, published May 3, 2018, updated May 5, 2018, https://gothamist.com/arts-entertainment/new-diverse-childrens-books-that-actually-reflect-the-lives-of-nyc-kids.

[40]"FCPS Reinstates Two Books, Reaffirming Commitment to Supporting Diversity in Literature," Fairfax County Public Schools, November 23, 2021, https://www.fcps.edu/news/fcps-reinstates-two-books-reaffirming-commitment-supporting-diversity-literature.

[41]Colin Kaepernick, *I Color Myself Different* (New York: Kaepernick Publishing, 2022).

[42]"Castro, Guevara, and Commie Kids Books," *The Tuttle Twins* (blog), June 25, 2021, https://tuttletwins.com/blog/castro-guevara-and-commie-kids-books/.

[43]Joy Pullman, "Scholastic's New Catalog Hawks Books to Saturate Kids with Identity Politics," *The Federalist*, August 21, 2019, https://thefederalist.com/2019/08/21/scholastics-new-school-catalog-hawks-books-to-indoctrinate-kids-with-identity-politics/.

[44]Pullman, "Scholastic's New Catalog Hawks Books to Saturate Kids with Identity Politics."

[45]Interview with librarian, February 18, 2022.

[46]Interview with Kiri Jorgensen, January 11, 2022.

[47]Interview with librarian, January 6, 2022.

[48]Interview with Josh, January 6, 2022.

[49]Interview with Christine, January 6, 2022.

[50]Alexandra Alter, "Y.A. Author Pulls Her Debut After Pre-Publication Accusations of Racism," *The New York Times*, January 31, 2019, https://www.nytimes.com/2019/01/31/books/amelie-wen-zhao-blood-heir-ya-author-pulls-debut-accusations-racism.html.

[51]This and the preceding two quotations are all from an interview with Christine, January 6, 2022.

[52]"I Am Every Good Thing," Kirkus Reviews, June 30, 2020, https://www.kirkusreviews.com/book-reviews/derrick-barnes/i-am-every-good-thing/.

[53]"I Am Every Good Thing."

[54]Abe Greenwald, "Yes, There is a Counter-Revolution," *Commentary*, February 2022, https://www.commentary.org/articles/abe-greenwald/counter-revolution-to-anti-american-revolution/.

[55]Alexandra Alter, "Y.A. Author Pulls Her Debut After Pre-Publication Accusations of Racism," *The New York Times*, January 31, 2019, https://www.nytimes.com/2019/01/31/books/amelie-wen-zhao-blood-heir-ya-author-pulls-debut-accusations-racism.html.

[56]Alter, "Y.A. Author Pulls Her Debut After Pre-Publication Accusations of Racism."

[57]Josephine Bartosch, "Inside the Trans Publishing Purge," *UnHerd*, December 9, 2021, https://unherd.com/2021/12/inside-the-trans-publishing-purge/.

[58]Bartosch, "Inside the Trans Publishing Purge."

[59]Bartosch, "Inside the Trans Publishing Purge."

[60]Bartosch, "Inside the Trans Publishing Purge."

[61]Interview with librarian, January 16, 2022.

[62]Rod Dreher, "'Mommy, What's A Pansexual?,'" *The American Conservative*, February 12, 2021, https://www.theamericanconservative.com/blues-clues-pride-flags/.

[63]Rod Dreher, "What's Happening To America?," *The American Conservative*, June 1, 2021, accessed July 8, 2022, https://www.theamericanconservative.com/america-decline-and-fall-hungary/.

[64]Scottie Andrew, "Nonbinary Characters like 'Gonzo-Rella' Are Lighting up Children's TV and Encouraging Self-Acceptance," CNN, accessed July 8, 2022, https://www.cnn.com/2021/09/25/entertainment/gonzorella-nonbinary-childrens-tv-cec/index.html.

[65]Andrew, "Nonbinary Characters like 'Gonzo-Rella' Are Lighting up Children's TV and Encouraging Self-Acceptance."

[66]"We Created the First-Ever Searchable Database of 259 LGBTQ Characters in Cartoons That Bust the Myth That Kids Can't Handle Inclusion," *Insider*, accessed May 4, 2022, https://www.insider.com/lgbtq-cartoon-characters-kids-database-2021-06?page=see-the-data.

[67]We Created the First-Ever Searchable Database of 259 LGBTQ Characters in Cartoons That Bust the Myth That Kids Can't Handle Inclusion."

[68]Elisha Krauss, "Netflix Slips Transgender Propaganda Into 'Baby-Sitters Club,'" *The Federalist*, July 15, 2020, https://thefederalist.com/2020/07/15/netflix-slips-transgender-propaganda-into-baby-sitters-club-targeted-at-tweens/.

[69]Interview with Neera Deshpande, April 26, 2022.

[70]Douglas Blair, "Cartoons Are the Left's New Weapon to Target Your Kids," *The Daily Signal*, December 22, 2020, https://www.dailysignal.com/2020/12/22/cartoons-are-the-lefts-new-weapon-to-target-your-kids/.

[71]Blair, "Cartoons Are the Left's New Weapon to Target Your Kids."

[72]Aryn Zombolas, "Nickelodeon Equality Commercial 2021," YouTube, May 10, 2021, video, 1:03, https://www.youtube.com/watch?v=EAPEBdSsDGc.

[73]Zombolas, "Nickelodeon Equality Commercial 2021."

[74]Andy P (@andyrogyny), Instagram photo, April 16, 2022, https://www.instagram.com/p/CccFpT7Ojz8/?igshid=MDJmNzVkMjY%3D.

[75]Ben Kew, "Watch—PBS's 'Arthur' Rolls Out Propaganda Video for Kids: 'It's Not Enough to Say, I'm Not Racist,'" *Breitbart*, August 11, 2020, https://www.breitbart.com/entertainment/2020/08/11/pbss-arthur-rolls-out-propaganda-video-for-kids-its-not-enough-to-say-im-not-racist/.

[76]Kew, "Watch—PBS's 'Arthur' Rolls Out Propaganda Video for Kids."

CHAPTER 5

[1]This and the preceding quotation are from an interview with Alexandra, October 11, 2021.

[2]Margot Sanger-Katz, "Your Surgeon Is Probably a Republican, Your Psychiatrist Probably a Democrat," *The New York Times*, October 6, 2016, https://www.nytimes.com/2016/10/07/upshot/your-surgeon-is-probably-a-republican-your-psychiatrist-probably-a-democrat.html.

[3]Brooke Singman, "American Academy of Pediatrics Sides with Teachers Unions, Rips Funding Threats Cited by White House," Fox News, July 10, 2020, https://www.foxnews.com/politics/american-academy-of-pediatrics-sides-with-teachers-unions-rips-funding-threats-after-cited-by-white-house.

[4]Anya Kamenetz, "U.S. Pediatricians Call For In-Person School This Fall," NPR, June 29, 2020, https://www.npr.org/sections/coronavirus-live-updates/2020/06/29/884638999/u-s-pediatricians-call-for-in-person-school-this-fall.

[5]Anya Kamenetz, "Nation's Pediatricians Walk Back Support For In-Person School," NPR, July 10, 2020, sec. The Coronavirus Crisis, https://www.npr.org/sections/coronavirus-live-updates/2020/07/10/889848834/nations-pediatricians-walk-back-support-for-in-person-school.

[6]Kamenetz, "Nation's Pediatricians Walk Back Support For In-Person School."

[7]PoliMath, (@politicalmath), "Here is it: The American Academy of Pediatrics Published a Flyer 'Face Time and Emotional Health' They Unpublished it in the Middle of the Pandemic but Told a @Reuters Fact Checker That it was Just Part of a Site Migration & Would Be Republished it Never Was," Twitter, January 25, 2022, https://twitter.com/politicalmath/status/1486172185983131653.

[8]"Do Masks Delay Speech and Language Development?," HealthyChildren, accessed May 4, 2022, https://www.healthychildren.org/English/health-issues/conditions/COVID-19/Pages/Do-face-masks-interfere-with-language-development.aspx.

[9]"Should Children Wear a Mask?," UNICEF, September 10, 2020, https://www.unicef.org/northmacedonia/stories/should-children-wear-mask.

[10]"Face Masks and Other Prevention Strategies," American Academy of Pediatrics, accessed July 8, 2022, http://www.aap.org/en/pages/2019-novel-coronavirus-covid-19-infections/clinical-guidance/face-masks-and-other-prevention-strategies/.

[11]This and the preceding two quotations are all from an interview with Kristen Walsh, October 4, 2021.

[12]Bethany Mandel, "Perspective: Don't Blame Governors for Treating Kids like Criminals. It's the CDC," *Deseret News*, September 20, 2021, https://www.deseret.com/2021/9/19/22683342/dont-blame-governors-for-treating-kids-like-criminals-its-the-cdc-mask-mandate-new-york-daycare.

[13]"FSMB: Spreading COVID-19 Vaccine Misinformation May Put Medical License at Risk," Federation of State Medical Boards, July 29, 2021, https://www.fsmb.org/advocacy/news-releases/fsmb-spreading-covid-19-vaccine-misinformation-may-put-medical-license-at-risk/.

[14]Interview with Alexandra, October 11, 2021.

[15]"About – FAIR," Foundation Against Intolerance and Racism, accessed October 25, 2021, https://www.fairforall.org/about/.

[16]Foundation Against Intolerance and Racism, "Pediatricians' Professional Organization Commends Segregated Education," YouTube, September 1, 2021, video, 4:35, https://www.youtube.com/watch?v=cBJ1isHbx3c.

[17]Foundation Against Intolerance and Racism, "Pediatricians' Professional Organization Commends Segregated Education."

[18]"Fighting Racism to Advance Child Health Equity - AAP," American Academy of Pediatrics, accessed July 10, 2022, https://shop.aap.org/fighting-racism-to-advance-child-health-equity/.

[19]Interview with Erica Li, October 11, 2021.

[20]"Fighting Racism to Advance Child Health Equity – AAP."

[21]"Fighting Racism to Advance Child Health Equity – AAP."

[22]"AAP Equity Agenda," American Academy of Pediatrics, accessed May 4, 2022, http://www.aap.org/en/about-the-aap/american-academy-of-pediatrics-equity-and-inclusion-efforts/aap-equity-agenda/.

[23]"AAP Equity Agenda."

[24]This and the preceding quotation are from an interview with Erica Li, October 11, 2021.

[25]"PAS 2021 Virtual Event," accessed May 4, 2022, https://virtual2021.pas-meeting.org/2021/PAS/fs-Popup.asp?efp=WldIRlFRV1gxNDAzOA&PresentationID=857450&rnd=0.3820107&mode=sessionInfo.

[26]Erica Kaye (@EricaKayeMD), "More than 70% of Pediatricians are Women. More than One-Third of Neonatologists are Women. Yet @AmerAcadPeds Can't Find a Single Woman to Speak on or Moderate this National Panel? #MedTwitter #WomenInMedicine #AcademicTwitter 1/," Twitter, May 14, 2021, https://twitter.com/ericakayemd/status/1393300270650646533

[27]Erica Kaye (@EricaKayMD), "@AmerAcadPeds Nor a Single Black Physician, to Speak on a Topic that Disproportionately Affects Black Women? WTAF are These Optics? #MedTwitter #maternalhealth #BlackLivesMatter 2/," Twitter, May 14, 2021, https://twitter.com/EricaKayeMD/status/1393300272223510529.

[28]PASMeeting (@PASMeeting), "Thank you, Erica. PAS Acknowledges and Apologizes for this Error. This Session has been Canceled. It Does Not Align with our Values & Commitment to No Manels and to a Diverse and Inclusive Program. We Must - and Will - do Better," Twitter, May 15, 2021, https://mobile.twitter.com/PASMeeting/status/1393613899367395331.

[29]Rhea Liang (@LiangRhea), "Advocacy Works. The Meeting has been Cancelled. I Think This is the Big Change in the Last Couple of Years- that Orgs Understand the Social Signalling a #Manel Sends. It's a Shame We have to Keep Calling it Out Though," Twitter, May 15, 2021, https://twitter.com/LiangRhea /status/1393732299921920001.

[30]"Fighting Premature Birth: The Prematurity Campaign," March of Dimes, accessed July 10, 2022, https:// www.marchofdimes.org/mission/prematurity-campaign.aspx.

[31]This and the preceding quotations are from an interview with Fred, October 11, 2021.

[32]Colin P. Hawkes and Terri H. Lipman, "Racial Disparities in Pediatric Type 1 Diabetes: Yet Another Consequence of Structural Racism." Pediatrics 148, no. 2 (August 2021), https://doi.org/10.1542/peds.2021 -050333.

[33]Asheley Cockrell Skinner et al., "Implicit Weight Bias in Children Age 9 to 11 Years," Pediatrics 140, no.1 (July 2017), doi: 10.1542/peds.2016-3936.

[34]This and the preceding quotation are from an interview with Fred, October 11, 2021.

[35]Richard Bosshardt, "No Longer a Fellow – Why I am Leaving the American College of Surgeons," Musings on Medicine and Life (blog), WordPress, April 19, 2021, https://rtbosshardt.com/2021/04/19/no-longer-a -fellow-why-i-am-leaving-the-american-college-of-surgeons/2/.

[36]Bosshardt, "No Longer a Fellow – Why I am Leaving the American College of Surgeons."

[37]"The AMA's Strategic Plan to Embed Racial Justice and Advance Health Equity," American Medical Association, accessed July 8, 2022, https://www.ama-assn.org/about/leadership/ama-s-strategic-plan- embed-racial-justice-and-advance-health-equity.

[38]"New APA Poll Shows Sustained Anxiety Among Americans; More than Half of Parents are Concerned about the Mental Well-Being of their Children," American Psychiatric Association, May 2, 2021, https:// www.psychiatry.org/newsroom/news-releases/new-apa-poll-shows-sustained-anxiety-among-amer- icans-more-than-half-of-parents-are-concerned-about-the-mental-well-being-of-their-children #:~:text=More%20than%20half%20of%20adults,and%20major%20problems%20for%2019%25.

[39]"New APA Poll Shows Sustained Anxiety Among Americans; More than Half of Parents are Concerned about the Mental Well-Being of their Children."

[40]"U.S. Pediatricians, Psychiatrists Declare 'Emergency' in Child Mental Health," U.S. News & World Report, October 19, 2021, https://www.usnews.com/news/health-news/articles/2021-10-19/us-pediatricians- psychiatrists-declare-emergency-in-child-mental-health.

[41]"AAP-AACAP-CHA Declaration of a National Emergency in Child and Adolescent Mental Health," American Academy of Pediatrics, October 19, 2021, https://www.aap.org/en/advocacy/child-and-ado- lescent-healthy-mental-development/aap-aacap-cha-declaration-of-a-national-emergency-in-child- and-adolescent-mental-health/.

[42]"AAP-AACAP-CHA Declaration of a National Emergency in Child and Adolescent Mental Health."

[43]"APA Apologizes for Longstanding Contributions to Systemic Racism," American Psychological Association, October 29, 2021, https://www.apa.org/news/press/releases/2021/10/apology-systemic-racism.

[44]"APA Apologizes for Longstanding Contributions to Systemic Racism."

[45]"APA GUIDELINES for Psychological Practice with Boys and Men," American Psychological Association, August 2018, https://www.apa.org/about/policy/boys-men-practice-guidelines.pdf.

[46]Megan Trimble, "'Traditional Masculinity' Is Harmful to Boys, Men," U.S. News & World Report, January 9, 2019.

[47]Trimble, "'Traditional Masculinity' Is Harmful to Boys, Men."

[48]Interview with Alice, October 8, 2021.

[49]Harry Kazenoff, "The American Psychological Association has Lost Its Mind," Capital Research Center, March 8, 2019, https://capitalresearch.org/article/the-american-psychological-association-has-lost -its-mind/.

[50]Kazenoff, "The American Psychological Association has Lost Its Mind."

[51]"Ethical Principles of Psychologists and Code of Conduct," American Psychological Association, March 2017, https://www.apa.org/ethics/code.

[52]Interview with mental health professional, October 20, 2021.

[53]This and the preceding quotation are from an interview with Kyle, October 20, 2021.

[54]Interview with Sam, October 20, 2021.

[55]Interview with Alice, October 8, 2021.

[56]Interview with spouse of medical school applicant, October 25, 2021.

[57]"University of Minnesota Medical School Secondary Questions," Prospective Doctor, accessed August 12, 2022, accessed November 7, 2021, https://www.prospectivedoctor.com/university-of-minnesota-medical-school-secondary/.

[58]"Loyola University Chicago Stritch School of Medicine Secondary Questions," Prospective Doctor, accessed November 7, 2021, https://www.prospectivedoctor.com/loyola-university-chicago-stritch-school-of-medicine-secondary/.

[59]"University of Kentucky College of Medicine Secondary Questions," Prospective Doctor, accessed November 7, 2021, https://www.prospectivedoctor.com/university-of-kentucky-college-of-medicine-secondary/.

[60]Interview with Jonathan, October 24, 2021.

[61]"HMS Adds New Significant Supporting Activity to Promotion Criteria: Diversity, Equity, and Inclusion (DEI)," *Perspectives* 21, no. 4 (2021), https://www.childrenshospital.org/sites/default/files/2022-04/perspectives-2021-september.pdf.

[62]This and the preceding quotation are from an interview with Jonathan, October 24, 2021.

[63]Angira Patel, "It's Time for More Physicians to Embrace Advocacy," *Scientific American*, March 13, 2018, https://blogs.scientificamerican.com/observations/its-time-for-more-physicians-to-embrace-advocacy/.

[64]Krista Conger, "Pay it Forward: Including Social Justice in Curriculum," *Stanford Medicine*, May 10, 2021, http://stanmed.stanford.edu/2021issue1/medical-school-racial-justice-curriculum.html.

[65]Conger, "Pay it Forward: Including Social Justice in Curriculum."

[66]"DRAFT The Essentials: Core Competencies for Professional Nursing Education," American Association of Colleges of Nursing, November 5, 2020, https://www.aacnnursing.org/portals/42/downloads/essentials/essentials-draft-document.pdf.

[67]"Faculty Advisors & State Consultants," National Student Nurses' Association, accessed November 7, 2021, https://www.nsna.org/faculty.html.

[68]Robert I. Field, "Independent Doctors' Offices are Disappearing as More Physicians Work for Hospitals and Companies," *The Philadelphia Inquirer*, August 7, 2021, https://www.inquirer.com/business/doctors-practice-health-corporate-20210807.html.

[69]Naomi Schaefer Riley, *No Way to Treat a Child: How the Foster Care System, Family Courts, and Racial Activists Are Wrecking Young Lives* (New York: Bombardier Books, 2021).

[70]Schaefer Riley, *No Way to Treat a Child*, 15.

[71]Brian Kennedy, Alec Tyson, and Cary Funk, "Americans' Trust in Scientists, Other Groups Declines," Pew Research Center, February 15, 2022, https://www.pewresearch.org/science/2022/02/15/americans-trust-in-scientists-other-groups-declines/.

[72]Benjamin Mueller and Jan Hoffman, "Routine Childhood Vaccinations in the U.S. Slipped During the Pandemic," *The New York Times*, April 21, 2022, https://www.nytimes.com/2022/04/21/health/pandemic-childhood-vaccines.html.

[73]Mueller and Hoffman, "Routine Childhood Vaccinations in the U.S. Slipped During the Pandemic."

CHAPTER 6

[1]Lisa Gershkoff-Stowe et al., "Categorization and Its Developmental Relation to Early Language," *Child Development* 68, no. 5 (October 1997): 843-859, https://doi.org/10.2307/1132037.

[2]Abigail Shrier, "When Your Daughter Defies Biology," *Wall Street Journal*, January 6, 2019, https://www.wsj.com/articles/when-your-daughter-defies-biology-11546804848.

[3]Abigail Shrier, back cover of *Irreversible Damage: The Transgender Craze Seducing Our Daughters* (Washington, DC: Regnery Publishing, 2020).

[4]Jacqueline Ruttimann, "BLOCKING PUBERTY in TRANSGENDER YOUTH," Endocrine News, January 2013, https://endocrinenews.endocrine.org/blocking-puberty-in-transgender-youth/.

[5]Abigail Shrier, "The Books Are Already Burning," *Common Sense* (blog), Substack Newsletter, June 21, 2021, https://bariweiss.substack.com/p/the-books-are-already-burning.

[6]Shrier, "The Books Are Already Burning."

[7]"Quick Guide to Gender Dysphoria," Child Mind Institute, accessed July 10, 2022, https://childmind.org/guide/gender-dysphoria-quick-guide/.

[8]Helen Joyce, *Trans: When Ideology Meets Reality* (London: Oneworld, 2021), 1.

[9]Jane Robbins, "Against the 'Feminine Essence,'" *Public Discourse*, October 23, 2019, https://www.thepublicdiscourse.com/2019/10/57293/.

[10]Robbins, "Against the 'Feminine Essence.'"

[11]William Malone, "Time to Hit Pause on 'Pausing' Puberty in Gender-Dysphoric Youth," Medscape, September 17, 2021, https://www.medscape.com/viewarticle/958742.

[12]"Our Aim is to Promote Safe, Compassionate, Ethical and Evidence-Informed Healthcare for Children, Adolescents, and Young Adults with Gender Dysphoria," Society for Evidence-Based Gender Medicine, accessed July 10, 2022, https://segm.org/home.

[13]"Our Aim is to Promote Safe, Compassionate, Ethical and Evidence-Informed Healthcare for Children, Adolescents, and Young Adults with Gender Dysphoria."

[14]"Our Aim is to Promote Safe, Compassionate, Ethical and Evidence-Informed Healthcare for Children, Adolescents, and Young Adults with Gender Dysphoria."

[15]Interview with Alexandra, October 11, 2021.

[16]William Malone, "Time to Hit Pause on 'Pausing' Puberty in Gender-Dysphoric Youth," Medscape, September 17, 2021, http://www.medscape.com/viewarticle/958742.

[17]Christina Jewett, "Drug Used to Halt Puberty in Children May Cause Lasting Health Problems," STAT, February 2, 2017, https://www.statnews.com/2017/02/02/lupron-puberty-children-health-problems/.

[18]The World Professional Association for Transgender Health, *Standards of Care for the Health of Transsexual, Transgender, and Gender Nonconforming People*, vol. 7, (WPATH, 2021), https://www.wpath.org/media/cms/Documents/SOC%20v7/SOC%20V7_English.pdf.

[19]Interview with Alexandra, October 11, 2021.

[20]"Gender Affirming Hormone Therapy," accessed July 10, 2022, https://www.plannedparenthood.org/planned-parenthood-mar-monte/patient-resources/gender-affirming-care.

[21]Maureen Kelly, *Providing Transgender and Non-Binary Care at Planned Parenthood: A Best Practices Guide and Start-Up Action Kit* (Southern Finger Lakes: Planned Parenthood, 2018), https://www.plannedparenthood.org/uploads/filer_public/00/0b/000b0b36-c257-446d-a63b-453efe9298c1/providing-transgender-nonbinary-care-book-2018.pdf.

[22]Kelly, *Providing Transgender and Non-Binary Care at Planned Parenthood.*

[23]Becky McCall, "WPATH Draft on Gender Dysphoria 'Skewed and Misses Urgent Issues,'" Medscape, December 10, 2021, http://www.medscape.com/viewarticle/964604.

[24]Laura Edwards-Leeper and Erica Anderson, "The Mental Health Establishment Is Failing Trans Kids," *The Washington Post*, November 24, 2021, https://www.washingtonpost.com/outlook/2021/11/24/trans-kids-therapy-psychologist/.

[25]Abigail Shrier, "Top Trans Doctors Blow the Whistle on 'Sloppy' Care," *Common Sense* (blog), Substack Newsletter, October 4, 2021, https://www.commonsense.news/p/top-trans-doctors-blow-the-whistle.

[26]Edwards-Leeper and Anderson, "The Mental Health Establishment Is Failing Trans Kids."

[27]Edwards-Leeper and Anderson, "The Mental Health Establishment Is Failing Trans Kids."

[28]"The AAP Silences the Debate on How to Best Care for Gender-Diverse Kids," SEGM, August 9, 2021, https://segm.org/AAP_silences_debate_on_gender_diverse_youth_treatments.

[29]"The AAP Silences the Debate on How to Best Care for Gender-Diverse Kids."

[30]Lisa Nainggolan, "AAP 'Silencing Debate' on Gender Dysphoria, Says Doctor Group," Medscape, August 16, 2021, http://www.medscape.com/viewarticle/956650.

[31]"The AAP Silences the Debate on How to Best Care for Gender-Diverse Kids."

[32]"The AAP Silences the Debate on How to Best Care for Gender-Diverse Kids."

[33]The White House, "Press Briefing by Press Secretary Jen Psaki, April 7, 2022," press release, April 7, 2022, https://www.whitehouse.gov/briefing-room/press-briefings/2022/04/07/press-briefing-by-press-secretary-jen-psaki-april-7-2022/.

[34]The United Stated Department of Justice, "Justice Department Reinforces Federal Nondiscrimination Obligations in Letter to State Officials Regarding Transgender Youth," press release, March 31, 2022, https://www.justice.gov/opa/pr/justice-department-reinforces-federal-nondiscrimination-obligations-letter-state-officials.

[35]Steven Nelson, "Biden Says Trans People 'Made in Image of God,' Parents Must 'Affirm' Identity," *New York Post*, March 31, 2022, https://nypost.com/2022/03/31/biden-says-trans-people-made-in-image-of-god-during-video/.

[36]Suzy Weiss, "The Testosterone Hangover," *Common Sense* (blog), Substack Newsletter, April 19, 2022, https://www.commonsense.news/p/the-testosterone-hangover.

[37]Weiss, "The Testosterone Hangover."

[38]Helen Joyce, *Trans: When Ideology Meets Reality* (London: Oneworld, 2021), 79.

[39]Joyce, *Trans: When Ideology Meets Reality*, 79.

[40]Joyce, *Trans: When Ideology Meets Reality*, 81.

[41]This and the preceding two quotations are all from an interview with Dr. Jeffrey, December 24, 2021.

[42]*LCS Lesbian, Gay, Bisexual, Transgender, Gender Nonconforming and Questioning Guide*, Leon County School, accessed January 2, 2022, https://www.politico.com/f/?id=0000017f-d30b-d9e9-a57f-d38b05900000.

[43]Julie Montanaro, "Parents Sue Leon County Schools over Its LGBTQ Policies," WCTV, November 3, 2021, https://www.wctv.tv/2021/11/03/parents-sue-leon-county-schools-over-its-lgbtq-policies/.

[44]Steve Stewart, "Tallahassee Mom: 'Gender ideology Almost Ruined My Family,'" Tallahassee Reports, December 2, 2021, https://tallahasseereports.com/2021/12/02/tallahassee-mom-gender-ideology-almost-destroyed-my-family/.

[45]Jeremiah Poff, "Florida Parents Sue after School Clandestinely Orchestrated Daughter's Gender Transition," *Washington Examiner*, November 12, 2021, https://www.washingtonexaminer.com/restoring-america/community-family/florida-parents-sue-after-school-clandestinely-orchestrated-daughters-gender-transition.

[46]This and the preceding quotation are from an interview with January Littlejohn, January 2, 2022.

[47]This and the preceding quotation are from Joyce, *Trans: When Ideology Meets Reality* (London: Oneworld, 2021), 120.

[48]This and the preceding quotation are from an interview with Kay, December 9, 2022.

[49]This and the preceding four quotations are all from Joyce, *Trans: When Ideology Meets Reality* (London: Oneworld, 2021), 103.

[50]Interview with Dr. Jeffrey, December 24, 2021.

[51]This and the preceding quotation are from an interview with Arielle Scarcella, December 6, 2021.

[52]Joyce, *Trans: When Ideology Meets Reality* (London: Oneworld, 2021), 113.

[53]Sanchez Manning, "Breastfeeding Charity Sparks Outrage by Allowing Men Who Identify as Female to Attend Meetings for Mothers Struggling to Feed their Babies," *Daily Mail*, November 28, 2020, https://www.dailymail.co.uk/news/article-8997405/Breastfeeding-charity-sparks-outrage-allowing-men-identify-female-attend-meetings.html.

[54]Luke Rosiak, "Loudoun County Schools Tried to Conceal Sexual Assault Against Daughter in Bathroom, Father Says," *Daily Wire*, October 11, 2021, https://www.dailywire.com/news/loudoun-county-schools-tried-to-conceal-sexual-assault-against-daughter-in-bathroom-father-says.

[55]Bruce Leshan, "Loudoun Teen Pleads 'No Contest' to High School Sexual Battery that Ignited Political Firestorm," WUSA, November 15, 2021, https://www.wusa9.com/article/features/producers-picks/loudoun-teen-admits-to-sexual-touching-not-violent-rape-at-broad-run-high-school/65-3d2cc68d-d9fe-4b36-9b13-53cb08db6319.

[56]Ryan T. Anderson, "Sex Reassignment Doesn't Work. Here is the Evidence," The Heritage Foundation, March 9, 2018, https://www.heritage.org/gender/commentary/sex-reassignment-doesnt-work-here-the-evidence.

[57]Melissa Block, "Americans are Deeply Divided on Transgender Rights, a Poll Shows," NPR, June 29, 2022, https://www.npr.org/2022/06/29/1107484965/transgender-athletes-trans-rights-gender-transition-poll.

[58]CS/CS/HB 1557: Parental Rights in Education, 2022-22 L.O.F. (2022), https://www.flsenate.gov/Session/Bill/2022/1557/?Tab=Citations.

[59]"'Don't Say Gay' Is Popular? You Don't Say: One poll shows backing from suburbs, parents and . . . Democrats," *Wall Street Journal*, April 1, 2022, https://www.wsj.com/articles/dont-say-gay-is-popular-you-dont-say-ron-desantis-florida-law-elementary-school-11648849131.

[60]Corey DeAngelis, "Parents Are Schooling Democrats," *Washington Examiner*, January 27, 2022, https://www.washingtonexaminer.com/restoring-america/community-family/parents-are-schooling-democrats.

CHAPTER 7

[1]Marie Doezema, "France, Where Age of Consent Is Up for Debate," *The Atlantic*, March 10, 2018, https://www.theatlantic.com/international/archive/2018/03/frances-existential-crisis-over-sexual-harassment-laws/550700/.

[2]Rachel Aviv, "The German Experiment That Placed Foster Children with Pedophiles," *The New Yorker*, July 19, 2021, https://www.newyorker.com/magazine/2021/07/26/the-german-experiment-that-placed-foster-children-with-pedophiles.

[3]Aviv, "The German Experiment That Placed Foster Children with Pedophiles."

[4]Jennifer Oriel, "Protect Kids from Marxist Sexualisation Programs," *The Weekend Australian*, April 18, 2016, https://www.theaustralian.com.au/opinion/protect-kids-from-marxist-sexualisation-programs/news-story/2d4f796c2c53c26c22320df709719f7a.

[5]Sarah Schmidt, "'Blasphemy' from the Book they Tried to Stop: A 9-Year Old Trapped in Sex-Therapy Hell," *National Post*, April 20, 2002, https://sites.ualberta.ca/~fchriste/LawsuitDocA/Article%20from%20Levine.htm.

[6]Judith Levine, *Harmful to Minors: The Perils of Protecting Children from Sex* (Minneapolis: University of Minnesota Press, 2002).

[7]Bumpus, "What the Smart Parents Know," review of *Harmful to Minors: The Perils of Protecting Children from Sex*, Amazon, October 8, 2016, https://www.amazon.com/Harmful-Minors-Perils-Protecting-Children/dp/1560255161.

[8]Bumpus, "What the Smart Parents Know Parents."

[9]Christopher Rufo, "The War on Innocence: A Kentucky Camp Teaches 'Sex Liberation,' 'BDSM,' and 'Self-Pleasure' to Minors," *City Journal*, March 16, 2022, https://www.city-journal.org/kentucky-summer-camp-teaches-sex-liberation.

[10]Rufo, "The War on Innocence: A Kentucky Camp Teaches 'Sex Liberation,' 'BDSM,' and 'Self-Pleasure' to Minors."

[11]Rufo, "The War on Innocence: A Kentucky Camp Teaches 'Sex Liberation,' 'BDSM,' and 'Self-Pleasure' to Minors."

[12]Grooming: Know the Warning Signs," Rape, Abuse, & Incest National Network. July 10, 2020, https://www.rainn.org/news/grooming-know-warning-signs.

[13]"Grooming: Know the Warning Signs."

[14]Buck Angel® Transsexual (@BuckAngel), "Number One Rule! Never Teach Children to Keep Secrets from Parents!! This is Groomer Tactics You F*cking Morons," Twitter, November 15, 2021, https://twitter.com/BuckAngel/status/1460385288249757699.

[15]Roberto Wakerell-Cruz, "Ottawa-Carleton Schoolboard Will Allow Students to Change Names without Parents' Knowledge," *The Post Millennial*, November 15, 2021, https://thepostmillennial.com/ottawa-carleton-schoolboard-change-names-without-parents-knowledge.

[16]Abigail Shrier, "How Activist Teachers Recruit Kids," *The Truth Fairy* (blog), Substack Newsletter, November 18, 2021, https://abigailshrier.substack.com/p/how-activist-teachers-recruit-kids.

[17]Shrier, "How Activist Teachers Recruit Kids."

[18]Brad Jones, "Parent Says Daughter Was 'Coached' on LGBTQ Identity at California School," *The Epoch Times*, December 14, 2021, https://www.theepochtimes.com/mkt_app/parent-says-daughter-was-coached-on-lgbtq-identity-at-california-school_4156865.html.

[19]Jones, "Parent Says Daughter Was 'Coached' on LGBTQ Identity at California School."

[20]Jonathon Van Maren, "Furious Mother Tears into School Board after Teacher Convinces Her Daughter She's Transgender," *The Bridgehead*, December 20, 2021, https://thebridgehead.ca/2021/12/20/furious-mother-tears-into-school-board-after-teacher-convinces-her-daughter-shes-transgender/.

[21]Van Maren, "Furious Mother Tears into School Board after Teacher Convinces Her Daughter She's Transgender."

[22]Brad Jones, "Parent Says Daughter Was 'Coached' on LGBTQ Identity at California School," *The Epoch Times*, December 14, 2021, https://www.theepochtimes.com/mkt_app/parent-says-daughter-was-coached-on-lgbtq-identity-at-california-school_4156865.html.

[23]This and the preceding two quotations are all from an interview with Libs of TikTok Twitter account owner, November 14, 2021.

[24]Marianne Garvey, "TikTok Surpasses YouTube in Viewing Time per User," CNN, September 7, 2021, https://www.cnn.com/2021/09/07/entertainment/tiktok-youtube/index.html.

[25]Salvador Rodriguez, "TikTok Usage Surpassed Instagram This Year among Kids Aged 12 to 17, Forrester Survey Says," CNBC, November 18, 2021, https://www.cnbc.com/2021/11/18/tiktok-usage-topped-instagram-in-2021-among-kids-12-to-17-forrester-.html.

[26]Rob Barry et al., "How TikTok Serves Up Sex and Drug Videos to Minors," *Wall Street Journal*, September 8, 2021, https://www.wsj.com/articles/tiktok-algorithm-sex-drugs-minors-11631052944.

[27]Barry et al., "How TikTok Serves Up Sex and Drug Videos to Minors."

[28]This and the preceding quotation are from an interview with Brian Willoughby, November 15, 2021.

[29]Office of the Texas Governor Greg Abbott, "Governor Abbott Directs TEA to Investigate Criminal Activity Involving Pornography In Texas Public Schools," press release, November 10, 2021, https://gov.texas.gov/news/post/governor-abbott-directs-tea-to-investigate-criminal-activity-involving-pornography-in-texas-public-schools.

[30]Olly MacNamee, "Previewing Oni Press's 'Gender Queer' Graphic Novel," Comicon, June 24, 2022, https://www.comicon.com/2022/06/24/previewing-oni-presss-gender-queer-graphic-novel/.

[31]Sharon T. Reviewier, "Member Reviews," NetGalley, accessed July 10, 2022, https://www.netgalley.com/book/255289/reviews?=r.updated&direction=desc&page=2.

[32]Erika Sanzi, "School Officials Must Pull Porn from Library Shelves," The Valley Breeze, accessed July 10, 2022, https://www.valleybreeze.com/opinion/school-officials-must-pull-porn-from-library-shelves/article_5c120a9c-365d-11ec-b199-f7ad31594170.html.

[33]Sanzi, "School Officials Must Pull Porn from Library Shelves."

[34]Noah Berlatsky, "'That Stigma Itself Can Lead to Harm,' An Interview with Researcher and Author Allyn Walker," Prostasia Foundation, November 7, 2021, https://prostasia.org/blog/that-stigma-itself-can-lead-to-harm-an-interview-with-researcher-and-author-allyn-walker/.

[35]"Protecting Children by Upholding the Rights and Freedoms of All," Prostasia, accessed November 21, 2021, https://prostasia.org/.

[36]Jesse Singal and Katie Herzog, "Episode 80: Because God Hates Us Or Is Dead, Here's A Whole Episode About Noah Berlatsky And Pedophilia," September 2, 2021, in Blocked and Reported, produced by Permabanned Media LLC, podcast, MP3 audio, 1:13:38, https://www.blockedandreported.org/p/because-god-hates-us-or-is-dead-heres-90c.

[37]Anna Slatz, "Prostasia's Goal Is to Normalize Pedophilia," 4W - Feminist News, August 29, 2021, https://4w.pub/prostasia-normalize-pedophilia/.

[38]"Our Campaigns against Doll Bans," Prostasia Foundation, accessed July 10, 2022, https://prostasia.org/sex-doll-laws/.

[39]Singal and Herzog, "Episode 80."

[40]Singal and Herzog, "Episode 80."

[41]James Lindsay (@ConceptualJames), "The Most Obvious Way Wokeness Goes after the Innocence of Children Is in the Queer Variant of Trans Activism, Especially by Having Trans Strippers Perform for Children in Schools, for Example. Why Would They Do This?" Twitter, July 9, 2022, https://twitter.com/conceptualjames/status/1281416775498969088.

[42]Lindsay, "The Most Obvious Way Wokeness Goes after the Innocence of Children."

[43]Lindsay, "The Most Obvious Way Wokeness Goes after the Innocence of Children."

[44]James Lindsay, "Groomer Schools 1: The Long Cultural Marxist History of Sex Education," November 19, 2021, in New Discourses, podcast, MP3 audio, 1:17:35, https://newdiscourses.com/2021/11/groomer-schools-1-long-cultural-marxist-history-sex-education/.

[45]"Understanding Gender Identity and Gender Expression," Geneseo, accessed July 10, 2022, https://www.geneseo.edu/lgbtq/gender-identity.

[46]Austin, Texas, parent group, letter shared with the author, May 2021.

[47]Houston Keene, "Judge Who Headed 'Drag Queen Story Hour' Sponsor Arrested on Child Porn Charges," Fox News, March 18, 2021, https://www.foxnews.com/politics/milwaukee-brett-blomme-arrested-drag-queen-story-hour-sponsor.

[48]"Drag Queen Storytime Reader Once Charged with Child Sex Assault," ABC13 Houston, March 16, 2019, https://abc13.com/houston-public-library-drag-queen-story-time-albert-garza-reader-charged-with-child-sex-assault/5197176/.

[49]Jonathon Van Maren, "Drag Performer Flashes Children at Drag Queen Storytime," The Bridgehead, October 31, 2019, https://thebridgehead.ca/2019/10/31/drag-performer-flashes-children-at-drag-queen-storytime/.

[50]Van Maren, "Drag Performer Flashes Children at Drag Queen Storytime."

CHAPTER 8

[1]"Florida Student Emma Gonzalez to Lawmakers and Gun Advocates: 'We Call BS,'" CNN, February 17, 2018, https://www.cnn.com/2018/02/17/us/florida-student-emma-gonzalez-speech/index.html.

[2]Brianna Sacks, "The FBI Was Warned about a School Shooting Threat from a YouTube User Named Nikolas Cruz in September," BuzzFeed News, February 15, 2018, https://www.buzzfeednews.com

/article/briannasacks/the-fbi-was-warned-about-a-school-shooting-threat-from.

[3]Chelsea Bailey, "Three Sheriff's Deputies Remained Outside During Parkland Shooting," NBC News, February 24, 2018, https://www.nbcnews.com/news/us-news/three-sheriff-s-deputies-remained-outside-school-during-parkland-shooting-n850946.

[4]Emanuella Grinberg and Steve Almasy, "Students at Town Hall to Washington, NRA: Guns are the Problem, Do Something," CNN, February 22, 2018, https://www.cnn.com/2018/02/21/politics/cnn -town-hall-florida-shooting/index.html.

[5]Caroline Glenn, "Supporters, Critics of Arming Schools with Guns Speak Up at Town Hall," Florida Today, April 25, 2018, https://www.floridatoday.com/story/news/2018/04/25/community-split-town -hall-discuss-arming-brevard-school-staff/542154002/.

[6]Scott Powers, "CNN Parkland Town Hall Crowd Expresses Powerful Gun-Control Message," Florida Politics, February 22, 2018, https://floridapolitics.com/archives/257071-cnn-parkland-town-hall -crowd-expresses-powerful-gun-control-message/.

[7]Powers, "CNN Parkland Town Hall Crowd Expresses Powerful Gun-Control Message."

[8]Interview with Dana Loesch, February 16, 2022.

[9]"Transcript: Stoneman Students' Questions to Lawmakers and the NRA at the CNN Town Hall," CNN, February 22, 2018, https://www.cnn.com/2018/02/22/politics/cnn-town-hall-full-video-transcript /index.html.

[10]"Transcript: Stoneman Students' Questions to Lawmakers and the NRA at the CNN Town Hall."

[11]CNN, "Survivor to Rubio: Will You Reject NRA Money?," YouTube, February 21, 2018, video, 4:49, https://www.youtube.com/watch?v=Lo52BObqCds.

[12]Evan Osnos, "CNN's Town Hall on Guns and the Unmaking of Marco Rubio," The New Yorker, February 22, 2018, https://www.newyorker.com/news/news-desk/cnns-town-hall-on-guns-and-the-unmaking -of-marco-rubio.

[13]Powers, "CNN Parkland Town Hall Crowd Expresses Powerful Gun-Control Message."

[14]Powers, "CNN Parkland Town Hall Crowd Expresses Powerful Gun-Control Message."

[15]Interview with Dana Loesch, February 17, 2022.

[16]Barack Obama, "Cameron Kasky, Jaclyn Corin, David Hogg, Emma González and Alex Wind," Time, accessed May 4, 2022, https://time.com/collection/most-influential-people-2018/5217568/parkland -students/.

[17]Obama, "Cameron Kasky, Jaclyn Corin, David Hogg, Emma González and Alex Wind."

[18]Kyle Kashuv, "KASHUV: We Need To Stop School Shootings And Here's How," Daily Wire, June 7, 2018, https://www.dailywire.com/news/kashuv-we-need-stop-school-shootings-and-heres-how-kyle-kashuv.

[19]Kashuv, "KASHUV: We Need To Stop School Shootings And Here's How."

[20]This and the preceding quotation are from an interview with Kyle Kashuv, February 17, 2022.

[21]Laurie Mansfield Reiter, "At #PS321 in #Brooklyn, Students Tie Orange Ribbons on the School Fence to Spell out 'NO PLACE FOR HATE.' #NationalWalkoutDay," Twitter, March 14, 2018, https://twitter.com /lauriemansfield/status/973927981721833474.

[22]Susannah Cullinane, "Marches, Walkouts and Sit-Ins: Gun Control Battle Heads to the Street," CNN, February 19, 2018, https://www.cnn.com/2018/02/19/us/florida-parkland-shooting-marches/index .html.

[23]Simon Hattenstone, "The Transformation of Greta Thunberg," The Guardian, September 25, 2021, https://www.theguardian.com/environment/ng-interactive/2021/sep/25/greta-thunberg-i-really-see -the-value-of-friendship-apart-from-the-climate-almost-nothing-else-matters.

[24]"Greta Thunberg Ted Talk Transcript: School Strike For Climate," Rev, accessed July 8, 2022, https:// www.rev.com/blog/transcripts/greta-thunberg-ted-talk-transcript-school-strike-for-climate.

[25]"Greta Thunberg Ted Talk Transcript: School Strike For Climate."

[26]Hattenstone, "The Transformation of Greta Thunberg."

[27]Brent Lindeque, "Greta Thunberg: School Strike for Climate and to Save the World!," Good Things Guy, May 5, 2019, https://www.goodthingsguy.com/opinion/greta-thunberg/.

[28]Hattenstone, "The Transformation of Greta Thunberg."

[29]Hattenstone, "The Transformation of Greta Thunberg."

[30]PBS NewsHour, "WATCH: Greta Thunberg's Full Speech to World Leaders at UN Climate Action Summit," YouTube, September 23, 2019, video, 5:19, https://www.youtube.com/watch?v=KAJsdgTPJpU.

[31] Oliver Milman, "Greta Thunberg Stares down Trump as Two Cross Paths at UN," *The Guardian*, September 23, 2019, sec. Environment, https://www.theguardian.com/environment/2019/sep/23/greta-thunberg-trump-stare-video-moment-un-summit.

[32] Eliza Barclay and Brian Resnick, "How Big Was the Global Climate Strike? 4 Million People, Activists Estimate," *Vox*, updated September 22, 2019, https://www.vox.com/energy-and-environment/2019/9/20/20876143/climate-strike-2019-september-20-crowd-estimate.

[33] Scott Neuman and Bill Chappell, "Young People Lead Millions To Protest Global Inaction on Climate Change," NPR, September 20, 2019, https://www.npr.org/2019/09/20/762629200/mass-protests-in-australia-kick-off-global-climate-strike-ahead-of-u-n-summit.

[34] Tosin Thompson, "Young People's Climate Anxiety Revealed in Landmark Survey," *Nature* 597, no. 605 (September 2021), https://doi.org/10.1038/d41586-021-02582-8.

[35] Thompson, "Young People's Climate Anxiety Revealed in Landmark Survey."

[36] Andrew Gregory, "'Eco-Anxiety': Fear of Environmental Doom Weighs on Young People," *The Guardian*, October 6, 2021, https://www.theguardian.com/society/2021/oct/06/eco-anxiety-fear-of-environmental-doom-weighs-on-young-people.

[37] Gregory, "'Eco-Anxiety': Fear of Environmental Doom Weighs on Young People."

[38] William K. Stevens, "Worst Fears on Acid Rain Unrealized," *The New York Times*, February 20, 1990, https://www.nytimes.com/1990/02/20/science/worst-fears-on-acid-rain-unrealized.html.

[39] Peter Parisi, "Al Gore's Carbon Footprint Hypocrisy," *The Daily Signal*, August 15, 2017, https://live-daily-signal.pantheonsite.io/2017/08/15/al-gores-carbon-footprint-hypocrisy/.

[40] James Freeman, "What Else Did Al Gore Get Wrong?," *Wall Street Journal*, July 25, 2017, https://www.wsj.com/articles/what-else-did-al-gore-get-wrong-1501021804.

[41] Karol Markowicz, "My 6yo Learned in School Today That the Earth Will Soon Flood and Came Home with a Plan to Stop It Involving Helicopters on Autopilot to Antartica. You Wanted My 1st Grader on It, He's on It," Twitter, September 19, 2019, https://twitter.com/karol/status/1174813343674241025.

[42] Michael Sanera, "Facts Not Fear," Competitive Enterprise Institute, September 1, 1999, https://cei.org/studies/facts-not-fear/.

[43] Sanera, "Facts Not Fear."

[44] Corey A. DeAngelis, "Here Is the Business Item #39 from 2021 That Was Adopted," Twitter, July 6, 2021, https://twitter.com/deangeliscorey/status/1412509541032464385.

[45] Mary Grabar, "Howard Zinn's Assault on Historians and American Principles," Real Clear Public Affairs, March 9, 2020, https://www.realclearpublicaffairs.com/articles/2020/03/09/howard_zinns_assault_on_historians_and_american_principles_486279.amp.html.

[46] Zinn Education Project, "Teaching People's History," Zinn Education Project, accessed July 10, 2022, https://www.zinnedproject.org/.

[47] Karol Markowicz, "Got This from My Son's Elementary School. Local (Park Slope) Middle School Will Be Teaching Kids How to Protest and Use a Bullhorn and My Kindergartner Is Invited! There Aren't Enough Eyeroll Emojis," Twitter, January 22, 2019, https://twitter.com/karol/status/1087788954022264833.

[48] Luke Rosiak, "Whoops: Leftist 'Teen' Group Says Teachers Union Is Behind Protest Asking Kids To Skip School," *Daily Wire*, January 10, 2022, https://www.dailywire.com/news/whoops-leftist-teen-group-says-teachers-union-is-behind-protest-asking-kids-to-skip-school.

[49] Rosiak, "Whoops: Leftist 'Teen' Group Says Teachers Union Is Behind Protest Asking Kids To Skip School."

[50] Nico Voigtländer and Hans-Joachim Voth, "Nazi Indoctrination and Anti-Semitic Beliefs in Germany," *PNAS* 112, no. 26 (June 2015): 7931-7936, https://doi.org/10.1073/pnas.1414822112.

[51] John H. McWhorter, *Woke Racism: How a New Religion Has Betrayed Black America* (New York: Portfolio/Penguin, 2021), x.

[52] "Co-Founder Of March For Our Lives Cameron Kasky Explains The Mistakes He's Made & Why He Left March For Our Lives," Fox News Radio, September 19, 2018, https://web.archive.org/web/20181010120708/https://radio.foxnews.com/2018/09/19/co-founder-of-march-for-our-lives-cameron-kasky-explains-the-mistakes-hes-made-why-he-left-march-for-our-lives/.

[53] "Co-Founder Of March For Our Lives Cameron Kasky Explains The Mistakes He's Made & Why He Left March For Our Lives."

CHAPTER 9

[1] Interview with Josh, October 12, 2021.

[2] Interview with friend of author, February 1, 2022.

[3] The Based Librarian (@BasedLibrarian), "Time for Another Woke Librarian TikTok...@libsoftiktok" Twitter, February 2, 2022, https://twitter.com/BasedLibrarian/status/1488861801047543817.

[4] "TikTok Statistics – Updated July 2022," Wallaroo Media, July 14, 2022, https://wallaroomedia.com/blog/social-media/tiktok-statistics/.

[5] Sophie Mellor, "'Munchausen by Internet' and the Dangers of Self-Diagnosing Mental Health Issues on TikTok," *Fortune*, September 4, 2021, https://fortune.com/2021/09/04/tiktok-mental-health-self-diagnose-videos/.

[6] This and the preceding two quotations are all from an interview with Charlie Jacobs, April 26, 2022.

[7] Benjamin A. Boyce, "Diagnosing Woke Therapies | with Seerut Chawla," YouTube, November 17, 2020, video, 1:05:28, https://www.youtube.com/watch?v=yXPeTSh-31k.

[8] Boyce, "Diagnosing Woke Therapies | with Seerut Chawla."

[9] Robert Pondiscio, "The Unbearable Bleakness of American Schooling," *Commentary*, February 8, 2022, https://www.commentary.org/articles/robert-pondiscio/american-schooling-bleak-broken/.

[10] Pondiscio, "The Unbearable Bleakness of American Schooling."

[11] Interview with Josh, October 12, 2021.

[12] This and the preceding quotation are from an interview with John Rosemond, December 31, 2021.

[13] Susan Bolotin, "The Disciples of Discipline," *The New York Times*, February 14, 1999, https://www.nytimes.com/1999/02/14/magazine/the-disciples-of-discipline.html.

[14] Bolotin, "The Disciples of Discipline."

[15] Boyce, "Diagnosing Woke Therapies | with Seerut Chawla."

[16] Boyce, "Diagnosing Woke Therapies | with Seerut Chawla."

[17] Erika Sanzi (@esanzi), "Add In the Covid Stuff: Kids Being Told They are Viral Vectors, that They Shouldn't be High-Fiving or Hugging their Friends, that They Can't Let that Mask Slip or Else. Hysterical Adults with No Sense of Costs/Benefit have Projected their Neurosis onto Children," Twitter, February 6, 2022, https://twitter.com/esanzi/status/1490462169959436294.

[18] Jonathan Rosenblum, "No Fourth Vaccine For Me," Jewish Media Resources, January 26, 2022, https://www.jewishmediaresources.com/2157/no-fourth-vaccine-for-me.

[19] Rosenblum, "No Fourth Vaccine For Me."

CONCLUSION: BETHANY

[1] United States Government, "Census Bureau's Household Pulse Survey Shows Significant Increase in Homeschooling Rates in Fall 2020," United States Census Bureau, accessed July 11, 2022, https://www.census.gov/library/stories/2021/03/homeschooling-on-the-rise-during-covid-19-pandemic.html.

[2] United States Government, "Census Bureau's Household Pulse Survey Shows Significant Increase in Homeschooling Rates in Fall 2020."

[3] Charlotte Mason, *Parents and Children* (Australia: Living Book Press vol. 2, 2017), 163.

[4] Karen Glass and David V. Hicks, *Consider This: Charlotte Mason and the Classical Tradition*, (CreateSpace, 2015), 20.

[5] Karen Glass and David V. Hicks, *Consider This.*

[6] Steve Warren, "Nickelodeon Ratings Drop Dramatically - Is It Tied to Cable Network Pushing LGBTQ Agenda to Kids?," CBN News, June 15, 2021, https://www1.cbn.com/cbnnews/entertainment/2021/june/nickelodeon-ratings-drop-dramatically-as-cable-network-pushes-lgbtq-agenda-to-kids.

[7] Brittany Bernstein, "Poll: 68 Percent of Americans Less Likely to Do Business with Disney over Sexualized Content," April 12, 2022, https://news.yahoo.com/poll-68-percent-americans-less-211429571.html.

[8] "National Issues Survey," Trafalgar Group, April 2022, https://www.thetrafalgargroup.org/wp-content/uploads/2022/04/COSA-DisneyBusiness-Full-Report-0410.pdf.

[9] Naomi Schaefer Riley, *Be the Parent, Please: Stop Banning Seesaws and Start Banning Snapchat: Strategies for Solving the Real Parenting Problems* (West Conshohocken, PA: Templeton Press, 2018).

[10] Matt Richtel, "'It's Life or Death': The Mental Health Crisis Among U.S. Teens," *The New York Times*, published April 24, 2022, updated May 3, 2022, https://www.nytimes.com/2022/04/23/health/mental-health-crisis-teens.html.

[11] This and the preceding three quotations are all from an interview with Mary, April 27, 2022.

CONCLUSION: KAROL

[1]Rod Dreher, book jacket of *The Benedict Option: A Strategy for Christians in a Post-Christian Nation* (New York: Penguin Random House LLC, 2018).

[2]Mark Lungariello, "Banned, 'Problematic' Florida Math Textbooks Include Racial-Bias Graph," *New York Post*, April 22, 2022, https://nypost.com/2022/04/22/floridas-banned-math-textbooks-include-racial-bias-graph/.

[3]This and preceding quotation are from an interview with Will Johnson, February 18, 2022.

A division of The Daily Wire
www.dailywire.com